ANOTHER
EGO

ANOTHER
EGO

*The Changing View of Self and Society in the
Work of D. H. Lawrence*

BARUCH
HOCHMAN

UNIVERSITY OF SOUTH CAROLINA PRESS
Columbia, South Carolina

Acknowledgments

The publishers gratefully acknowledge permissions to reprint quotations from the works of D. H. Lawrence.

From *Sons and Lovers*, copyright 1913 by Thomas Seltzer, Inc., all rights reserved; reprinted by permission of The Viking Press, Inc.

From *The Rainbow*, copyright 1915 by David Herbert Lawrence, renewed 1943 by Frieda Lawrence; reprinted by permission of The Viking Press, Inc.

From *Women in Love*, copyright 1920, 1922 by David Herbert Lawrence, renewed 1948, 1950 by Frieda Lawrence; reprinted by permission of The Viking Press, Inc.

From *Psychoanalysis and the Unconscious*, copyright 1921 by Thomas Seltzer, Inc., renewed 1949 by Frieda Lawrence; reprinted by permission of The Viking Press, Inc.

From *Fantasia of the Unconscious*, copyright 1922 by Thomas Seltzer, Inc., renewed 1950 by Frieda Lawrence; reprinted by permission of The Viking Press, Inc.

From *Kangaroo*, copyright 1923 by Thomas Seltzer, Inc., renewed 1951 by Frieda Lawrence; reprinted by permission of The Viking Press, Inc.

From *Apocalypse*, copyright 1931 by The Estate of David Herbert Lawrence, all rights reserved; reprinted by permission of The Viking Press, Inc.

From *Etruscan Places*, originally published by The Viking Press, Inc., in 1932, all rights reserved; reprinted by permission of The Viking Press, Inc.

From "Corot," "Red Moon-Rise," and "Renascence" in *The Complete Poems of D. H. Lawrence*, Vol. I, edited by Vivian de Sola Pinto and F. Warren Roberts, copyright 1920 by B. W. Huebsch, Inc., renewed 1948 by Frieda Lawrence; reprinted by permission of The Viking Press, Inc.

From "Study of Thomas Hardy," "Education of the People," "Introduction to These Paintings," "New Mexico," "Democracy," "John Galsworthy," "Autobiographical Fragment," and "The Good Man" in *Phoenix: The Posthumous Papers of D. H. Lawrence*, edited by Edward D. McDonald, copyright 1936 by Frieda Lawrence, copyright © renewed 1964 by the Estate of the late Frieda Lawrence Ravagli, all rights reserved; reprinted by permission of The Viking Press, Inc.

From "Reflections on the Death of a Porcupine" in *Phoenix II: Uncollected, Unpublished, and Other Prose Works by D. H. Lawrence*, edited by Warren Roberts and Harry T. Moore, copyright 1925 by Centaur Press, renewed 1953 by Frieda Lawrence, all rights reserved; reprinted by permission of The Viking Press, Inc.

From *The Collected Letters of D. H. Lawrence*, edited by Harry T. Moore, copyright © 1962 by Angelo Ravagli and C. Montague Weekley, Executors of the Estate of Frieda Lawrence Ravagli; 1932 by The Estate of D. H. Lawrence, and 1934 by Frieda Lawrence; © 1933, 1948, 1953, 1954, and each year 1956–1962 by Angelo Ravagli and C. Montague Weekley, Executors of the Estate of Frieda Lawrence Ravagli; all rights reserved; reprinted by permission of The Viking Press, Inc.

From *The Plumed Serpent*, Copyright 1933 by The Albatross Verlag (William Heinemann, Ltd., 1955); reprinted by permission of Alfred A. Knopf, Inc.

From "A Propos of Lady Chatterley's Lover" from *Sex, Literature and Censorship*, edited by Harry T. Moore (Viking Compass Books, 1959); reprinted by permission of Twayne Publishers, Inc.

FIRST EDITION

For my parents
who made everything possible

ACKNOWLEDGMENTS From Lionel Trilling
I have learned many
of the things that in-
form this study. I am
grateful to him, too, for the characteristic kindness with
which he received it.

I wish to thank Robert Gorham Davis and John Unterecker
for their patience in directing the dissertation that was its
basis.

My friend Ilja Waches has provided—here, as in so much
else—a degree and a kind of moral and intellectual support
that beggars gratitude. And I stand grateful to all the friends,
especially to my sister Ruth, whose kindness nudged this
study onto paper and into the light.

For permission to quote extensively from Lawrence's writings, I wish to thank Laurence Pollinger Limited and the
Estate of the late Mrs. Frieda Lawrence.

PREFACE

A sense of the tension between self and society pervades the work of D. H. Lawrence. Lawrence was struck by the harshness of that tension and by the way that "progress" seemed to aggravate it. Throughout his career he was committed to exploring its grounds, to seeking ways to allay it. In a sense, his effort was avowedly utopian: to conceive of some way of obviating such tension altogether. Lawrence attempted, in the language of a formulation he once used to describe his novelistic technique, to apprehend "another ego"—an ego opposed to "the social and moral ego of character," within which the antagonism between self and society could be eliminated.

There is something at once foolhardy and toughminded in his effort. Lawrence often flew in the face of the obvious and violated the strictures of common sense. Yet his speculations have somehow worn well. They are firmly rooted in his time, his place, and the peculiarities of his sensibility. But they

seem fresh and vital, as relevant to our times as to his. Though
excessive, they continue to suggest ways of thinking about our
lives. And where they fail completely, they point to the proto-
typical dangers of the utopianism they espouse.

Lawrence never, to be sure, confronted the world that we
have had to learn to live in. Having died in 1930, he was
spared the final nightmares of Hiroshima and Auschwitz and
the ultimate thrust of the totalitarianism that begat them. Indeed, his entire vision was colored by much the lesser of the
two Great Wars that have shaped our century's experience.
The standards by which he judged what he saw reflected a
hopefulness accessible only to the heir, however skeptical, of
a specifically English, specifically nineteenth-century faith in
man's capacity to make a world.

But Lawrence's hopefulness issued, not in a pollyanna's
vision of the glorious future, but in a full-blown vision of
doom for the West. That vision was informed, however, by
a countervision of salvation. Lawrence was one of those whose
expectations were pulled up short by the Great War. But he
also took up the task of confronting the civilization whose discontents had so deeply engaged him before the war. The result
was a death-vision more dire than any our latter-day prophets
have achieved, but also a more vivid glimpse of possible redemption.

By Lawrence's admission, what he achieved were the mere
"stutterings of a . . . life wisdom." Yet his speculations continue to bear a certain authority, even in times so rich in apocalyptic stammering as our own. Even if we reject his particular
doctrines, his anatomy of the modern malaise continues to
bear upon our own condition. And even if we wholly reject his
prophetic pretensions, his art remains opaque unless its doctrine is clarified.

My purpose is to clarify the grounds and development of
Lawrence's vision. I neither attempt to press the Lawrencean

anatomy of self and society to its most radical conclusions, nor finally to relate them to other views of the modern condition. Rather, I try to define its governing conceptual framework, with a view to exposing its underlying assumptions and to clarifying the logic of its development. For, unlike many of Lawrence's readers, I believe that Lawrence's ideas do bear examination. Despite eccentric habits of language and idiosyncratic turns of thought, Lawrence maintains a consistent interest in the problems of self and society, and his ideas develop in terms of relatively clear conceptions of both. Even where his responses are most nakedly personal, they tend to be couched in terms that reflect principles as well as preferences. And it can be shown that the very contradictions that animate his evolving world-view are a logical outgrowth of the underlying assumptions of his initial position. Lawrence moves from a radical individualism to what I term a radical (if qualified) communalism—not out of waywardness, but out of a sustained engagement with the issues and observations that underlie his initial individualism.

Indeed, a good part of this essay is concerned with tracing the steps involved in this movement. I deal with both Lawrence's fiction and his speculative writings with a view to elucidating the inner development of his vision. After sketching the central problem with which Lawrence engages—the problem of a denatured world, and of its renaturalization by vital individuals who transcend common morality (Chapter I)—I examine the unfolding of his views of nature (Chapter II) and history (Chapter III). Then I engage at length (Chapters IV and V) with his sense of the impasse into which man's historical development has driven him, scrutinizing his effort to imagine a way out of that impasse and analyzing in detail the one novel (*The Plumed Serpent*) where he attempts to project an image of that solution in its practical consequences. Finally, in an Afterword, I attempt—only tentatively—to suggest Lawrence's affinities among utopian speculators from the Romantic period to the present.

There are a number of studies dealing with Lawrence's visionary thrust. The most notable is Eugene Goodheart's *The Utopian Vision of D. H. Lawrence,* which effectively placed Lawrence in his intellectual context and related him to the traditions of utopian speculation as no earlier study has done. The present essay tries to go a step further both in exploring Lawrence's critique of the modern world and in exploring the logic (and illogic) of its unfolding.

Were I to start all over again, I would wish further to probe Lawrence's sense of the self and its possibilities. Lawrence's utopianism assumes that an economy of plenty is around the corner, and plays with notions of a selfhood that need not be subject to the demands of a repressive reality-principle. There is a sense, in fact, in which Lawrence stands between the Romantic visionaries, who turned their attention to the workings of the deepest subjectivity, and such contemporary thinkers as Herbert Marcuse and Norman O. Brown, who envision possibilities of a nonrepressive mode of being that would free man from the negative, destructive burden of civilization. I am not sure just what the examination of Lawrence's work—fiction, essays, and poetry together—would yield, in the end. But there is no doubt that it promulgates a set of images, at least, of essential modes of being that would assert their valence alongside those of poets and seers from, say, William Blake, to the present. Examined in this context, they would surely cast some further light on the malaise of self and society which have become, for some of us at least, a subject of constant concern.

CONTENTS

ANOTHER
EGO

You mustn't look in my novel for the old stable ego of character. There is another ego, *according to whose action the individual is unrecognisable, and passes through, as it were, allotropic states which it needs a deeper sense than any we've been used to exercise, to discover. . . .*

D. H. Lawrence

1

The Radical Individualist

The ordinary claims of conventional morality are, in a sense, on trial in Lawrence's early work. From the very outset, Lawrence is concerned with examining the claims of family and society, and with evolving grounds for rejecting them. By the time of *Women in Love* (drafted 1914–1916), he had come to repudiate all the commonplace pieties, placing the autonomous individual not only at the center of human history, but of the creative universe as well.

The struggle toward such a view is evident in the early novels, which portray heroes engaged in freeing themselves from the limitations of their backgrounds. Paul Morel, the hero of *Sons and Lovers* (1913), outgrows his mother's nonconformist pieties. Ursula Brangwen, in *The Rainbow* (1915), moves beyond the bounds of the church at Cossethay into the spacious gothic halls of Nottingham University and then into the "great world" of the modern, emancipated consciousness. And Rupert Birkin of *Women in Love* (published 1920) touches the "entire pulse of social England" and leaves it behind. At the conclusion of the novel he and Ursula leave industrial England, seeking the south, "wo die Citronen blühen," as well as a "condition" of freedom within the "yoke and leash of love" into which they have entered.

These protagonists grow toward a complete rejection of the traditional grounds of morality. In the course of depicting their growth, Lawrence erects a rival system designed to affirm the radical values of civilization without sacrificing individual life and happiness. Lawrence wants civilization without the price men pay for it in renunciation and repression of instinct, and without the wasteful subordination of individual creativity to social necessity. As one critic puts it: "The basis of Lawrence's 'social criticism' is a passionate quarrel . . . with the dualism presupposed by life in society. The opposition between impulse and obligation, personal right and law—which is the preoccupation of so much of Western literature and thought—is dissolved in Lawrence's conception of spontaneous being."[1]

The call for "spontaneous being" is Lawrence's affirmation of the spontaneous impulses of the personality. He seeks to eliminate not only the dualism of impulse and obligation, but also the antagonism between flesh and spirit which, in the West, tends to parallel the first antinomy. Lawrence's affirmation of impulse is also an affirmation of the flesh and a negation of all that would deny the flesh. Even religion, for so long a vehicle of repressive morality, must be redeemed and transformed. It must be recognized as a simple mode of being, as the living organism's palpable relation to the living universe. Arguing with Miriam Lievers about the value of churches and of ritual obligations, Paul Morel points to a crow flying in the sky and asks whether its religiosity does not lie just there: in its "being" as it moves through the sky.[2]

Essential to this concept is Lawrence's assertion that there is no necessary contradiction between the impulsive, passion-

[1] Eugene Goodheart, The Utopian Vision of D. H. Lawrence (Chicago: University of Chicago Press, 1963), p. 9.
[2] D. H. Lawrence, Sons and Lovers (New York: Modern Library, n.d.), p. 294.

ate life of the body and the life of the human community. On the contrary, the human community is a direct outgrowth of the body's life and needs. The "utopian vision" Lawrence promulgates in his work reveals a redeemed world in which the schism between passion and reason, between flesh and spirit, between nature and history, and between individual and society will be healed. It is a vision of men who, in their integral humanity, walk with each other in an instinctive harmony of impulse—a harmony, to be sure, that emerges out of incessant conflict. Lawrence writes: "One craves that his life should be more individual, that I and you and my neighbour should each be distinct in clarity from each other, perfectly distinct from the general mass. Then it would be a melody if I walked down the road; if I stood with my neighbour, it would be a pure harmony."[3]

The vision is necessarily utopian, literally a "no where" vision, because of the actual state of the present world. This state is symbolized in the last third of *The Rainbow*, in *Women in Love*, and in much of Lawrence's later fiction. In general, "society" is identified with twentieth-century industrial England.

The world of these novels is marked by a stultifying ugliness that blights the landscape with scaly slate roofs, smoking pitheads, and filthy, sprawling factories. This is a world of coal and iron, of machines and metals, peopled by the "elementals" who mine the metals and the "operatives" who run the machines. The "deadness" of this mechanical world is contrasted with the pulsing life of the "green" and "organic" world of nature. Its stoniness is set against the supple "life" of wild and startled things. Deformed and decayed by this ugliness, the realm of life has been "reduced" to chaos. But this is

[3] D. H. Lawrence, "Study of Thomas Hardy," *Phoenix* (London: William Heinemann Ltd., 1936; reprinted 1961), p. 432.

a stony chaos, of red brick and blue slate and the beetle-like iridescence of coal.[4]

Obviously, the physical ugliness of the industrial landscape is not a moral quality. It does not in itself testify to inner corruption. But for Lawrence, the quality and appearance of the human world within the natural world provides a metaphor, or rather an elaborate set of interlocking metaphors, for the relationship between the natural and the social in the human soul. The green world of nature is identified with the natural, presocial, nonmoral man; the black, stony world of industrial society with the social and moral man. Society has been mechanized; the feeling life of men has become petrified, and man's soul has become a self-enclosed realm where noxious and corrosive elements are perpetually at work. This dark, ugly, mechanical world has been superimposed upon the green world of nature, alive with feeling, with spontaneous being.

Actually, this image figures most dramatically in the "Study of Thomas Hardy," which was written in 1914, between "The Sisters" and the final draft of The Rainbow. Hardy was, in a sense, Lawrence's fictive mentor. He provides Lawrence with an occasion for defining directly that tension between individual and society which Lawrence's own fiction tends to circumvent. In Hardy, Lawrence finds a novelist with an unexampled sensitivity to the tension between individual passion and social demands and a deep awareness of the abyss that lies between the civilized consciousness and the primordial world of nature. Hardy's "feeling, his sensuous understanding," Lawrence writes, "is . . . very great and deep, deeper than that, perhaps, of any other English novelist."[5] This responsiveness to sensual experience led Hardy to depict social forms as

[4] These images are most vividly rendered in Lady Chatterley's Lover, The Rainbow, and Women in Love.
[5] Lawrence, Phoenix, p. 480.

a prison to individual desire. When individual desire is urgent, these forms cannot contain it. Again and again in the Hardy novels, Lawrence writes, the individual is forced to burst the shell of social self. In doing so, he makes contact with the greater energies of life itself.[6]

The realm of life itself is the realm of nature, but nature in Hardy is not the green world of Lawrence's early fiction.[7] It is rather an awesome, cruel, majestically indifferent entity, virtually beyond the comprehension of man. Hardy insists that man can neither apprehend the full range and richness of life nor attune himself to its will. Nature is eternally outside man and eternally beyond him.

This is a constant revelation in Hardy's novels: that there exists a great background, vital and vivid, which matters more than the people who move upon it. Against the background of dark, passionate Egdon, of the leafy, sappy passion and sentiment of the woodlands, of the unfathomed stars, is drawn the lesser scheme of lives. . . . Upon the vast, incomprehensible pattern of some primal morality greater than ever the human mind can grasp, is drawn the little, pathetic pattern of man's moral life and struggle.[8]

The Return of the Native projects a crucial metaphor for Lawrence. Man is opposed to nature. Hardy does not refer, however, to man the individual, but to social man, banding together with other men to beat back the "wilderness." In The Return of the Native, the human community is described as a "little walled city" which man has built to "defend himself from the vast enormity of nature," against the "vast, unexplored morality of life itself, what we call the immorality of nature."[9] Moreover, Lawrence points out, man is constrained by more than the walls of the city. Society

---

[6] See Chap. II.

[7] I refer to the view of nature in The White Peacock and the Love Poems. See Chap. II.

[8] Lawrence, "Study of Thomas Hardy," Phoenix, p. 419.   [9] Ibid.

forces him to play confining "roles." Hence the metaphor, probably drawn from the Christmas mummery in *The Return of the Native*, of the life of society as a play. Within the Wessex community, man enacts what Lawrence describes as a "little . . . morality play," whose triviality we can apprehend only against the larger backdrop of projected life in the "heath" or "nature." All of life in society, as it unfolds in the Wessex communities, is a stilted drama, "with its queer frame of morality, and its mechanized movement." Within the drama men assume masks, not in accord with their natures, but in keeping with arbitrary roles defined in the social scenario.[10]

Because these constraining *personae* are unable to embody all the energies which the "real, vital, potential self" engenders, each nascent personality must inevitably "explode out of the convention," bursting "independently, absurdly, without mental knowledge or acquiescence" out of its imprisoning form. What it seeks is fulfillment, or "being." In Lawrence's account, "the *via media* to being for man or woman, is love, and love alone." Motivated by the need for love, Hardy's "people are always bursting suddenly out of bud and taking a wild flight into flower, always shooting suddenly out of a tight convention. . . . And from such an outburst, . . . the tragedy usually develops."[11]

In effect, Lawrence finds that in the Hardy novels the individual's passional needs are identified with and symbolized by the "greater world of nature," which is made evident through the actual heaths and moors of the Hardy landscape. Nature, the great mover and the primordial source of life, is identified with "nature" in the sense of the great outdoors, with "human nature," and with the presocial, unconditioned aspects of the self. When man looks to the heath, he looks to the place where the "instinctive life heaves up" and where, in

[10] *Ibid.*   [11] *Ibid.*, pp. 410–11.

the phrase of the later essays on the unconscious, "life bubbles up in us, prior to any mentality."[12] At that source, savage and incomprehensible, the instinctive life of man and the primordial life of the cosmos are joined.

Although it announces itself as a work of literary criticism, the "Study of Thomas Hardy" is in large part a militant manifesto of Lawrence's values. In it, Lawrence calls for a leap out of bud into flower and challenges any "tight convention" that cuts man off from his "real, potential self," a self whose deep affinities are in nature rather than history. What must be transcended if man is to reach down into the real sources of his vitality is not merely convention, but the entire mentality that affirms the "communal adhesion." Lawrence holds that in the nineteenth century at least, such adhesion is rooted in the need to justify industrialism. "For what is the moral system," he writes, "but the ratified form of the material system?" And the material system, with its stony rigidity, can prevail only because of man's irrational fear of extinction.

Lawrence's anthropology reveals this bias. "All of human history," he writes at the opening of the Hardy "Study," "ever since man first discovered himself exposed between sky and land, belonging to neither," has been marked by the "mighty struggle to feel at home on the face of the earth." But he has never really succeeded.

Though he has roofed-in the world with houses and though the ground has heaved up massive abundance and excess of nutriment to his hand, still he cannot be appeased . . . In his anxiety he has evolved nations and tremendous governments to protect his person and his property; his strenuous purpose . . . has brought to

---

[12] *Ibid.,* p. 415; D. H. Lawrence, *Psychoanalysis and the Unconscious* and *Fantasia of the Unconscious* (New York: The Viking Press, 1960), p. 13. (When I refer to either work in later notes, I shall name either the one or the other of the treatises in this volume. All references to the treatises on the unconscious will refer to this volume.)

pass the whole frantic turmoil of modern industry . . . that he may
have enough to eat and wear, that he may be safe.[13]

Lawrence insists that even man's religion has had "for the
systole and diastole of its heart-beat, propitiation of the Unknown God who controls death and the sources of nourishment." Lawrence does not argue with the problem of survival
itself. Nor does he challenge the conventions that are necessary to insure survival. What he challenges is the nineteenth-
century, Carlylean obsession with work and productivity and
the sense that life is vindicated by work.

We must work to eat, and eat to work—that is how it is given out.
But the real problem is quite different. "We must work to eat, and
eat to—what?" Don't say "work," it is so unoriginal.
   In Nottingham we boys began learning German by learning
proverbs. "Mann muss essen um zu leben, aber Mann muss nicht
leben um zu essen," was the first. "One must eat to live, but one
must not live to eat." A good German proverb according to the
lesson-book. Starting a step further back, it might be written, "One
must work to eat, but one must not eat to work." Surely that is
just, because the second proverb says, "One must eat to live."[14]

Lawrence insists that society must provide each individual
with the means of survival. Indeed, he anticipates the ease
with which industrial technology can relieve man of the burden of back-breaking and soul-destroying labor. And he feels
free to regard society as no more than a vast catering service, a mere "self-preservation scheme" or "cook-housekeeper
scheme."[15] His argument—aggressively presented by Rupert
Birkin in *Women in Love*[16]—is with those who demand a

[13] Lawrence, "Study of Thomas Hardy," *Phoenix*, p. 398.
[14] *Ibid.*, pp. 422–23.
[15] D. H. Lawrence, "Democracy," *Phoenix*, pp. 702–703.
[16] D. H. Lawrence, *Women in Love* (New York: Modern Library,
n.d.), pp. 61–62 and 115–17.

greater acquiescence in the claims of society than mere survival necessitates.

The ground of Lawrence's radical individualism is his sense
of the rich possibilities opened up by an imminent economy
of plenty. Hence his indignation at the fact that the freest
spirits of the nineteenth century submit to the "communal
adhesion." Of Hardy he writes: "His private sympathy is
always with the individual against the community." But because Hardy is himself not free of unconscious communal
bondage, "he must select his individual with a definite weakness, . . . a certain inevitable and inconquerable adhesion to
the community" and let him be destroyed owing to his inability to act in such a way as to "disintegrate the community,
either in its moral or its practical form."[17] Hardy betrays his
rebellious protagonists, who have had the courage to burst out
of "the tight convention" and "out of bud and into flower."
He does so because he lacks the courage to imagine ways out
of the "social encampment," with its "little morality play,"
and into the greater life of the heath outside. In effect, Hardy
fails morally because he is not able to imagine himself out of
history. He cannot envision individuals whose roots are in
nature rather than history and whose destinies are a value for
themselves alone, and not for mankind in general.

Lawrence insists on the urgency of such envisionment. Man
must learn to make life take precedence over work and come
to understand that society as constituted—with its political
arrangements, its legal systems, and its "plausible ethics of
productivity"—is averse to life and the life-bearers. If the life
of society, not to speak of the life of individuals, is to be
renewed, then potentially vital men must free themselves
from the trammels of both the "moral system" and the "material system" that is "ratified" by the moral system.

The issue is the renaturalizing of a denatured world. So-

[17] Lawrence, "Study of Thomas Hardy," *Phoenix*, pp. 439 and 441.

ciety, as Lawrence perceives it at the time of the Hardy "Study," is cut off from nature: it isolates its denizens from the wonder and vitality of nature itself. Lawrence insists that strong individuals, whom he terms the "natural aristocrats," must break down the stony walls of the social encampment and re-establish communication between encampment and wilderness. This is possible because the stony walls of society and the glassy encrustations of the "social ego" are themselves aberrant.

There is, in this view, no inherent contradiction between nature and civilization. Rather, civilization is a spontaneous outcropping of nature; art (or artifice) is—if we wish—man's nature, so long as he remains in harmony with his deepest nature and with "objective" nature in the cosmos around him. Conflict within men, as between them, is natural and inevitable. Such conflict, however, should be between the inherent components of each individual's nature, not between his social or civilized self and his "natural" or spontaneous one. If Western (or European, or English) civilization is to be "re-sourced," men must venture outside convention and encampment, into the wilderness of the self. The Lawrencean "call to the wilderness" is a call for a return to nature—though for a special kind of return to a special kind of nature. Like the Romantic Genius or the Nietzschean Overman, the natural aristocrat, in Lawrence's conception, must overleap all the constraints of the encampment morality and find the point where, symbolically at least, inner and outer nature meet: where "life springs up at the source."

2.

Lawrence's "call to the wilderness" echoes the traditions of Romantic individualism. It is no surprise, therefore, that it is made to hinge, not so much on the material conditions that might sustain the enterprise, but on a grandiose metaphysical vision of nature itself. Vitalist in essence, the Lawrencean vision of nature, especially as projected in the Hardy "Study," constitutes a full-front rebuttal of the nineteenth-century materialist (and moralist!) view. In it, prodigality supersedes economy and the individual takes precedence over the species. Its imperatives are "Live" and "Be," and on those imperatives the vital world depends.

Nature, in Lawrence's view, as in Goethe's, is alive, not dead. She is a teeming prodigal who casts up life and life forms in bewildering profusion. Such prodigality is not an aberrant or instrumental aspect of her being, but her essence. "The excess," Lawrence writes, "is the thing itself, at the maximum of being. If it had stopped short of this excess, it would not have been at all. If the excess were missing, darkness would cover the face of the earth."[18]

Creation itself hinges on the superfluity of being. Yet "being" exists only in highly individuated creatures who exist not for the world but for themselves. "It seems," Lawrence writes,

as though one of the conditions of life is, that life shall continually and progressively differentiate itself, almost as though this differentiation were a purpose. Life starts crude and unspecified, a great Mass. And it proceeds to evolve out of that mass ever more distinct and definite particular forms, and ever-multiplying number of separate species and orders, as if it were working always to the production of an infinite number of perfect individuals, the individual so thorough that he should have nothing in common with any other individual.[19]

Thus, life has a direction; a kind of latent will would seem to guide it. Individuals are "leading shoots" on the Tree of Life. Yet individual existence is not governed by a Bergsonian

[18] *Ibid.*, p. 402. [19] *Ibid.*, p. 431.

life-force or a Schopenhauerian life-will. Lawrence insists on the randomness and gratuitousness of each moment of self-assertion and self-fulfillment. The individual springs into being and blossoms for itself, in the exuberant abandon of its self-hood. "The final aim of every living thing, creature, or being is the full achievement of itself. . . . Not the fruit . . . but the flower is the culmination and climax."[20] "The final aim," Lawrence writes, "is the flower, the fluttering, singing nucleus which is a bird in spring, the magical spurt of being which is a hare all explosive with fullness of self . . . ; the real passage of a man down the road, no sham, no shadow, no counterfeit. . . ."[21]

Indeed, of all creatures man would seem to be the most exuberantly creative. Man may, in a sense, be seen as the advance-guard of life in its movement toward ever greater individuality. He is "in his normal state . . . like a palpitating leading shoot of life, where the unknown, all unresolved, beats and pulses, containing the quick of all experience, as yet unrevealed, not singled out."[22] That unknown is in man but also outside him, in the realm of nature. He enters it when he breaks the habitual patterns of conformity within the social pale—patterns imposed in the name of self-preservation. He does this chiefly when he succeeds in immersing himself in the darkness of authentic erotic experience. Love, as in Lawrence's formulation with regard to the Hardy novels, is the via media to being. Man is born into his real selfhood through love. And by love is meant "the love of a man for a woman and a woman for a man."

Such love is unequivocally sexual; it is in the experience of sexuality that man enters the "unknown," whose medium is woman, but whose locus is in both the mysterious darkness within himself and the cosmos without. That darkness is below the conscious mind and beyond the socially condi-

[20] *Ibid.*, p. 403.   [21] *Ibid.*   [22] *Ibid.*, p. 424.

tioned will, "within" the realm of sensual oblivion into which man descends in the erotic act—a realm symbolically but also in a sense literally continuous with nature.

More concretely, what is explored in the sex act is the duality of each individual's nature. For, within Lawrence's system, men are at once male and female by nature, as are women. The sexual encounter elicits both terms of their natures and facilitates a resolution of that duality. The male experiences his feminine, fleshly nature in the sex act, even while he is purified into utter maleness by his mate's absorption of his feminine component. At the same time, his mate experiences her masculine, spiritual, intellectual component, but has it purified out of her as well. And by undergoing this simultaneous exploration and purification, the individual is able to flower as an integral identity—as a self in its fullness of being.

There are many obscurities and ambiguities in Lawrence's conception of the self and in his formulations with regard to its birth out of the matrix of sexuality. I shall return to some of them. All I wish to call attention to at the moment is the fact that "love," meaning sexual love, is the matrix of the true self in its flowering. That self is the "Holy Ghost" of individual and cosmic Being, generated within each individual and between the parties to the erotic act. Thus, utter unadulterated individuality is precipitated in the darkness of the sexual journey into the unknown. Such individuality is *the* cosmic, vital, ontological essence. In this way, man, "merely" seeking his own satisfaction, accomplishes the aim of the cosmos itself, whose final end is perfect individuation "till, in the future, wonderful, distinct individuals, like angels, move about, each one being himself, perfect as a complete melody or a pure colour."[23]

And such individuality directly contravenes the ordinary
[23] *Ibid.*, p. 432.

social and moral schemes. For, "working in contradiction to the will of self-preservation, from the first man wasted himself begetting children, colouring himself and dancing and howling and sticking feathers in his hair, in scratching pictures on the walls of his cave, and making graven images of his unutterable feelings."[24] The passional self, with its phoenix-like, poppy-like waste, is antagonistic to the instrumental productive self affirmed by the "cook-housekeeper scheme." One need not renounce, repress, labor to produce. Production itself is rooted in passional being, not moralistic negation of being. "Not the work I shall produce, but the real Me I shall achieve, that is the consideration; of the complete Me will come the complete fruit of me, the work, the children."[25]

Lawrence, one must note again, does not negate the "cook-housekeeper" or the "great preservation" scheme: food, clothing, and shelter are real, legitimate needs, and man must have them to survive. But the vital human reality on which the universe depends—as it depends on the song of a bird or a poppy's flowering—springs from "complete Me," and the "complete Me" is a product of the "journey into the Unknown" of sexuality. That "Me"—which Lawrence terms the Holy Ghost of the Self—is beyond the demands and limitations of the social system and its moral "ratifications." It is somehow contiguous and consanguineous with the "greater realm of nature," where "life springs up at the source." Indeed, out of this realm there springs not only the radical, irreducible self and the ultimate individuality, but also all that man has produced which is of value in civilization. It is in the "wasteful" overflow of his passional exuberance that he "scratches pictures on the walls of his cave, and makes graven images of his unutterable feelings."[26]

Clearly, passional striving does not subvert the body politic,

[24] *Ibid.*, p. 398.   [25] *Ibid.*, p. 403.   [26] *Ibid.*, p. 398.

THE RADICAL INDIVIDUALIST 15

it strengthens it. Social creativity is the product not of social controls but of radical self that comes into being in the course of the "journey into the Unknown." Indeed, failure to embark upon that journey is lethal, for society as well as the self. Here Lawrence's view echoes Blake's proverbs of Hell: "Sooner strangle an infant in its cradle than nurse unacted desires"; "standing water breeds pestilence"; and so on. Man, being a "wellhead" springing from the "Unknown," must let the waters of his being play, lest they stagnate and breed corruption. He must—to shift from the hydraulic to a botanical metaphor of which Lawrence is inordinately fond—allow his energies to flow into the "leading shoot" that "reaches into the Unknown." Otherwise he will rot like a bud that has failed to burst "out of bud into blossom." Lawrence likes to speak of the self as a rose or a poppy that has burst into blossom. And he insists that the "rose" that lacks the "courage" to blossom becomes a "fat cabbage, going rotten at the core." Indeed, modern society is a "cabbage patch" full of the stench of rotting cabbages—that is, full of energies that have turned on themselves and begun to corrupt both cabbages and garden. And the process of corruption, as Lawrence envisions it, is not one of vegetable passivity, but of violent, noxious thrashing that emits deadly poisons and lethal death-rays.

Hence the urgency of Lawrence's "call to the wilderness," which involves a movement utterly beyond all the aims and values of the social and moral ego. This means a refusal, not only of the "thou shalt nots" of repressive morality, but also of all programs for reforming present society. To attempt to change a dead, materialistic society is to remain subject to the values of that society; to set oneself against something is in some sense to validate it. This is essentially the position reached by Paul Morel in considering the "woman question": the issue is one of personal being and fulfillment, not of legal and social action. "Where," Lawrence asks in the Hardy

"Study," "is the source of all money-sickness, and of all sex-perversion? It lies in the heart, and not in conditions."

The crucial need is a change of heart, a change that can only come from within. And this can be achieved only through a Faustian leap into the "Unknown." Man must strive to approximate in his consciousness some viable relation to "the greater morality of life, which we call the immorality of Nature." The courageous individual must face the wilderness: "Come away from the crowd and the community. . . . Your business is to produce your own real life. . . ."[27] The wilderness into which one withdraws is not a place of isolation, however; it holds out the promise of a more comprehensive community, the community of life: "If sufficient people came out of the walled defenses, and pitched in the open, then the very walled city would be dependent on the free tents of the wilderness. . . ."[28]

3.

Lawrence's claims are radical indeed; and they fly in the face of the Western moral tradition. If one insists that sexuality is the ground of individuation and that individuation is the goal of life, then one obviously cannot "do one's duty" by life through productivity, which only contributes to the "great self-preservation scheme." Moreover, it contradicts psychological traditions as well. Lawrence holds that the natural moment of passional fulfillment, rather than the pattern of habitual behavior in society, is the center and source of life. The early Lawrence thinks of sexuality as a sort of "reservation." Within it, man can achieve a naturalness and a creativity which the social self cannot attain.[29] This self springs from a

[27] *Ibid.*, p. 429.   [28] *Ibid.*

[29] Raymond Williams speaks of sexuality as a "reservation" in the Lawrencean world. See Williams, *Culture and Society* (New York: Doubleday Anchor Books, 1960), pp. 230ff. I use the term "reservation" in a somewhat different way.

world of "outsideness" that is totally uncontaminated by the moods and motives of social man. Sexuality is the guide to another world, within which the self realizes itself and ascends into being—into a paradisal state of individuality.

Lawrence's celebration of sexuality as both the seat and the vehicle of emergent life is radical, and its radical nature becomes evident if we contrast his treatment of sexuality, and of the relationship between sexuality and society, with Freud's. Freud, like the classical moralists—and like Lawrence himself —regards sexuality as the aspect of experience least amenable to social regulation. Yet Freud holds that sexuality is necessarily socialized and shaped in the course of the individual's development. It is this shaping that leads to an inevitable modification of the sexual life in accordance with the demands of the repressive social world. Individuality, ultimately, depends on this process.

Freud held that pleasure is the end toward which men strive. The life-history of each individual is the history of successful and unsuccessful pursuit of pleasure. What the psychoanalyst terms "adult genital sexuality"—and this is, fundamentally, the only kind of sexuality that Lawrence accepts—is the end of a long process. The whole history of individual development, bearing with it the complexity of social relationships, feeds into the process of sexual fulfillment.

Lawrence, on the other hand, treats sexuality as though it had engendered itself and relates it, not to the internal history of the individual, but to the external life of nature. The moment of orgastic fulfillment is cut off from the past and from the complications of consciousness. What Lawrence had called, in Sons and Lovers, the "baptism of fire in passion" has no rationally apprehendable roots in the past and no predictable relation to the future. It is an epiphanal moment wherein the individual confirms his being. The crucial moment is one in which the individual is carried beyond time and space into the realm of the "absolute"—of what Lawrence later called "heaven," or the "fourth dimension."[30]

It is to the transcendental nature of the self that critics refer when they speak of Lawrence's "mysticism." This conception is one of the most problematical elements in Lawrence's work. If it seemed radical in relation to Freud, it appears virtually apocalyptic when juxtaposed with other representatives of the humanistic tradition.

Christopher Caudwell sharply summarizes a traditional view as formulated in the nineteenth century by thinkers like Marx and even Hegel. Attacking what he takes to be Lawrence's primitivism, Caudwell insists that individuation is made possible only through social adaptation, which is in turn necessitated by the differentiation of roles in society.[31] He maintains that the high degree of individuation in modern society stems from its complicated division of labor. Individuals are merely variants of the social types which have in turn been determined by variegated economic roles. In addition, Caudwell implies that individuation depends upon obstacles that must be overcome before the individual can gratify himself. Man comes into being through adaptation to a resistant environment.

Lawrence, to be sure, does not believe that impulsive self-expression results in growth or individuation. As one critic writes: "By spontaneity Lawrence does not mean giving free rein to the impulses. He means rather a dialectic within the spontaneous mode itself between impulse and resistance."[32] This would seem to conform to Caudwell's notion of individuality as fostered by resistance and conflict. The congruity is merely formal, however, since Lawrence assumes that the

[30] See Chap. II, pp. 52–64.
[31] Christopher Caudwell, *Studies in a Dying Culture* (New York: Dodd, Mead & Co., 1958), pp. 62 and 119ff.
[32] Goodheart, *The Utopian Vision*, p. 10.

essential tensions without which development is impossible
are personal and passional, built into the very nature of the
organism itself. For Caudwell, institutional relationships of
an objective historical order are the ground of individuation.
For Lawrence, the order of causation is reversed: individuality, *sui generis*, becomes the ground of the objective, institutional, historical order.

Even while Lawrence breaks with more normative conceptions of the self and its development, he looks forward to
certain midcentury and utopian views, and especially those
discussed by Norman O. Brown and Herbert Marcuse. Both
Brown and Marcuse posit the existence of a "Dionysian" or
"narcissistic" ego, whose coherence and creativity do not depend on social control, and which can constellate itself con-
structively around its own inherent aims and instincts. Like
them, Lawrence insists that there is no necessary conflict
between nature and civilization or between culture and the
instincts. Hence, he can argue so vehemently for enactment of
man's spontaneous desires without threat to the civilized community.

4.

Lawrence's claims, to be sure, remain highly abstract. The
desiderated ends and the actual process of the "journey into
the Unknown" are largely prefigured in vague and rhapsodic
images that sometimes defy precise interpretation. As novelist, Lawrence is most trenchant in portraying the negativity of
social selfhood within the conventional moral schemes. But
he strives at the same time to enunciate the Way into Being,
and—not surprisingly—it sustains much of the imaginative
force of his work.

That Way, moreover, is rooted in the vision of nature and
history that is implied by the "call to the wilderness" of the

Hardy "Study." Indeed, Lawrence's novels, like his manifes-
toes and calls to action, reflect the metaphysic of self and
nature which underlies all of his work. This is reflected in a
letter written at about the time that Lawrence was working on
the Hardy "Study" and *The Rainbow*. In it he says that "that
which is physic—non-human, in humanity, is more interesting to me than the old-fashioned human element—which
causes one to conceive a character in a certain moral scheme."
Lawrence insists that instead of attempting to depict the "old
stable ego of character," he would like to attempt recording
his intuition of "another ego, according to whose action the
individual is unrecognizable." Lawrence conceives of that ego
in elemental terms. Specifically, he notes that the aspects of
feeling in a particular individual can be regarded as manifestations of his "being" even as diamonds and coal are allotropic
forms of carbon.[33]

Lawrence is, to be sure, speaking in this letter of a specific
artistic endeavor, namely, the effort at a special mode of
characterization in *The Rainbow*. But the terms of the formulation are revealing. He wants to conceive of the human
personality as a *natural* entity and to project images of it that
undercut the manifest social surfaces. He wants, moreover, to
conceive of the coherence of such an entity without reference
to the moral scheme or to the mechanisms of adjustment to
the forms of prescribed behavior. Beyond that, in *The Rainbow* and its sequel, one must note that he strives to imagine a
way of integrating and organizing the elemental components
of the self without reference to social and repressive controls.
He seeks, in other words, to create a perspective on the self
that would permit us to glimpse it in its "wilderness" elementality, at a level where, quite unconditioned, "life springs up
at the source."

[33] Aldous Huxley, ed., *The Letters of D. H. Lawrence* (New York:
The Viking Press, 1936), pp. 99–100.

Such an imaginative effort informs all of the early work, and much of the late. Implicit in it is both the metaphysic of nature and the metaphysic of history in which both novels and "calls to the wilderness" are rooted. Any adequate reading of either the novels or the utopian speculations must come to grips with the imagery and the ideas in which that metaphysic is grounded—including the notion that self and society *can* be regenerated by venturing into the wilderness.

It is this metaphysic, initially formulated in the "Study" and developed in "The Crown" essays of the following year and the postwar *Fantasia of the Unconscious*, that I wish to consider in the following chapter. Then I will turn to Lawrence's embryonic theory of history.

11

The Self and Nature

The notion that self and society can both be regenerated through simple sexuality could not survive even within Lawrence's slipshod ideological system. Lawrence soon came to see that sexuality and perversity are intimately related. The problem of modern man is precisely that his sexuality no longer offers release, fulfillment, and a link to the cosmic life. Instead, it leads away from nature and into self-conscious artifice. For Ursula Brangwen, sexuality, marriage, and the marital battle that arises from sexuality do not unfold "naturally." Her relation to nature and to the rhythms of nature has been disrupted by an excess of self-consciousness; so has her relationship to her own deeper needs. A nearly ritual concentration is needed to put her back in "touch"—and even such contact as she achieves is precarious. For later characters, even ritual concentration does not work. The mystic community becomes the necessary medium of naturalization.[1]

Yet, throughout his early work Lawrence continues to regard love as the via media to being and expends considerable effort in constructing an elaborate "metaphysic" to validate his championship of sexual love.

He had written (1913): "My great religion is a belief in the

[1] See Chap. VI.

blood, the flesh, as being wiser than the intellect."² "Religion," to be sure, is used loosely here in the sense of deep devotion or commitment. Yet the language of religion, both pagan and Christian, figures centrally in the treatment of sexual experience. Sexuality becomes the path to transcend once, and the quest for fulfillment through sexual love becomes a way of salvation that culminates in a transfiguration of the parties to it.

The tendency to use the language of Christian tradition is evident even when Lawrence urges the free spirits of his time to leave the "walled city" and venture into the "wilderness." Jesus, John the Baptist, and Elijah had each gone into the wilderness to seek greater purity of soul by confronting the spirit that dwells only in deserts and on mountain tops. The modern individual, like the biblical prophet, was to venture outside the walled city of modern life and to seek a higher and more deific self in the uncharted and unseeded lands of the soul. The "final" self cannot come into being without the isolation and despair of ultimate confrontation which accompany a sojourn in the wilderness. Like the mystic or prophet, the Lawrencean individual must seek a dissolution of the commonplace self and its values, and then evolve a new self and new values. He does so by entering into communion with the transcendent "being" or energy that inhabits him and also inhabits nature itself. The ultimate, or final, self lies within but wells up out of sources that lie far deeper than those of ordinary consciousness. These sources are, in a sense, the deity, which is, in turn, life, or nature.

The wilderness is, in other words, a spatial metaphor for a state of soul. It lies, to pursue the terms of the metaphor, within the self in the great "unknown" which is to be found in the deepest strata of the preconscious soul. The way into

² Letter to Ernest Collings, Jan. 17, 1913, *The Letters of D. H. Lawrence*, ed. and with an introduction by Aldous Huxley (New York: The Viking Press, 1932), p. 96.

the hinterland of consciousness which lies there, and which is the home of the authentic, irreducible self, is the way of sexual love. Out of a thorough-going engagement in the struggle for love and into love one realizes the validated self. The condition for verification of being is the "baptism of fire in passion" which, in the formulation of Rupert Birkin in *Women in Love,* causes the "light of consciousness to go out." Then one is immersed in the great darkness in which one dies to oneself and "comes into being of another."[3]

The novels of the Hardy "Study" phase are taken up with the exploration of the process whereby the self comes into being. This process involves the yielding up of oneself to the "vast impersonal flood of passion." When the "light of consciousness" flickers out, and with it the glaring yet commonplace light of day, the individual can sink down into the luminescent mother-darkness from which life, achievement, and the ultimate self must spring. This is the wilderness in which and out of which the self is born in stark confrontation and in unremitting attendance upon the stirrings of fear and desire. Both the creativity of the self and the self's awareness of its primordial bond to nature depend upon it.

Not only life, but also a species of divinity dwells in the darkness below consciousness, within the wilderness of the soul. This divinity belongs to the "dark gods" who, as Rupert Birkin insists, "enter through the lower gates"—that is, through the gates of the flesh—when the light of consciousness goes out. "It is death to oneself—but it is the coming into being of another." The dark gods transform one into a demon lover. The demonic, however, is not a diabolical phenomenon, but rather a manifestation of creative life.

This entire process of union with deity through descent into the world of the senses is formulated in one of the "The Crown" (1915) essays. "I can become one with God," he

[3] For discussion of the theme, see Chap. I. See also *Sons and Lovers,* p. 373; *Women in Love,* p. 47.

writes, "consummated into eternity by taking the road down the senses into the utter darkness of power, till I am one with the darkness of initial power, beyond knowledge of any opposite."[4] And out of such immersion in the darkness of power, as well as in the refulgence of the fleshly "light," are born the self and all the values and entities that spring from the self.

Indeed, virtually all of Lawrence's work is marked by the double identification of the integral self with nature on the one hand and with some form of deific or demonic power on the other. Though particular individuals like Paul Morel or Tom Brangwen may indeed fail to bring themselves into being, Lawrence's novels of the Hardy "Study" period suggest that the self is consanguineous with nature, and that both self and nature, when fully actualized, partake of divinity. Sons and Lovers, The Rainbow, and Women in Love all suggest a radical affinity between the self and the cosmos and the possibility of actualizing one's being in the matrix of nature.

The notion of the self's consanguinity with nature is, to be sure, a metaphysical rather than a psychological one, and it resists representation in ordinary novelistic terms. Attempting to render it, Lawrence appropriates a number of strategies from the poetic rather than the novelistic tradition, in the manner of such romance novelists as Emily Brontë and Thomas Hardy.

Like the nineteenth-century English "nature" writers, Lawrence uses scenes from nature to symbolize man's experience of himself. The landscapes of The White Peacock or Sons and Lovers serve a function similar to that of the heath in Wuthering Heights or The Return of the Native or of mountain and storm in Byron's verse. Lawrence suggests a correspondence between outer scene and inner life, a correspondence made imaginatively viable by a more or less animistic view of nature. Scenes from nature are felt to be pervaded

[4] D. H. Lawrence, "The Crown," Reflections on the Death of a Porcupine (Philadelphia: The Centaur Press, 1925), p. 25.

by life while Nature, metaphysically grasped, is identified
with such life, as are the feelings of individual characters.
Analogues of the method are to be found in the traditions of
Romantic pantheism, where there is a tendency to blur the
distinction between subject and object.

In such work, it is often not clear whether the reality being
treated is a reality of the inner life or the outer world, and for
Lawrence it does not ordinarily matter. Nature, as in the
Romantic tradition, serves to signify human possibilities beyond the pale of civilized consciousness.[5] These possibilities
can be negative as well as positive; but their negativity, in
Lawrence, is subsumed under a larger pattern of positive
anticipations. Lawrence, even when he insists on the horror of
the destructive energies encompassed by nature, insists—like
Goethe or Wordsworth—on ultimate possible harmonies.

In the following section I shall examine Lawrence's strategies in representing the consanguinity of self and nature in the
novels, noting along the way the manner in which his conception of nature changes with his changing sense of the problems of the self. I shall then turn to the "systematic" treatment of self and nature in the discursive writings with a view
to structuring the imagery through which he strove to concep-
tualize his intuition of the self's affinities with nature.

Section I
Self and Nature in the Fiction and the Early Poetry

A. The Early Work: *Love Poems,*
The White Peacock, and *The Trespasser.*

The early Lawrence tended to conceive of the universe as
pervaded by an immanent divinity not unlike the spirit that

[5] George Lukacs, *Goethe und Seine Zeit* (Berlin: A Franke Verlag,
1947), pp. 21ff.

dwells within the Wordsworthian universe or that informs
the landscapes of Meredith's poems. Meditating on a painting
by Corot, he writes:

> The grey, phosphorescent, pellucid advance
> Of the luminous purpose of God, shines out
> Where the lofty trees athwart stream chance
> To shake flakes of its shadow about.
>
> The subtle, steady rush of the whole
> Grey, foam-mist of advancing God,
> As he silently sweeps to His somewhere, his goal,
> Is heard in the grass of the sod.
>
> Is heard in the windless whispers of leaves,
> In the silent labours of men in the fields,
> In the downward dropping of flimsy sheaves
> Of cloud the rain skies yield.
>
> . . . .
> For what can all sharp-rimmed substance but catch
> In a backward ripple, God's purpose, reveal
> For a moment His mighty direction, snatch
> A spark beneath His wheel.
>
> Since God sweeps onward dim and vast,
> Creating the channeled vein of Man
> And Leaf for his passage, His shadow is cast
> On all for us to scan.[6]

A more direct identification of nature, God, and man is made
in "Red Moon-Rise":

> . . like the fire that boils within this ball
> Of earth, and quickens all herself with flowers,
> God burns within the stiffened clay of us;
> And every flash of thought that we and ours
> Send up to heaven . . . does
> Fly like a spark from this God-fire of passion;

[6] D. H. Lawrence, *Love Poems* (London: Duckworth & Co., 1913),
pp. xxxiii–xxxiv.

And pain of birth and joy of the begetting,
and sweat of labour . . .
                    . . . (is) but the jetting
Of a trail of the great fire . . .
                    . . . a jet from the innermost fire . . .[7]

The sense of the consubstantiality of man and nature and
of the intertwinedness of man's life and that of the cosmos is
as strongly felt in *The White Peacock* (1911), Lawrence's
first novel. It is pervaded by a sense of nature's life, which is
alternately felt to be a tender mother and a cruelly indifferent
stepmother. The imagery of the novel swarms with personifi-
cations of nature-as-woman, and its characters are animated
by a craving for fusion with mother-nature and baffled rage at
her remoteness and imperturbability. One critic has observed
that the novel treats nature as a screen onto which to project
sentiment and fantasy—somewhat along the lines foreshad-
owed by one of the early poems:

> . . . I see the valley
> Fleshed all like me
> With feelings that change and quiver:
> And all things seem to tally
> With something in me. . . .[8]

To insist on this, however, is to overlook the ever-present wish
to experience nature as alive, and the consistent quest for
images to convey the intuition of the shared life of man and
the cosmos.[9]

The history of Lawrence's development may in fact be said
to be a history of increasing skill in objectifying his basic

---

[7] *Ibid.*, p. xxvii.   [8] *Ibid.*, p. xxxix.
[9] Elizabeth Hess, *Die Naturbetrachtung in die Prosawerk von D. H.
Lawrence* (Bern: University of Bern English Studies, 1957). This is
probably the best and the least pretentious study of Lawrence's treatment of nature.

intuition of shared life. *The Trespasser* (1912), his second novel, is more coherent in mood and theme than the earlier one. It is marred, however, by exacerbated sensibility and an increased tendency to blur the distinction between the inner world of self and the outer world of nature. Within the year Lawrence was to write of *The Trespasser* that it was a "florid prose poem," even as he was to say of *The White Peacock* that it was "a decorated idyll running to seed in realism." Its floridity lies largely in a heavy-handed rendering of intense subjective responses to an overwhelmingly beautiful, sun-flushed stretch of beach on the Isle of Man. The hero of the novel is a musician, one who carries the score of Wagner's *Tristan* with him on his love tryst on the island. And a Wagnerian emotionalism is in fact the distinguishing trait of the novel. Everything is experienced through the turgid sensibility of characters in the grip of inchoate, pseudo-heroic passions; the outer world billows in the coercive rhythm of the characters' feeling. The novel is rooted in the intensity of desire and frustration in a man whose passions are doomed by the form his life has taken, and whose life is doomed by the passions it cannot contain. Wagner's cosmic feeling, but also the overwrought sensibility of Goethe's *Werther*, has its echo in the novel. *The Trespassers* embarrasses with its excess of sensibility. It appals with a sort of overwriting that comes of the effort uncritically to represent the hectic world of subjectivity at the point of its disintegrative interaction with the natural world of sun, sand, and sea.

B. *Sons and Lovers*: Nature, and the Metaphors of Birth and Rebirth Through Nature

One of the great advances marked by *Sons and Lovers* (1913) lies in the rendition of an objective world apart from the subjectivity of the characters. The characters of the novel live their lives intensely, and they live it in relation to their environment. As Dorothy Van Ghent points out, no other novel is so rich in natural images, most of them apprehended in the context of a character's intense experience of himself or of his world. In some instances, a neutral object, more often than not a natural one, serves to reveal the inwardness of characters and their relation to each other, in communion scenes.[10] It is, in fact, such communion scenes that form the structural units of the novel. The novel may be said to be organized in terms of movement toward crucial communion scenes. In these, characters move toward fuller selfhood as they come to experience the world and the independent life that is in the world.[11]

The pulling of subjectivity back into the characters seems to be one of the conditions for the achievement of *Sons and Lovers* in this regard. Since the objective world is no longer contaminated at every point by the feeling and wishes of his characters, it seems to become possible for Lawrence to make clear statements about his characters and their world, and for him to present a consistent view of the life of the world and of his characters' relation to that life. As a result, we have, in *Sons and Lovers* the first clear depiction of the process of self-realization as conceived and enunciated in the Hardy "Study": the process of coming-into-being on the high road of love and of its unfolding in relation to the greater life of nature. As Mark Spilka has shown, *Sons and Lovers* is concerned with the birth of an individual.[12] This process is enacted against a set of landscapes heaving and pulsing with a kind of life that is akin to the life of the realized individual.

The condition for Paul Morel's coming into being is emancipation from his mother, that is, from the maternal world of

[10] Dorothy Van Ghent, *The English Novel: Form and Function* (New York: Rinehart & Co., 1953), pp. 247ff.
[11] Mark Spilka makes this point in *The Love Ethic of D. H. Lawrence* (Bloomington, Ind.: Indiana University Press, 1957), p. 24.
[12] *Ibid.*, Chap. III.

origins, which in Lawrence's vision, encysts the individual and cuts him off from his real nature and possibilities. *Sons and Lovers* traces Paul's movement out of the closed world of origins into an open world of potentially self-posited ends. He moves out of a state of dependence on the ultimately corruptive sources of his life into an ever greater autonomy of being in relation to the cosmos and to other men. Predictably, woman—or rather the experience of the "unknown" in woman—is the medium in which that movement becomes possible. To be free—that is, to be—Paul must learn to abandon himself to the drift of the unknown in another. This, as when he turns his back on death at the end of the novel, involves deliberate choice. But here the choice is one of suspending the ordinary will, which is the social will, and learning to strive with a will-beyond-will to come into contact with the "larger life" of self and cosmos. And, predictably, sexuality is the medium for making such contact.

Paul describes the process in formulating his own sense of his mother's "quickness" of being: "but my mother, I believe, got *real* joy and satisfaction out of my father at first. . . . She had a passion for him. . . . That's what one *must have* . . . , the real, real flame of feeling through another person—once, only once, if it lasts only three months. See, my mother looks as if she's *had* everything that was necessary for her living and developing. There's not a tiny bit of a feeling of sterility about her."[13]

Paul goes still further in generalizing about such experience. Gertrude has had the "real thing; she knows, she's been there." He cannot, to be sure, articulate what it is she has had and where she has been. But he is certain that it has enabled her to "ripen" as she has ripened—that she has had "something big and intense that changes you when you really come

[13] Lawrence, *Sons and Lovers*, p. 372.

together with somebody else. It almost seems to fertilize your soul."[14]

Paul, clearly, is describing his mother's "baptism of fire in passion." He himself must undergo such a baptism before he can come into being. And a good part of the novel is concerned with Paul's adolescent quest for satisfaction, a quest that, as the novel renders it, succeeds in sweeping him into the passional tide of life and creates the possibility, however qualified, for him to realize the "quickness" of his creative self.

This initiation is in two stages. The first, with Miriam, is negative. Miriam cannot follow him into the darkness of the "unknown" and hence he feels nullified, quiescent, death-like after he has had sexual intercourse with her. Yet, even in this negative state, a new mode of being is revealed to him: "Now, life seemed a shadow, day a white shadow; night, and death, and stillness, and inaction, this seemed like *being*. To be alive, to be urgent and insistent—that was *not-to-be*. The highest of all was to melt out into the darkness and sway there, identified with the great Being."[15]

Later, with Clara, who gives herself to him without restraint, his experience of the "great Being" is larger, richer, and more concrete. Urgent in his need, he loses all sense of the particular woman: "Clara was not there for him, only a woman, warm, something he loved, and almost worshiped, there in the dark."[16] The woman accepts his impersonality, however; she is carried along by "the naked hunger and inevitability of his loving her, something strong and blind and ruthless in its primitiveness. . . ."[17] His experience of her is a submission for him as well. His passing-beyond-himself is absolute, so that, himself a seeming blank, he is able to experience both her and the reality that lies behind her and is mediated through her: the reality of the cosmic life.

[14] *Ibid.*, p. 373.   [15] *Ibid.*, p. 337.   [16] *Ibid.*, p. 414.
[17] *Ibid.*

All the while the peewits were screaming in the field. When he came to, he wondered what was near his eyes, curving and strong with life in the dark, and what voice it was speaking. Then he realized it was the grass, and the peewit was calling. The warmth was Clara's breathing heaving. He lifted his head, and looked into her eyes. They were dark and shining and strange, life will at the source staring into his life, . . . that breathed with his in the darkness through this hour. It was all so much bigger than themselves that he was hushed. They had met, and included in their meeting the thrust of the manifold grass-stems, the cry of the peewit, the wheel of the stars.[18]

Something in Lawrence's love scenes reminds us of the most garish of *True Romances:* the surge and slush of feeling, the cosmic interpenetrations, the ennoblement of commonplace emotion with the language of religious transcendence, and so forth. Yet, quite obviously, the love scenes cannot be isolated from the pattern of the works in which they occur, and within this pattern, their excesses take on meaning as evocations of a process of growth and relationship. Thus, the moment just cited represents, not a transient moment in the experience of the lovers, but a validation of being which they bear with them as part of the sacrament of their souls and which marks the consecration of what is experienced as a permanent and final bond to nature and to life:

It was for each of them an initiation and a satisfaction. To know their own nothingness, to know the tremendous living flood which carried them always, gave them rest within themselves. If so great a magnificent power could overwhelm them, identify them altogether with itself, so that they knew they were only grains in the tremendous heave that lifted every grass blade its little height, and every tree, and living thing, then why fret about themselves? They could let themselves be carried by life, and they felt a sort of peace each in the other. There was a verification which they had had together. Nothing could nullify it, nothing could take it away; it was almost their belief in life.[19]

[18] *Ibid.,* pp. 414–15.   [19] *Ibid.,* p. 415.

Part of the unique imaginative achievement of *Sons and Lovers* lies in the projection through passages like these of the reciprocal relationship between the ultimate being of such individuals as Paul and Clara and the life that moves in the peewit, the grass-stems, and the stars. Paul's validated being puts him in touch with the living universe; its life not only touches his but is also fulfilled in his life and in his apprehension of the life they share in common. Journeying into the unknown within himself, he discovers the universe and becomes aware of his sacramental unity with it—a unity, or community, out of relation to which his essential individuality can develop.

The sacramental sense of the unity of life plays its part in Paul's fulfillment, and hence it is necessary that Lawrence project within the scene of the novel's action some sense of the reality of the life, or of the divinity, that pervades nature. This Lawrence does by projecting what in the Hardy "Study" he had called a "background, vivid and vital, where the instinctive life heaves up," a background that evokes a sense of the power that governs the fate of the individuals. Lawrence casts a spell of coruscating light and shimmering darkness over his landscapes, infusing the novels with a visionary magic which is the characteristic quality of his mature work.

I do not mean to suggest that a mere "baptism of fire in passion" is the sole condition for an individual's "coming into Being." Quite the contrary: the novel's total impact in part contradicts Paul's assessment of his mother's vitality; we often feel her to be cramped and moralistic, a negative force, and especially in relation to her husband. And Paul's "validation" with Clara does not free him from the death-hold his mother has upon him. That can only be achieved through a series of deliberate acts: through the literal (but also symbolic) killing-off of his mother, and his awareness—at the very end—that he must reject the lure of the great darkness which his mother inhabits. That darkness is death and is directly opposed to the lights of the town, toward which he *chooses* to move—"quickly."

Yet the suggestion of the novel clearly is that Paul's capacity to make such choices is almost magically derived from an inward exploration and discovery. The context of such exploration is not the daylight world of men, but the darkness of the minepits and the chiaroscuro of sunset and darkness. Ultimately, the glowing embers in the trunk of the pine trees that Paul draws at one point in the novel are a kind of metaphor for the luminosity of his own radical being. Paul speaks of embers rather than outline as the essence of the thing he depicts and articulates his will to capture the protoplasmic stuff of life in the trunk of the pine. It is out of such protoplasmic "stuff," evoked by the entire movement of the novel, that Paul's choices are felt to spring.

C. The Rainbow
and Women in Love

What is true of *Sons and Lovers* is still more true of *The Rainbow* and of *Women in Love*. Both novels depend for their effect on a poetically realized vision of the living universe as the matrix of being for men, and both depict the process which individuals must undergo if they are to experience anything resembling the primordial harmony with life which is the condition for creation and fulfillment. Both novels complicate the problem beyond anything that is suggested by *Sons and Lovers*, yet an underlying sense of life in nature unifies the three works.

The Rainbow opens with a vision of an almost complete harmony between man and nature and with an image of a "natural" life that is lived in the autonomous rhythm of nature. The farmers at Cossethay live in a state of "blood" unity with nature; they have not fallen out of harmony with pulsating nature. Trapped in the density of what Lawrence was later to celebrate as blood-consciousness, the farmers of Cossethay experience life in terms of a primordial unity with the rhythms of life in the cosmos.

The vision is impressively rendered:

They felt the rush of the sap in spring, they knew the wave which cannot halt, but every year throws forward the seed to begetting, and, falling back, leaves the young-born on the earth. They knew the intercourse between heaven and earth, sunshine drawn into the breast and bowels. . . . Their life and interrelations were such; feeling the pulse and body of the soil, that opened to their furrow for the grain, and became smooth and supple after their ploughing. . . . The young corn waved and was silken, and the lustre slid along the limbs of the men who saw it. They took the udder of the cows, the cows yielded milk and pulse against the hands of the men, the pulse of the blood of the teats of the cows beat into the pulse of the hands of the men.[20]

The women are different; they want something more. But the men are satisfied with the heave and surge of life as it pulses in furrow and teat: "So much warmth and generating and pain and death did they know in their blood, earth and sky and beast and green plants, so much exchange and interchange they had with these, that they lived full and surcharged, their senses full fed, their faces always turned to the heat of the blood, staring into the sun, dazed with looking towards the source of generation, unable to turn round."[21]

Lawrence seems to be writing a paean to the blood-unity of the farmer. Yet the peasant harmony with nature and blood is not conceived as a final good. It represents a passive enwombing in the matrix of nature and precludes realization of the individual self. In a sense, the farmers at Cossethay relate to

[20] D. H. Lawrence, *The Rainbow* (New York: Modern Library, n.d.), p. 2.
[21] *Ibid.*, p. 3.

the rhythms and urgencies of nature much as the adolescent
Paul had related to his mother. Just as Paul must break out of
his symbiotic relationship with the mother who is the source
of his being and come to experience his independent erotic
relation to self and world, so the people of Cossethay are
forced to evolve toward a "finer life" which the women see in
the ministers of the church and in the gentry who visit the
church. They must achieve a more highly individuated, self-
conscious personal existence through a more complicated intellectual and social awareness than any they had previously
known. It is the paradox of their existence—as it is, in Lawrence's view, the paradox of all life in history—that such
awareness, although fulfilling the purposes of nature as it
presses toward individuation, nonetheless threatens to cut
man off from his own nature and from the life of objective
nature.

The problem is posed in *The Rainbow*, but the rudiments
of an answer are to be found only in Lawrence's next novel,
Women in Love. There Lawrence insists on the presence of
life in the natural world and in the natural self as conceived in
the early poems and in *Sons and Lovers*. That life is merely
harder to reach and more given to perverse forms of expression. The hideous trappings of the barbaric civilization which
prevails at Beldover and the brittle and effete appurtenances
of the deadened past that survives at Breadalby are superimposed on the vital world of nature. Similarly, the barbarism of
values and attitudes that typify relationships within that
world shuts out the vital possibilities of the vital, organic self.
Yet the living universe is *there*, behind what Lawrence refers
to as the "painted flats" of civilization that shut out the great
heavens and the teeming earth; so is the integral self, beneath
the fixed ideas and roles of the social world. The problem is,
again, how to "contact" and to tap that life productively and
to realize one's own intrinsic wealth of being.

The way remains essentially the way of the senses, of love
or sexuality, but the way is complicated in a manner that is
unimaginable in the "Study." Each generation of lovers in
The Rainbow achieves a partial breakthrough. What complicates the matter is that, just as Gertrude's experience of marriage could not redeem her from the limitations of her personal history and culture, so sexuality cannot free the
characters in *The Rainbow* from the circumstances of their
selves and societies. Even their sexuality is colored by those
circumstances. Though Paul's prospects for fulfillment may
be positive owing to his validated selfhood, we do not see it
realized. Lawrence merely concludes the novel on a note of
possibility. In *The Rainbow* we follow each of several generations far beyond the point of initial breakthrough. Each time
some obstacle is reached. The selves in question are unable to
yield themselves utterly to the innocent self-consciousness and
self-containment demanded by modern sexuality.

All the vital characters experience the mysterious life of the
cosmos and the life that they share with it. This is evident, for
example, in the great moonlit sheaf-stacking scene in *The
Rainbow*, or in the scene in *Women in Love* where Birkin,
half-dead, abandons himself to contact with primroses and
fir-shrubs, to the sheer satisfaction of sensing the "coolness
and subtlety of vegetation traveling into his blood." The
moonlight and the cornfield in the sheaf-stacking scene are
symbolic of elements in each of the participants, and of
elements of their relationship with each other. Yet there is a
pervasive sense of their having a life of their own. Indeed,
even the "dead" and devitalized characters in these novels
experience the splendor and awe of life beyond themselves.
Both contain scenes of communion-in-violence in which, mur-
derously struggling, characters feel an affinity with the greater
life.[22]

[22] I am thinking of Hermione, Gerald, and Gudrun in *Women in
Love,* and of Ursula and Skrebensky in *The Rainbow.*

The momentary violence of abandonment to experience is not enough to provide sustained fulfillment or satisfaction, however. It is merely the condition within which fulfillment is possible. In the conditions of conflict and opposition rendered in *Women in Love*, it is not possible to fulfill oneself by being "natural"—that is, by succumbing to impulse. Even though spontaneity is preached by Birkin, it becomes clear that simple spontaneity is impossible even for Birkin himself. Birkin experiences the wonder and awe of nature; he acknowledges the Creative Mystery. But this mystery is not simply the subjective experience of having the greenness of vegetation running in one's veins, or of allowing one's consciousness to pass down the path of the senses into demonic darkness where one is part of the mystery. It is something far more complex, mediated through consciousness and representing nearly total self-awareness in a mode different from ordinary civilized consciousness. It is, ultimately, the sensation of "having one's pulse beat from the heart of the mystery"—a mystery that is in nature but is achieved through a yoga-like discipline of consciousness in sensuality itself.

D. The Evolving Concept of "Nature" in *Sons and Lovers*,
  The Rainbow, and *Women in Love*

Nature has, in other words, been identified with a metaphysical entity to which the unconscious self is related in direct experience, but which also seems to dictate values and attitudes through the medium of consciousness. In effect, there is a progression in the three novels. We move from Paul's sense of the cosmos as the great "all" in which he is engulfed in the tide of passion, to the Cossethay farmers' sense of nature as the blood-rhythm. From this, the "inevitable" pattern of peasant life as lived in the cycle of the vegetative year, we move to the glimpse of a more expansive "life" beyond the threshold and arch of each of the Brangwens' experience, and then to Birkin's sense of a metaphysical entity

—the Creative Mystery. The mystery dwells "out there" in the evening, among the trees, but it also works through man to produce "creative surprises" and functions in a way that is akin to the Bergsonian Life Force, so that an elaborate ritual of consciousness must be cultivated if one is to make contact with it.

In all three cases, the "great mystery" is said to reside in nature. Yet the implications of that life, and even its qualities, differ for each of the individuals who comes into contact with it. Paul Morel experiences wonder at the "cry of the peewit, the wheel of the stars"; he also experiences mixed terror and exhilaration at his own insignificance in the surging life of the world. The farmers at Cossethay experience neither wonder nor exhilaration. They experience only immediate satisfaction and a sluggish, turgid pleasure. But their children and grand-children, when they break through to a vision of life and an intuition of the greater life of nature, know satisfaction. They are like Paul in that they feel validated. They differ from Paul in that their conjugal satisfactions give them a sense of fulfill-ment and of a place in a human world that is final, natural, and valid. At the same time, they are uncertain and insecure about themselves and about the meaning of their achieve-ment and vision; in a sense, their very susceptibility to their vision reflects a certain incompleteness, a lack of wholeness: their vision gives them no certainty within their actual lives. Even Tom Brangwen, the oldest and most tradition-bound of the characters in the novel, suffers from a sense of not having lived his own life—of not having undergone his own experi-ence fully.

Birkin, on the other hand, achieves a measure of certainty. He learns, however, that the only final certainty is certainty as to the permanence of risk. There is no retreat from the inces-sant challenge of a nature intent on change and surprise, a nature that becomes the medium of death the moment one tries to arrest it. Birkin has a vision of peace and harmony still greater and more intense than Paul's. He too knows the greenness of vegetation in his veins; like Wordsworth, he conceives of the possibility of rendering himself utterly passive to experience. But the complement to this vision is an awareness of violence and change Nature is dual in its aspect, just as man's nature and his needs are dual.

In this we have the second innovation of *Women in Love* and a further complication of nature. Man must not only struggle toward a harmonic relationship with something not directly evident in the pattern of his spontaneous impulses, he must also struggle toward a nature that contains violence, danger, and death. One might say that implicit in Paul's experience and that of the farmers at Cossethay—even of Will and Anna Brangwen— is a bucolic vision of peace and harmony. Nature is not a wild heath where the violent life heaves up at the source; it is, rather, a placid farmland, a place of pastoral repose, where men need only reach down toward their best impulses to do their duty by life. In the depiction of Ursula Brangwen's adolescence, however, the "unknown," associated with nature, is a place of wildness and danger. It is separate from the "merely" human world, related to it as Hardy's heath is to the social encampment.

In his rendering of Ursula's experience, Lawrence affirms the image of wild nature which he had found in Hardy and renders it in his own terms. Civilized man, trammeled by his stonily civilized consciousness, looks out of the encampment into the "greater life" of the world and of his deeper consciousness—a wild, rich world, utterly at odds with the domesticated sensibility of supposedly rational man. In the imagery of Ursula's reflections, at the end of *The Rainbow*: "That which she was, positively, was dark and unrevealed, . . . it was like a seed buried in dry ash. This world in which she lived was like a circle lighted by a lamp. This lighted area, lit up by

man's completest consciousness, she thought was all the
world: that here all was disclosed forever. Yet all the time,
within the darkness she had been aware of points of light,
like the eyes of wild beasts, gleaming, penetrating, vanish-
ing. . . ."[23]

Ursula's intuition that nature is full of wild beasts was to
become central to Lawrence's later work. The development of
this idea is interesting. Already in *The White Peacock* Lawrence had stressed, crudely and in a manner directly imitative
of Hardy, the wildness, cruelty, and inhumanity of nature.[24]
This soon gives way to a more pacific view of nature—the
view of *Sons and Lovers,* where death and violence are seen as
an integral part of life, but where nature nonetheless itself
seems essentially benign and accommodating. The same vision pervades the first two-thirds of *The Rainbow.* Only with
Ursula do we begin to perceive nature as a place where wild
beasts lurk. Her experience is borne out by the experience of
characters in the later work. Birkin, in whom the theme is
pursued, sees in human nature the possibility of cruelty, disintegration, and destructiveness; he feels that man has the alternatives of creation and destruction, of civilization and barbarism, and that these alternatives are part of his nature.

In Birkin's case, there is no scene to embody the significance of death and destruction. Even the great white waste
of ice and snow which engulfs Gerald at the end of the novel
is mainly a setting that is symbolically appropriate to the
events that take place "in" it, rather than a synecdochical representation of nature itself, or a vehicle for its essential energy.
The negative conception of nature in *Women in Love* is
enunciated largely at a metaphysical, analytical level: it is the

[23] P. 413.

[24] See, for example, the scene in which Lawrence renders Annable's
funeral, or the reflections that follow upon the finding of a dead cat
in a trap. See D. H. Lawrence, *The White Peacock* (London: William
Heinemann Ltd., 1955), pp. 156ff. and 76.

"Creative Mystery," distant and indifferent, and it is represented in the play of possibilities in man. In later work, and especially in the work of the New Mexico phase, however, a wild, inhuman scene comes to symbolize a violence that is not only in man but in nature also. St. Mawr, the landscape surrounding Lou Carrington's ranch, the volcanic underworld of *The Plumed Serpent*, the mountain heights of "The Woman Who Rode Away," the terrain into which "The Princess" and Romero ride, all represent the quality of nature itself, and an aspect—perhaps the central aspect—of the Creative Mystery.

These scenes and animals are, to be sure, symbolic of something in man; but they are also an expression of some essential, ultimate quality in nature—of a quality that man naturally shares with nature. If we seek to interpret them, we find they are radically ambiguous. They seem at times to be a nightmarish dream scene on which man enacts the compulsions of his repressed and resentful passions; as part of the dream they represent an aspect of the dreamer and of the dreamer's nature. It seems as though Lawrence sought out the scenery of New and Old Mexico because it afforded suitable images for the kinds of feelings and actions which he wished to represent at that time in his life. Yet there is always the suggestion that the nature in question is objectively alive and cruel, that St. Mawr, the stallion, or Las Chivas, the ranch outside Taos, literally embodies some spirit of place, whose correlative is the violence in man. We have, in other words, another version of the Hardy heath, where "life springs up at the source"; the instinctive life.

And yet, even the objective life of nature has its ambiguous side, an ambiguity it shares with the demonic element in the life of the feelings. St. Mawr is not intrinsically destructive; he merely embodies the fierce energy of spontaneous life. The energy of nature is nonhuman—that is, nonmoral. To man, huddled in the encampment, within the stone walls designed to keep out the vital energies of life, those energies *look* violent, destructive, and evil; Ursula's wild beasts, in the passage cited from *The Rainbow*, are like Blake's devils in *The Marriage of Heaven and Hell*: their beastliness lies only in the way they are regarded by fear-ridden man. The hell man creates in his moral imagination is merely the experience of those energies which, for the man who entertains them without restraint, is eternal delight—what the religious call "heaven." The dangerousness of life is the dangerousness of energy, of the passions; this dangerousness, for Lawrence as for Blake, cannot be eliminated or tamed without creating a "poison tree" of repression and hate. It must be lived through on the way to heaven.

To the negativity and destructiveness of nature itself I shall return in a later chapter. What I wish to observe here is the fact that positive or negative, creative or destructive, the "greater world" of nature is identified with the "greater world of life," and that both are associated with the greater life of the passional self. The greater world of nature is, moreover, more and more openly identified with divinity. As Elizabeth Hess has observed, nature undergoes an apotheosis in *Kangaroo* and *The Plumed Serpent*, so that Lawrence no longer speaks in elaborate metaphysical and theological metaphors. He treats nature as "God," as a potentially demonic deity to which man must achieve some immediate, satisfactory relationship, lest he die either of inanition or of the violent passions he represses.[25]

By the time such a conception of nature emerges, however, Lawrence is no longer concerned exclusively with the individual and the imperious demands of his experience, nor with sexuality as the medium through which man experiences the deific quality of nature. The community moves to the center of interest, offering a medium through which man manages to

[25] Hess, *Die Naturbetrachtung*, pp. 101 and 106.

live "breast to breast with the cosmos." In *The Plumed Serpent*, the novel in which such notions are most fully explored, the landscapes of the novel—i.e., the world of nature—no longer play the part that they had played in the earlier work. Unless we read the novel as a Jungian allegory of Kate Forrester's individuation, which seems to me a wrong approach, the landscapes represent something alien and impersonal—something related to a sort of collective or communal unconscious, rather than to the highly differentiated potentialities of the individuals we meet in the earlier novels.

Section II

The Lawrencean "Systems"

Lawrence's sense of the interfusion of self and nature is in part enunciated in the novels through the kind of "landscape painting" I have described. Lawrence juxtaposes —at times he even telescopes- –intense representations of human experience with coruscating evocations of concomitant, mana-like energy felt to pervade the cosmos. The peculiar rhythmic and repetitive qualities of Lawrence's prose make such telescoping possible. So does his employment of a transpersonal idiom and imagery to render the preconscious levels of recognition and response that are involved.[26]

Part of the effect, however, hinges on the evocative use, in the fiction, of the imagery and terms of the metaphysics that were developed at various times in Lawrence's career. It would seem that his intuition of the "greater life of the cosmos," and of its affinities in the affective life of man, found expression both in the intuitive rendering of experience in the

[26] Mark Spilka touches on this effect in his introduction to *The Love Ethic of D. H. Lawrence*. A telling analysis of the evocative quality of Lawrence's rendering of consciousness is to be found in H. M. Daleski, *The Forked Flame* (Evanston: Northwestern University Press, 1965), pp. 77–79.

novels, and in the quasi-philosophic formulations of his discursive writings. The latter, which hover in the no-man's-land between metaphysics and incantation, strive for a precision of positive statement that the novels tend to avoid. They represent a fanciful embroidery on this theme, sometimes frankly playful and frivolous, sometimes solemn and urgently hortatory, presented in a tone that suggests a wish to hypnotize us out of thought.

It is hard to imagine that Lawrence took any of the systems in question so seriously as to believe them to be literally true. I suspect that they served him as a way of enunciating and elaborating ideas that were central to his thought, but they had no clear terms of reference in commonplace experience. At the same time, they served him in the polemical game that he played with his antagonists, a game in which his rage was often real, even when he could hardly have meant his arguments to be taken seriously.

The value of the arguments, in fact, lies in their structure as poetic articulations of the governing ideas of his work. They are, in a sense, homemade myths, private scientific systems, and chewing-gum-and-wire structures of faith concocted in lieu of a "given" system to which he could adhere. They are, we might say, Lawrence's whimsical alternatives to the Aquinian philosophy in Dante's work or the Epicurean in Lucretius'. And they are whimsical not because the truths they enunciate are finally untrue but because they are so far removed from the common world of scientific discourse that he must propose them as the gamesome hypotheses of a pugnacious, provocative clown.[27]

[27] William York Tindall, in D. H. *Lawrence and Susan His Cow*, holds that Lawrence's speculations reflected a quest for religious certainty and that he was enunciating a private religion in his writings. [See William York Tindall, D. H. *Lawrence and Susan His Cow* (New York: Columbia University Press, 1939), especially Chapter I.] Tindall does not take into account the tone of delighted provocativeness

The more recondite constructs have in common not only the basic assumption about the affinity of self and world, but also the tendency to conceive of the contact between self and world in terms of magical, mystical, and parascientific categories. Specifically, Lawrence imagines the relationship between the self and the world in terms of erotic affinity, tidal interplay, electrical circuits, magnetic exchange, and homological correspondence. In virtually all the systems, he employs the almost purely verbal device of using the same categories to deal with nature and the self. The deific quality of both nature and self is associated with their dynamic movement. In each case, the play of elements in the one reality—whether of self or of nature—is congruous with the play of elements in the other. In each case, identical terms are used to describe the elements at play in both.

A. The Shared Sexuality of Man and Nature

In the "Study" Lawrence defines the inner processes of the self in erotic terms and employs the same categories to characterize the objective world. He distinguishes between the integral, or true self, which is the unconscious self, and the social self. Within the integral, unconscious self, he distinguishes two basic modes, a masculine one and a feminine one. He is not completely consistent in his exposition of these matters, but his view develops more or less in the following way. The radical "nuclear" self is an entity that emerges out of the struggle between the polarized elements that make up the self. The self is the configuration that arises from moment to

in works like *Studies in Classic American Literature* and *Fantasia of the Unconscious*. It seems to me that Lawrence was struggling to enunciate a truth that he knew he would never find and that he was fully aware of his limitations in enunciating it. All of this does not make him any the less a crackpot, as some of the "systems" I shall outline in this section should indicate.

moment in the balance and reconciliation of the two radical elements. This reconciliation is, in its constant qualities, the self, and it is also "being"—the final reality. The elements which are at play within (and "before") the self are conceived along the lines of the dualism of flesh and spirit, as these categories are embodied in sexual terms.

In Lawrence's scheme, flesh and spirit do not represent dichotomous opposites, nor do they represent the sort of antagonism into which they tend to fall in Christianity. The Christian view, following the Platonic, tends to hold that the spirit is in principle separate from the flesh, that it descends into it from without, and that it must struggle to gain ascendancy over its sin-disposed, spirit-resisting antagonist. For Lawrence, on the other hand, flesh and spirit are aspects of the same substance which resides in the flesh, but which is ultimately identical with "life" itself. Both terms, moreover, represent not so much elements or entities as tendencies that are manifest in the radical, quasi-somatic consciousness which is the basis of all life. From this point of view, the material element which we term the flesh is not an organization of matter so much as a manifestation of life; as a result it is endowed with the latent will and consciousness which are properties of life itself and, therefore, of all living things.

This is not by any means the sole basis of the kinship of self and cosmos, however. The self, in its absolute existence, not only touches on the absolute (to be exact, the "relative absolute") of life, in nature, but in the course of doing so it re-enacts the process whereby life itself produces further life, and whereby nature itself subsists. The self is never a final and complete thing, even in its absolute form. Its very being is the outcome of becoming and a manifestation of becoming. It is the outcome of a process, though never the end of a process, since process is conceived as having no temporal end.

In this, it is like life itself, which is conceived as a Heraclitean flux wherein opposites coexist in external conflict. Movement, conflict, antiphonal balance are the principle of life as well as of self. Since all things in the vital universe are aspects and manifestations of life and of the life will, all things are necessarily caught up in the restless play of energy which is the cosmos.

The cosmos, to employ the Bergsonian distinction,[28] is not a fixed, spatial structure of relationships but a fluid, temporal play of energies which, at their most rigid and compulsive— the laws of nature—represent nothing but the "fixed habits" in the body of life.[29] As Lawrence writes in a passage already cited, life is not a fixed, finished system. Nature is not made, but always in the process of making other things, and of being itself made only in the process of making them.

The parallel between cosmic life and psychic life is strengthened by the fact that life is made up of the very principles which constitute the self. The cosmos itself is constructed along principles directly analogous to those which govern the self, the principles of masculinity and femininity. In the course of their struggle for dominance within the individual psyche, these principles give rise to the spontaneous uniqueness of the self in its disparate epiphanal moments. Sexuality pervades the universe and engenders everything that exists: "Why do we consider the male stream and the female stream as being only in the flesh? It is something other than physical. The physical, what we call in its narrowest meaning, the sex, is only a definite indication of the great male and female duality and unity. It is that part which is settled into an almost mechanized system of detaining some of the life which otherwise sweeps on and is lost in the full adventure."[30] Lawrence goes on to insist: "There is female apart from

[28] I return to this point later in this chapter, pp. 54ff.
[29] Lawrence, *Fantasia of the Unconscious*, p. 182.
[30] Lawrence, "Study of Thomas Hardy," *Phoenix*, p. 443.

Woman, as we know, and male apart from Man. There is male and female in my poppy plant, and this is neither man nor woman. It is part of the great twin river, eternally each branch resistant to the other, eternally running each to meet the other."[31]

To make such a formulation Lawrence substantially extended the range of significations attached to his terms. The female, as he defines her in this context, is the principle of things that enclose and contain; the male is that which strives to break out of containment. "The male exists in doing, the female in being. The male lives in the satisfaction of some purpose achieved, the female in the satisfaction of some purpose contained."[32]

Whereas the female comes into possession of things by generating them and then by refusing to release them, the male comes into possession by appropriation and direct mastery. The male must direct his energies at things and in a sense transform them by mixing his will or his energy with them. In a manner of speaking, he volatilizes the given elements of the world by infusing his protean energy into them. The essential quality of the two principles is conveyed in an elaborate metaphor for the relation between men and women (not, directly, masculinity and femininity) in the sex act.

As in my flower, the pistil, female, is the centre and swivel, the stamens, male, are close-clasping the hub, and the blossom is the great motion outwards into the unknown, so in a man's life, the female is the swivel and centre on which he turns closely, producing his movement. . . . The supreme effort each man makes, for himself, is the effort to clasp as a hub the woman who shall be the axle, compelling him to true motion, without aberration. . . . And the vital desire of every woman is that she shall be clasped as axle to the hub of her man, that his motion shall portray her

[31] *Ibid.*   [32] *Ibid.*, p. 481.

motionlessness, convey her static being into movement, complete and radiating out into infinity. . . .[33]

Woman is the principle of stability: "Every man seeks in woman for what is stable, eternal."[34] Man is the principle of motion. In this sense, if pressed to the most abstract definition, the masculine principle may be formulated as the dynamic principle—the principle of energy, movement, and change, or as the will-to-power over things and beings. The feminine principle, on the other hand, may be formulated as the static principle of containment; personified, "she" is the Will-to-Inertia. Lawrence enunciates this directly, employing just this terminology: "Life consists in the dual form of the Will-to-Motion and the Will-to-Inertia, and everything we see and know and are is the resultant of these two Wills."[35] And, again:"The dual Will we call the Will-to-Motion and the Will-to Inertia. These cause the whole of life, from the ebb and flow of a wave, to the stable equilibrium of the whole universe, from birth and being and knowledge to death and decay and forgetfulness. And the Will-to-Motion we call the male will or spirit, and the Will-to-Inertia the female."[36]

The imagery in question not only suggests a homological correspondence between psyche, cosmos, and civilization. It also helps to project a vision of the universe as a "creature" in perpetual motion and conflict and to convey Lawrence's sense of the fluidity and the almost "protoplasmic" vitality of the natural world. Its protoplasmic vitality is manifest despite the appearance of solidity and static depth. The dead world of

[33] *Ibid.*, p. 444. If one were to read the implicit imagery of this passage in the context of, say, Gerald Crich's experience of Gudrun or, more explicitly, Mellors' experience of Bertha Coutts, the image of the phallic female that emerges would bear significantly on much of Lawrence's fiction and on his cosmic speculations as well. Obviously, this genetic aspect of the problem does not concern me here.
[34] *Ibid.*, p. 445.   [35] *Ibid.*, p. 447.   [36] *Ibid.*, p. 448.

things and of spatial immobility is "there." Yet we experience
it as compounded of the contending forces which "make" it,
and we perceive that it reveals itself to us as a frozen current
which is prepared to thaw into dramatic life at any moment,
or as a compound which may under our very eyes resolve itself
back into its constituent elements. The universe, like the self,
as rendered in the novels and as formulated in the treatises, is
made up of the push-and-pull of masculinity and femininity,
revealed in a Van-Gogh-like tendency to swirl into the stress
of energic movement which underlies the scene.

Indeed, the aesthetic quality of the novels reflects the sense
of the cosmic dynamism which is at the center of Lawrence's
vision of nature. The novels confirm in realized art the qualities that have been enunciated, but only sketchily, in the
"theoretical" works, and especially in the Hardy "Study."
However, there is more than aesthetic evidence of his notion
that the universe is governed by contending principles and
reproduces in its modes of being and of coming-into-being the
inward dialectic of the self.

This is most explicit in "The Crown" essays, where incanta-
tory effect and substantive statement combine to convey the
volatility of the natural world and the interrelatedness of
subjective experience in the self and the principles that constitute the objective world. Reality is rendered in the essays in
the figure of an ocean, whose tides flow in from opposite
"eternities": the eternity of the beginning, which is of the
flesh, and the eternity of the end, which is of the spirit. The
first is darkness, the second light; the first power, the second
love; the first "lion," and the second "unicorn." The tides of
the ocean seem to flow in a circular round, contained within
the living flesh. They are reached, in man, by plumbing the
impulses of the living flesh. Even spirit, as in the Hardy
"Study," is in and of the flesh. The tides within the circumfer-
ence of the circular reality of beginning and end come from
rival eternities, which, because they are two and because they

contend, are relative eternities. The Absolute (itself a relative absolute, as in the "Study") is formed at the clashing of the rival eternities.

The self itself is to be grasped as a rainbow that spans the two oceans, or as the foam that spumes at the clashing of the waves where the two oceans meet. Somewhat less felicitously, the self is the iris or the rose that is brought into being at the point where the two oceans meet, one flowing from a beginning, which is the beginning of all things and not of the self alone, and one from an end, which is the end of all things and not of the self alone. The iris and the rose of "The Crown" essays are obviously related to the rose and the poppy of the Hardy "Study": images of abundant, erotic beauty, flamboyant, fragile, and transient—a beauty that rashly and gratuitously flings itself into oblivion.

Within this scheme, the appearance of solidity and stability is illusory; so is the effort to achieve it. The term "nature" itself, in its denotation of "the fixed and permanent," becomes a negative category, as it was again to become in Lawrence's polemics against modern science. "This I, which I am, has no being in timelessness," Lawrence writes. "In my consummation, when that which came from the Beginning and that which came from the End are transfused into oneness, then I come into being, I have existence. Till then *I am only a part of nature*, I am not. But as part of nature, as part of the flux, I have my instrumental identity, my inferior I, myself-conscious [*sic*] ego. . . . Most men are just *transitory natural phenomena*. . . ."[37]

B. The Shared Divinity of Man
and the Cosmos

Given Lawrence's celebration of nature, it is rather striking that he should write that one is "*only* a part of nature" and that "most men are *just* transitory natural phenomena" (ital-

---

[37] Lawrence, *Reflections on the Death of a Porcupine*, pp. 37–39. Italics mine.

ics mine). It would seem that nature, heretofore the source of all good, becomes evil, or at least neutral, "the *mere* endurance of matter within the Flux." The implication is that there is another realm where life and individuality are consummated and that this is a realm of both permanence and transcendence, conditions that horrify Lawrence in their ordinary signification.

Such a negation of nature seems paradoxical in a naturalist thinker. Yet Lawrence's position is not quite so self-contradictory as it may seem.[38] Nature remains, here as elsewhere, a positive value for Lawrence. Even in his pejorative assertions there is an implicit distinction between creative nature and created nature, between "life" and the "time-space continuum" of the natural scientists. Bergson's formulations about science are illuminating here. The nature apprehended by science is essentially static and spatial. Within it time is a lifeless "endurance" of the graph-paper patterns reproduced in static lifeless sameness from identical moment to identical moment. Thus, in Bergson's understanding of physics, the natural world is predictable, since it has no will and never changes.

Bergson insists that all living things have the qualities of change and purpose, and are in this way distinguished from the world of the physical scientist. "Even in the humblest manifestation of life . . . [scientists] discover traces of effective psychological activity," of the purposive, creative, changing qualities that permit something more than mere self-perpetuation in a will-less flux of identical moments.[39]

In the construct under discussion, Lawrence extends the Bergsonian notion of the physical world. He sees it as a

[38] Graham Hough, *The Dark Sun* (New York: Viking, 1956), p. 223.

[39] Henri Bergson, *Creative Evolution*, trans. Arthur Mitchell (New York: The Modern Library, n.d.), p. 41.

possibility in human life. Vital things seem to have the choice between living and not living; they can belong to the static scheme of created nature or to the dynamic scheme of creative nature. When they belong to the first they belong to a world of meaningless transience, which is essentially static and which admits no form of transcendence. When they belong to the other, they remain within the flux of time, but they find within it a mode of timelessness which is both of and in nature, yet beyond nature. Without losing their individuality or temporal concreteness, they participate in a realm —"mode" might be a better term here—of individual essences which have achieved the flower of their being. "Being" is in this instance a quality that is both in time and beyond time—in a sense, the temporal absolutized, and a being that is absolute becoming. Such "being" is the equivalent of the creative Lawrencean deity, a deity whose transcendence is immanent, i.e., inheres in the sense world.

The immanent transcendence of the Lawrencean deity (one should perhaps say his godlike power) is treated explicitly, if not systematically, in the essays that were published with "The Crown" essays when they appeared in 1925 in a volume entitled *Reflections on the Death of a Porcupine*, and that Lawrence clearly regarded as doctrinally as well as imaginatively consistent with "The Crown" essays, which were written in 1915. In the title essay of that collection, Lawrence schematizes his paradoxical theses about time, space, nature, and life:

1. Any creature that attains to its own fullness of being, its own *living* self, becomes unique, a nonpareil. It has its place in the fourth dimension, the heaven of existence, and there it is perfect, it is beyond comparison.
2. At the same time, every creature lives in time and space. And in time and space it exists relatively to all other existence. . . .[40]

[40] Lawrence, *Reflections on the Death of a Porcupine*, p. 210.

There are, then, two realms: a phenomenal world, of time and space, and a noumenal one, the "God-realm" that exists in another dimension. This other world is not outside the manifest one, however. It is within it—hence the term "fourth dimension," a dimension implicated in the other three. This "other," fourth-dimensional world "is *not* ideal, as Plato will have it . . . it is a transcendent form of existence, and as much material as existence is. Only the matter suddenly enters the fourth dimension."[41]

The fourth dimension, Lawrence says, is a dimension which "men once called heaven." Just as the "other" world, or "God-realm," is not apart from matter, it is also not apart from time. For timelessness, or "eternity," is not "life-everlasting"[42] but rather the "utter relation between the two eternities" out of which all things emerge: "heaven itself" is created from the "flux of time" and subsists within that flux.[43]

Just as the realm of "timelessness" is not apart from time and matter, it is also not before time. The deity or force that brought both realms into being is not apart from the temporal, spiritual-material flux of the world but rather is in it and, in a manner of speaking, during it.

Religion and philosophy both have the same dual purposes: to get at the beginning of things, and at the goal of things. They have both decided that the serpent has got his tail in his mouth, and that the end is one with the beginning.

It seems to me time someone gave that serpent of eternity another dummy to suck.

They've all decided that the beginning of all things is the life-stream itself, energy, ether, libido, not to mention the Sanskrit joys of Purusha, Pradhana, Kala.

Having postulated the serpent of the beginning, now see all the heroes from Moses and Plato to Bergson, wrestling with him might and main, to push his tail into his mouth.[44]

[41] *Ibid.*, p. 211.   [42] *Ibid.*, p. 89.   [43] *Ibid.*, p. 95.
[44] *Ibid.*, p. 127.

The truth as Lawrence perceives it is that there is no temporal beginning, no generation of the world from without, and no deity who stands outside the world generating it. "The old dragon of creation who fathered us all," he says in the tone of calculated impiety that marks many of the *Porcupine* essays, "didn't have an ideal in his head."

Just as God is in the fourth dimension so is the creativity that the Western tradition has identified with God. "Creation is a fourth dimension, and in it there are all sorts of things, gods and what not."[45] Again, in the essay "Reflections on the Death of a Porcupine," "The force which we call *vitality,* and which is the determining factor in the struggle for existence, is . . . derived also from the fourth dimension. That is to say, the ultimate source of all vitality is in that other dimension, or region, where the dandelion blooms, and which men have called heaven, and which now they call the fourth dimension. . . ."[46]

Although he occasionally mocks Bergson in the essays under discussion, it is in these essays that he employs the Bergsonian notions sketched earlier in this chapter. He sees the world of the natural scientist, which is the world of strict causality, as a spatialized world, and he insists that there must be "a goal in the *creative,* not the *spatial* universe" (Italics mine). Lawrence seems, moreover, to reject the Bergsonian Life Force because, like the will that governs the Schopenhauerian universe, it is *tangent* to the world and manipulates men and things for purposes beyond their own. God, or creativity, or life is *within* the fourth dimension, which is implicated at all times in the other three. At moments God is identified with that dimension, at times it is merely the consciousness to which it is revealed that is so identified: "But the god-quick" which is vitality or creativity "is the constant within the flux . . . [it] is neither temporal nor eternal, it is

45 *Ibid.,* p. 135.   46 *Ibid.,* p. 210.

truly timeless. And this perfect body was a revelation of the timeless God. . . . This revelation of God *is* God."[47] Again, later in the same essay, we hear that "We cannot know God. . . . We can only know the *revelation* of God in the physical world. And the revelation of God is God."[48]

If God *is* the revelation, if he comes into being rather than is, then he is creature rather than creator. Lawrence states this explicitly: God is "created every time a pure relationship, or a consummation out of twoness into oneness takes place."[49] Hence God is not purposive; rather, like the creative principle itself, He is random and unpredictable. Each living thing must achieve its immortality, or its being, and this depends on its ability to struggle into being: "I am not immortal till I have achieved immortality. . . . It is not easy to achieve immortality. . . . It means undaunted suffering and undaunted enjoyment, both."[50]

The world, as Lawrence wrote in his Introduction to *Fantasia of the Unconscious* (1921), is susceptible to the "rainbow change of ever-renewed creative civilizations."[51] Hence, it goes in all directions at once—and hence Lawrence's mockery of the idea of orderly, directed, progressive evolution. He writes in another connection:

> We live in a multiple universe. I am a chick that absolutely refuses to chirp inside the monistic egg. . . .
> When the cuckoo, the cow and the coffee-plant chipped the Mundane Egg, at various points, they stepped out, and immediately stepped off in different directions. Not different directions of space and time, but different directions in creation: within the fourth dimension.[52]

The fourth dimension is the dimension of vivid existents: of things that have "come into being." Anything that comes into

[47] *Ibid.*, p. 92.   [48] *Ibid.*, pp. 96–97.   [49] *Ibid.*, p. 94.
[50] *Ibid.*, p. 90.
[51] Lawrence, *Fantasia of the Unconscious*, p. 56.
[52] Lawrence, *Reflections on the Death of a Porcupine*, pp. 133–34.

being is to be found there. "Any man who achieves his own being will, like the dandelion or the butterfly, pass into that other dimension which we call the fourth and the old people called heaven."[53]

What comes into being, however, also passes out of being; the great sin, in fact, lies in the effort to "tie a knot in time" and to render the impermanent permanent. "Only perpetuation is a sin. The perfect relation is perfect. But it is therefore timeless. And we must not think to tie a knot in Time, and thus to make the consummation temporal or eternal. The consummation is timeless, and we belong to Time, in our process of living . . . We can no more *stay* in . . . heaven than the flower can stay on its stem "[54]

Things that simply exist, like dandelions and butterflies, cannot stay in existence through the will to survive. Neither can man's conscious efforts to preserve his being and the record of his being. The efforts of art and of historical writing, which commemorate man's aspirations and fulfillments, exist for a while, but they too pass out of existence. Even art, which "outlasts the brazen monuments of time," is worn down by time. And yet though "it passes away . . . it is not in any sense lost." "Our souls are established upon all the revelations, upon all the timeless achieved relationships, as the seed contains a convoluted memory of all the revelation in the plant it represents. The flower is the burning of God in the bush: the flame of the Holy Ghost."[55] The same is true of man, but in an even larger sense: "And a man, if he win to a sheer fusion in himself of all the manifold creation, a pure relation, a sheer gleam of oneness out of manyness, then this man is God created where before God was uncreate. He is the Holy Ghost in tissue of flame and flesh, whereas before the Holy Ghost was but Ghost. It is true of a man as it is true of a dandelion or of a tiger or of a dove."[56]

[53] *Ibid.*, p. 218.   [54] *Ibid.*, pp. 93–96.   [55] *Ibid.*, p. 94.
[56] *Ibid.*

Lawrence implies, again paradoxically, the interrelatedness of the entire living cosmos. In the Hardy "Study" he had written that the universe depends on the cry of a bird and on the fulfillment of sheer being in each man. Similarly, here he implies that, despite their randomness and multifariousness, all the particular manifestations of being or life sustain and reinforce each other. "Each creature, by some mystery, achieved a consummation in itself of all the wandering sky and sinking earth, and leaped into the other kingdom, where flowers are, of the gleaming Ghost."[57] It is as though each living thing is a miniature of the entire creation and reflects it, as the microcosm mirrors the macrocosm—in this instance by recapitulating the radical processes and tensions of the cosmos itself. Specifically, in consummating "in itself . . . the wandering sky and the sinking earth," each being that has achieved the "gleam" of relatedness which is God, recapitulates, not the static being of static nature, but the dynamism—the becoming—of which nature itself is compounded. For God, at this point, is merely the "utter relation" between "two eternities."[58]

The precise nature of the relationship between the two realms of being—between the creature within which the "God-gleam" is consummated and the realm, or condition, of "heaven" which all consummated beings share—is, as always in Lawrence, unclear. On the one hand, "heaven" and "God" are God because, in a formulation already quoted, "The revelation of God is God." On the other, there seems to be some sort of objective seat of power in the world or in some indeterminate realm that mediates between the unconscious self and the world.

In the essay "Love Was Once a Little Boy," Lawrence, employing an image that he had already used in the Hardy "Study," writes that "The individual is like a deep pool, or

[57] *Ibid.*, p. 94.   [58] See Appendix A.

tarn, in the mountains, fed from beneath by unseen springs, and having no obvious inlet or outlet. The springs which feed the individual at the depths are sources of power, power from the unknown."[59] This power, emanating from mysterious depths, is at least in some sense outside man. "Life is the river, darkly sparkling, that enters into us from behind, when we set our faces towards the unknown."[60]

In another characteristic image, what was later to become the "dragon of power" at the heart of the cosmos, is conceived as the "nameless flame" that flickers behind individuals. "In every great novel, who is the hero all the time? Not any of the characters, but some unnamed and nameless flame behind them all. Just as God is the pivotal interest in the books of the Old Testament. . . . In the great novel, the felt but unknown flame stands behind all the characters, and in their words and gestures there is a flicker of the presence."[61] "The quick," Lawrence adds, "is the God-flame in everything." Defining it thus, he reinvokes the original notion of the "quick" or the deity as the multifarious life that is manifest in all things: "And if one tries to find out, wherein the quickness of the quick lies, it is in a certain weird relationship between that which is quick and—I don't know; perhaps all the rest of things. It seems to consist in an odd sort of fluid, changing, grotesque or beautiful relatedness."[63]

The diffuse indefinable quality of God is stressed, largely through metaphors of light: "God is the flame-life in all the universe; multifarious, multifarious flames. . . ."[63] "Character is a curious thing. It is the flame of a man, which burns brighter or dimmer, bluer or yellower or redder, rising or sinking or flaring according to the draughts of circumstance and the changing air of life. . . ."[64] Just as life is multifarious,

[59] Lawrence, *Reflections on the Death of a Porcupine*, p. 176.
[60] *Ibid.*, p. 133.   [61] *Ibid.*, pp. 109–10.   [62] *Ibid.*, p. 110.
[63] *Ibid.*, p. 121.   [64] *Ibid.*, p. 116.

so is God, or the gods. "All the gods that men ever discovered are still God. . . . Yet they are *all* God: the incalculable Pan."[65] God is not one, for if he were, he could not be perceivable: "Why, the gods are like the rainbow, all colours and shades. Since light itself is invisible, a manifestation has got to be pink or black or blue or white or yellow or vermilion or 'tinted.' "[66]

The God who is the source of the power that flows into men is dissipated and lost in the multiplicity of his manifestations. And yet there is in Lawrence the recurrent suggestion that there is a power, like the Creative Mystery Rupert Birkin speaks of in *Women in Love*, a power whose expression mankind is. For Birkin, it is man's goal in life to bring himself into harmony with the unknown, where the Creative Mystery dwells. And yet, even in *Women in Love* it is difficult to say whether the Creative Mystery is an active or a latent will, and whether it has existence as anything more than an idea in Birkin's head. The divinity of the "Mystery," of the "Will," is psychologically real, as is the divinity of the self for which it becomes real. But the objective nature of the two is unclear, as the brief account earlier in this chapter should indicate.

The obscurity, it may be noted, is an obscurity that Lawrence implicitly acknowledged in his last writings, first in the essay "Dragon of the Apocalypse" and then in the study published posthumously under the title *Apocalypse* (1930). In the first, Lawrence affirms imagination, which can carry man out into the vast expanses of the starry heavens and grant him a release of sorts in the adventure of starry contempla-

[65] *Ibid.*, p. 119.
[66] *Ibid.*, p. 120. In "Education of the People," a similar metaphor contrasts the oneness of the sun, which conceals the rich multiplicity of heavenly lights and the multitudinous variety of stars. The sun of the intellect, or consciousness, and the fixed faith of fixed consciousness serve to bleach out the light. Lawrence, *Phoenix*, pp. 634–36.

tion. Lawrence does not say the myths of The Book of Revelations are true. He insists only that they have imaginative reality, coherence, and relevance and that they induce desirable responses in men. Lawrence does not even go so far as Blake had gone in asserting that "Anything that can be imagined is an image of truth."[67] He merely says that anything that has been imagined has imaginative reality of a sort. Lawrence affirms that sort of reality because it affords release from the intellectual straitjacket imposed by the scientific mind, which sees the sun as nothing but a ball of blazing gas.

Apocalypse celebrates the emotional-imaginative response in which self and cosmos fuse, and in which the distinction between self and cosmos is blurred. How it is possible for "power" to be inside and outside at once is made clear by a passage in *Apocalypse*, which I cite elsewhere—a passage in which Lawrence attempts to describe the mythic mode of response in primitive religions:

To the ancient consciousness, Matter, Materia, or Substantial things are God. A pool of water is god. And why not? The longer we live the more we return to the oldest of visions. A great rock is god. I can touch it. It is undeniable. It is god. . . . The universe is a great complex activity of things existing and moving and having effect.

Today it is almost impossible for us to realize what the old Greeks meant by god, or *theos*. Everything was *theos*; but even so, not at the same moment. At the same moment, whatever *struck* you was god. If it was a pool of water, the very watery pool might strike you: then that was god; or a faint vapour at evening rising might catch the imagination: then that was *theos*; or thirst might overcome you at the sight of the water: then the thirst itself was god; or you drank, and the delicious and indescribable slaking of thirst was the god; or you felt the sudden chill of the water as you touched it: and then another god came into being, "the cold," and

[67] William Blake, "Proverbs of Hell," *The Marriage of Heaven and Hell*.

this was not a *quality*, it was an existing entity, almost a creature, certainly a *theos*.[68]

In another and no less striking passage in *Apocalypse*, Lawrence writes:

The Dragon is one of the oldest symbols of the human consciousness. . . . [it is] the symbol of the fluid, rapid, startling movement of life within us. That startled life which runs through us like a serpent, or coils within us potent and waiting, like a serpent. . . . From earliest times man has been aware of a "power" or potency within him—and also outside him—which he has no ultimate control over. It is a fluid, rippling potency. . . . *It is something beyond him, yet within him*. It is swift and surprising as a serpent. . . . Primitive man early recognized the half-divine, half-demonish nature of this "unexpected" potency within him. The Greeks would have called it "the god" in recognition of the superhuman nature of the deed, and of the doer of the deed, who was *within* the man. The "doer of the deed," the fluid, rapid, invincible, even clairvoyant potency that can surge through the whole body and spirit of a man, this is the dragon, the grand divine dragon of his superhuman potency, or the great demonish dragon of his inward destruction.[69]

C. Vital Circuits, or, Divinity Electrified

Power, in a meaning far more specific than the meaning accorded it in "The Crown" essays, in "Reflections on the Death of a Porcupine" and in the essays on the Book of Revelations figures in the system propounded next after the system of "The Crown" essays. In the first drafts of the essays that were later collected as *Studies in Classic American Literature* (1922), in the posthumously published essay on "The Education of the People" (1918), and in the two treatises on

---

[68] D. H. Lawrence, *Apocalypse* (New York: The Viking Press, 1932), p. 84.
[69] *Ibid.*, p. 143. Italics mine.

the unconscious (1920 and 1922) Lawrence conceives of the universe as a living organism whose parts are related to each other through a system of vital-electrical circuits into which man is plugged.

Especially in *Psychoanalysis and the Unconscious* and *Fantasia of the Unconscious* man is seen as embedded in the matrix of nature and as living his life in the rhythm of the cosmic life. The notion is similar to the vision which is projected in the opening chapter of *The Rainbow*. As in *The Rainbow*, moreover, history is seen as at once an outgrowth of nature and a divergence from it. The treatises on the unconscious may be distinguished from the other discursive works on the basis of their containing a more clearly defined historical dimension as well as on the basis of the elaboration in them of a scientific-vitalist myth. Talk of divinity disappears. What remains is a sense of the world as alive—of both history and nature as realms of "rainbow-varied" possibilities and of "creative" surprises.

The vision of the consanguinity of man and nature that is enunciated in the *Fantasia of the Unconscious* and the related works is based on a proposal alternative to scientific materialism, as Lawrence understood it. Lawrence spells out in detail the notion, already enunciated in the Hardy "Study," that dead nature is not really dead, but rather a "habit" that has been formed in the "living unconscious" of life itself. In the *Fantasia*, such a notion is transformed into a wildly comic, weirdly provocative, cosmogonic myth that literally grounds the material universe in life—that is, in protoplasm. "In the beginning was a living creature, its plasma quivering and its life-pulse throbbing. This little creature died, as little creatures always do. But not before it had young ones. When the daddy creature died, it fell to pieces. And that was the beginning of the cosmos."[70]

[70] Lawrence, *Fantasia*, p. 63.

The reversal of Western cosmogonies is, in a way, rather neat. Both modern scientists and ancient materialists assume that life has sprung from matter. Life has been thought to have evolved either by the combination of atoms, as in the system of Democritus, or by ever more complicated chemical processes, as in the account rendered by modern biology. Lawrence flips the account: in his view, life precedes matter. In his whimsical account of the origin of life, the "daddy creature" provided the materials for the cosmos as we know it by the following process:

Its little body fell down to a speck of dust, which the young ones clung to because they must cling to something. Its little breath flew asunder, the hotness and brightness of the little beast—I beg your pardon, I mean the radiant energy from the corpse—flew away to the right hand, and seemed to shine warm in the air, while the clammy energy from the body flew away to the left hand, and seemed dark and cold. And so, the first little master was dead and done for, and instead of his little living body there was a speck of dust in the middle, which became the earth, and on the right hand was a brightness which became the sun, rampaging with all the energy that had come out of the dead little master, and on the left hand a darkness which felt like an unrisen moon.[71]

Later, in a chapter entitled "Cosmological," Lawrence generalizes more widely: "When the living individual dies, then is the realm of death established. Then you get Matter and Elements and atoms and forces and sun and moon and earth and stars and so forth. In short, the outer universe, the Cosmos."[72] The realities which science investigates are part of that physical cosmos, i.e., that dead, material cosmos. "The Cosmos is nothing but the aggregate of the dead bodies and dead energies of bygone individuals. The dead bodies decompose as we know into earth, air, and water, heat, and radiant

[71] Ibid., p. 63.   [72] Ibid., p. 182.

energy and free electricity and innumerable other scientific facts."[73]

More interesting than the dead bodies are the dead souls, for these create the field of life, will, and energy which is the life of the cosmos. "The dead souls likewise decompose . . . into some psychic reality, and into some potential will." These dead souls enter into relation with the living. "They re-enter into the living psyche of living individuals." It is through such surviving soul-life that living men relate to the soul-inhabited cosmic realities to which the dead bodies gave rise. For the law of life is that living beings sustain a constant vital interchange of energy with the cosmic realities that sprang from the dead being of once-live individuals.

Lawrence does not pretend to understand the mechanism that governs the vital interrelatedness of all living things to each other and to the cosmic realities. He merely knows that "concerning the universe of Force and Matter we pile up theories and make staggering and disastrous discoveries of machinery and poison-gas, all of which we were much better without."[74] About life-wisdom—the wisdom that facilitates vital interchange wherein "the living soul partakes of the outer air, and the blood partakes of the sun"—we know almost nothing. It is the forgotten wisdom of such knowledge that Lawrence attempts to stammer out. "How it is contrived that the individual soul in the living sways the very sun in its centrality, I do not know. But it is so. It is the peculiar dynamic polarity of the living soul in every weed or bug or beast, each one separately and individually polarized with the great returning pole of the sun, that maintains the sun alive. For I take it that the sun is the great sympathetic centre of our inanimate universe."[75] Altogether, the universe is conceived as a constant fund of vital energy that is trans-

[73] *Ibid.*   [74] *Ibid.*, p. 183.   [75] *Ibid.*

formed into the modes that suit the beings that are caught in its movement. What makes the world live, move, and change is the circulation of interpenetrative energies among the crea- tures and planetary bodies that constitute the universe.

Such energies are conceived as a sort of static electricity, which circulates among individuals and elements. This energy traverses fixed routes among the central bodies of creation, such as the sun, the moon, the stars, and the sea, and more or less arbitrary routes among the lesser elements, such as human individuals and other human individuals, men and animals, and men and the places to which they have a purely individual or communal connection.

Each individual is, in this sense, a transmission station that receives impulses from men and things and that discharges impulses toward men and things. The universe is a complex system of such transmitters, whose balance-in-tension, like the balance-in-tension of the psyche, generates life. Within the human individual, the various neural centers serve as recep- tion and transmission stations for life-impulses. The peculiar quality of the individual—that is, his uniqueness, or the "fre- quency" on which he functions—is the product of the balance between dominance and recessiveness in the neural centers, as well as of the frequencies on which he "contacts" those indi- viduals who are capable of attunement to him.

All individuals, however, must participate in certain fre- quencies. Each man is "polarized" to some individuals to which others are not attuned. These include his parents, fa- vored members of the opposite sex, and members of his race, community, and so forth. The precise frequency of each indi- vidual is elicited and conditioned through the stimulation of the nerve centers in childhood by those like one's parents with whom one has intense and vital relationships. In all individu- als, however, the limits of possibility are quite clear. They have been set by the generic nature of life. These possibilities lend themselves to translation back into the terms of the old polarities of masculinity and femininity, light and darkness, spirit and flesh, love-oriented and power-oriented—that is, of the categories of the simpler psychological systems of the Hardy "Study" and "The Crown" essays. In the treatises on the unconscious, the "lower" centers are sensual, the upper spiritual. The former govern the movement of self-enclosed disjunction from others, the latter the effluent, out-going seeking-out of others.[76]

From the point of view of our present interests, the universal modes of "connection" are far more important than the particular, personal ones. The entire system of upper and lower centers, and even the division of the body, which is the seat of the unconscious, into the areas into which it falls in Lawrence's psychological system, is probably borrowed from Yoga psychology.

D. Yoga Scientized, or,
Electricity Homologized

Yoga divides the body into seven *chakras*, or circles, symbolized by lotuses. Each of these is homologous with various aspects of the cosmos. For the Yogin, each of the *chakras* is a "gate" through which the somatic psyche communicates with the cosmic body to which it corresponds. The communication, though mediated through consciousness, is a quasi-physical one, having to do with the circulation of energies that link man to the cosmos. There is, in other words, a materialized, quasi-magical system of correspondences between microcosm and macrocosm which is regarded as more than a set of symbolic equations. For there is a sense in which, for the Yogin, the individual contains the sun, moon, and stars by virtue of imaginative participation in the vast system of metabolically interrelated elements which is the universe.[77]

[76] See Chap. V, pp. 146ff., for a fuller account.
[77] Mircea Eliade, *Yoga: Immortality and Freedom*, translated by Willard R. Trask (New York: Pantheon Books, 1958).

Lawrence literalizes and further materializes the Yoga scheme by eliminating the element of imagination and by substituting for it the movement of the static electricity through which relationships are mediated. He assumes a fundamental system of correspondences, or identities, that hark back to participation in the original particle of protoplasm from which the universe emerged. He then assumes the continuance of polarization along the lines that were set down at the beginning by virtue of the organic or chemical affinity between aspects of the life in the original protoplasmic unit and the aspects of nature that sprang from it. In the human being, aspects of the body are polarized with fixed aspects of the universe. In this sense, his vital electrical life is "hooked up" to the animate force of sun, moon, sea, and earth.

Through his heels, for example, man draws in the effluence of the earth's center, to which his veins are polarized. In a variant of the old Antaeus myth, we are told that he must remain in touch with earth—literally in touch. This is so because his heels serve as the channel for communicating the life-element that man draws from the center of the earth. Hence, if he loses touch, he cannot sustain his vital life and begins to suffer from a thinning of the blood. At the same time he must remain in touch with the sun and the moon as well. The moon, old Cynthia, the inconstant goddess of change, governs the fixed transformations of sea and of tides which, in their saline elementality, are polarized to the tidal element of the blood. The blood itself is polarized to the moon and at the same time akin to the sea. Here lies the "logic" of the ancient relationship between the blood and its passions to Aphrodite, daughter of the bitter sea-salt-spume. In his chest, however, man knows "objective knowledge." He is polarized with the sun, the constant luminary. Thus, suspended between sun and moon, man lives in constant vital touch with the two celestial bodies and is polarized at the same time to the stability of the earth's center.[78] The problem is maintenance of a suitable flow of energy within the individual, the body of mankind, and the various aspects of the natural world.

Sexuality, which had been so important in the earlier scheme, retains its centrality here. Although the immediate sexual engagement of individuals with each other is mediated through the other great centers of somatic consciousness, the blood is the chief seat of the psychosomatic activity. And the blood is both the prime element of life and, in its chemical and electrical constitution, the lowest common denominator between the soul in its most concrete somatic aspect and what Lawrence terms the mechanical-material universe. The frequency of the blood is closest to that of objective nature itself, so that through it man remains in touch with the movement of life in its most elementary material manifestation. Through the rhythm of the blood within the body man enters into sympathetic harmony with the rhythm, the basal metabolism, as it were, of the universe. At the same time, the upheaving tide of the blood, as it rises to its sexual crisis—and it is the blood that is the element of sexuality, the penis being characterized as a "column of blood," the vagina as a "valley of blood"—cleanses the entire organism and renews it in the matrix of darkness: that is, of the blood and of the flesh.

Man is thus seen as embedded in nature. Orgastic experience is literally a retreat into the darkness of the blood, which is attuned to the most primitive cosmic realities. Indeed, the well-being of every man depends on his capacity to achieve an adequate attunement to the cosmos at this level. And that attunement is achieved in himself and through others. These others are not merely the immediate partners to his radical

[78] For discussion of such "polarization" at the purely psychological level, see pp. 146–53 below.

experience, but—in these later formulations—the generality
of men in his community, race, nation.

The vision of the postwar years, as formulated in the studies of the unconscious and the leadership novels, insists that
communities, like individuals, are natural entities and that
man's fulfillment depends on participation in the daylight life
of society as well as on the nighttime experience of *eros*. Man
must return from the blood-darkness of sexuality, where he is
submerged in nature, to the daylight world of history, there to
participate in the purposive activities of men. The world he
builds there is, ultimately, the outgrowth of the experience of
the blood; it is, with seeming irony, the historical world—
what Lawrence, in the Hardy "Study," had pejoratively
termed the "social encampment." And that world is, ideally,
the natural outcropping of "heath" and "blood."

With this, Lawrence would seem to have reversed the position he took in the "Study." There he rejected the encampment and called upon man to venture into the wilderness.
Suddenly, it would seem, the antagonism between encampment and wilderness abates, and the encampment becomes an
adjunct of the wilderness. Man has come to be thought of as
an unequivocally amphibious creature, whose being is submerged in nature but whose energies are expended in history.

The reversal, as it happens, is more apparent than real.
Even the Hardy "Study," as I have already suggested and as I
shall try to show in detail in my next chapter, implies a vision
of history which assumes the naturalness of history itself and
which views the phenomena of history as the spontaneous
manifestations of the "realized" self. In fact, the problem that
haunts Lawrence's speculations is not this reversal of his initial position, but a far more subversive question: how, granting the conception of history as the outgrowth of nature, does
history turn against nature? How can the sensitive "leading-
shoot of life" create (and not merely be trapped in) the stony

encampment that shuts out the life of the wilderness? And, granting the naturalness of both civilization and the "nuclear self," how can one explain the fact that in the early Lawrence civilization derives from the self, whereas in the later the self is seen to derive from civilization?

Before turning to these questions, we must first examine Lawrence's vision of history.

III

The Self and History

Strictly speaking, Lawrence does not merit treatment as either a historian or a philosopher of history. His only formal historical work, *Movements in European History*, is a secondary-school text, arbitrarily conceived and full of facile and often secondhand generalization. And the historical allusions and speculations scattered through his other works are unhistorical in the extreme: the fanciful images of a writer for whom the spectacle of history provided a repertory of provocative images to play with as mood or interests demanded.

Lawrence's stated view of history in a sense justifies his cavalier treatment of historical material, but it has little to recommend it as a systematic approach. History, in his view, is like nature. It follows no pattern and conforms to no preordained order or logic. With nature it shares the qualities of spontaneity, dynamism, and unpredictability. Lawrence emphatically does not "believe in evolution, but in the strangeness and rainbow-change of ever-renewed creative civilizations."[1] Historical events, like natural events, are to be understood as movements in a planless, causeless surge of life. *Movements in European History* itself represents "an attempt

[1] Lawrence, *Fantasia of the Unconscious*, p. 56.

to give some impression of the great, surging movements which rose in the hearts of men in Europe, sweeping them together in one great concentrated action, or sweeping them apart forever on the tides of opposition. *These are movements which have no deducible origin. They have no reasonable cause, and they are so great that we must call them impersonal.*"[2]

This view accords with the view, presented in "'The Crown" essays, of life as a fluid field of energies, in the midst of which some energies or constellations of energy flicker into the "fourth dimension" of vivid life, inexplicably and altogether without cause. History, in this sense, is an open-ended adventure in which all things are possible and in which there is always the possibility of life-assertion or the renewal of lapsed life. Such a view is in line with Lawrence's utopian mode. It permits him to reassert his faith in nature and in human possibilities, to rebut those who would enclose man in a "tight skin" of consciousness or circumstance, and to call for a meaningful "resourcing" of civilization through a movement into the "wilderness," which is the "unknown."

Yet Lawrence's early sustained confrontations with history undercut his fundamental position from two directions. On the one hand, history, in his account of it, falls into a progressive, highly structured, triadic pattern, very much like the pattern it forms in the work of Hegel, Vico, or Herbert Spencer. On the other, even such progressive open-endedness as his ideological account would seem to promise is undercut by the observed facts of history. Chief among these is the fact that a development which should have issued in freedom and vitality has instead led mankind into an impasse. History, which should be open-ended, has become a dead end. In the unfolding of time and events, man has come to be entrapped

[2] D. H. Lawrence, *Movements in European History* (Oxford: Oxford University Press, 1926), pp. ix–x. Italics mine.

in the tight skin of his civilized consciousness and the stony walls of the civilized encampment. The double entrapment precludes free movement into the unknown and the achievement of further, vital advances in civilization.

Lawrence, as I shall attempt to show, cannot wholly deal with the contradiction, though much of his later work is concerned with it. His initial formulations, however—presented chiefly in the "Study of Thomas Hardy" and the *Twilight in Italy* essays—hardly admit such difficulty. The "Study," in fact, makes a rather rigorous case for freedom and openness, a case that is immediately undercut only by the orderliness of the actual version of history sketched within it and the pattern of events presented within it.

The Ground of the Vision

Lawrence's vision of history more or less conforms to his vision of nature. It rejects the notion that civilization arises primarily out of the struggle for survival. Instead, it proposes waste and willful self-expression as the ground of human creativity in history. "Working in contradiction to the will of self-preservation," we recall, "from the very first man wasted himself begetting children, colouring himself and dancing and howling and sticking feathers in his hair, in scratching pictures on the walls of his cave, and making graven images of his unutterable feelings."[3] It is not merely in art and reproduction that he wastes himself, however; he also spends himself in work and thought.

Lawrence is explicit about this. Labor is not undergone for ulterior reasons, out of submission to the "self-preservation scheme." Rather, it is performed out of "an inherent passion . . . a craving to produce, to create, to be as God."[4] Thought, too—even the most rigorous, impersonal, scientific thought—

³ Lawrence, "Study of Thomas Hardy," *Phoenix*, p. 398.
⁴ *Ibid.*, p. 429.

is the outgrowth of instinctive mimetic and empathetic impulses. Man naturally wants to enter into empathetic rapport with nature. Hence he reproduces, mimetically, in his mind "the movement life made in its initial passage, the movement life still makes, and will continue to make, as a habit, the movement already made so unthinkably often that rather than a movement it has become a state, a condition of all life: it has become matter, or the force of gravity, or cohesion, or heat, or light."[5] This being the case, society need not ground itself in repression and self-subordination of individuals. Every civilization has its modes of labor and fund of scientific and technical knowledge; every civilization sustains itself on the basis of these. But neither labor nor knowledge is the true ground of history; they are its natural condition. Lawrence does not address himself to such issues. He does not take up the question of changing technologies and differential means of production in various ages and cultures. Nor is he interested in sociological distinctions. What does engage him is the "ideal" dimension of civilization: the dimension that involves art, philosophy, religion, and—peripherally—politics. And these, too, are treated in a coarse, off-handed way, so that —for example—everything before Christianity and out of the main line of its development is subsumed under a single, rather simplistic category.

Lawrence conceives of religion and art as direct expressions of man's deepest experience. The works and acts which constitute man's significant history represent the projection into event, relationship, and institution of the self's experience of itself and of the other in the course of its "journey into the unknown." The contents of history are engendered in the course of immersion in the realm of dynamic unconsciousness that is akin to nature. In this sense, the dynamic psyche, as experienced during the journey, is the domain of nature out of

[5] *Ibid.* For further formulations as to the "naturalness" of labor, see "Education of the People," *Phoenix*, pp. 648–50.

which civilization springs. The psyche, which is contiguous with nature, mediates nature and history; it is the channel through which "the greater life of nature" unfolds itself within history. This being the case, history is characterized by the same radical qualities as both nature and the psyche.

Lawrence offers conflicting explanations of how the ineffable inwardness of individual experience translates itself into outward and visible relationships and artifacts. On the one hand, he insists that the historical embodiments of man's experience are the effervescence of his integral self. A man's works and his children arise, not from the struggle toward anything, but rather from the overflow of his "being," as achieved in the medium love. On the other hand, it is suggested in the discussion of particular cultures and artists that the works of man in history represent an effort to make up for a defect ("defaulture") in the "being" he has striven toward in his journey into the unknown.

In the first notion, works and children are the spontaneous overflow of being. "With a natural male," Lawrence writes, "what he draws from the source of the female, the impulse he receives from the source, he transmits through his own being into utterance, motion, action, expression."[6] His experience becomes the ground of celebration, aspiration, and wonder.

Such a view accords with the activist bias of the "Study," with its call to the wilderness and its insistence on the spontaneity and naturalness of civilization. For the most part, however, the "Study" suggests that men are propelled into the active life of civilization owing to a lack, or failure: the failure to have fathomed the depths of the unknown. Man suffers because he cannot take full physical and imaginative possession of the mate who is the true complement of his being and who figures for him as the far shore of the un-

[6] Lawrence, "Study of Thomas Hardy," *Phoenix*, p. 484.

known. This failure is the correlative of his failure fully to articulate his own being in relation to his mate. Essentially, Lawrence holds, man wishes "that his movement, the manner of his walk, and the supremest effort of his mind shall be the pulsation outwards from stimulus received in sex, in the sexual act, *that the woman of his body shall be the begetter of his whole life. . . .*"[7] The wish, however, is usually frustrated, so that "A man must seek elsewhere than in woman for the female to possess his soul, to fertilize him and make him try with increase. And the female exists in much more than his woman. And the finding of it for himself gives a man his vision,—his God."[8]

Consciousness itself—the faculty which makes it possible for man to look before and after and pine for what is not—would seem to be a by-product of the necessary failure of sexual fulfillment. "Man is stirred into thought," Lawrence writes, "by dissatisfaction, or unsatisfaction, as heat is born of friction." Consciousness, he continues, "is the same effort in male and female to obtain perfect frictionless interaction, perfect as Nirvana. It is the reflex both of male and female from defect in their dual motion. Being reflex from the dual motion, consciousness contains the two in one."[9] The two-in-one of consciousness, as generated between a man and woman, would seem to be the exact counterpart of the Holy Ghost of the Self within the individual—the being, that is, which the individual, within himself, seeks to attain. Like being, moreover, it seems in its essence to be a recoil from absolute oneness and fusion—a product, again, of a fault in fulfilled relationship.

As a result, man seeks the complement in religious vision of what he had found in his relationship with woman. Religious vision is, in fact, the consequence of man's will to embody in

[7] *Ibid.*, pp. 444–45. Italics mine.   [8] *Ibid.*, p. 445.
[9] *Ibid.*, p. 446.

imaginative form the sensed potentialities of his ultimate relation to woman. Lawrence states this baldly: "Since no man and no woman can get a perfect mate, nor obtain complete satisfaction at all times, each man according to his need must have a God, an idea, that shall compel him to the movement of his own being."[10]

Art and religion, the chief aspects of man's life in history treated by Lawrence in the "Study," are the by-products of success and failure, of fulfillment and frustration, in the erotic relationship. In culture, and in the supreme effort of consciousness which the life of culture demands, man strives to create or to recreate what he has known and lost, or intuited and never really grasped, in the journey into the unknown.

This effort, as opposed to the effort of the great self-preservation scheme to wrest a livelihood from nature, constitutes the significant history of the race.

The religious effort is to conceive, to symbolize that which the human soul, or the soul of the race, lacks, that which it is not, and which it requires, yearns for. It is the portrayal of the complement to the race-life which is known only as a desire: it is the symbolizing of a great desire, the statement of the desire in terms which have no meaning apart from the desire.

Whereas the artistic effort is the effort of utterance, . . . of . . . that which has been for once, that which was enacted. . . . The artistic effort is the portraying of a moment of union . . . according to knowledge. The religious effort is the portrayal or symbolizing of the eternal union of the two wills according to aspiration.[11]

Desire and knowledge as they figure here are erotic desire and knowledge in the biblical sense, that is, knowledge of the erotic reality of the self and the other in the erotic encounter.

[10] *Ibid.*, p. 445. Note the similarity between Lawrence's idea that the energies of history stem from fragmentation of being and the notion of love that Plato puts in Aristophanes' mouth in *The Symposium*.   [11] *Ibid.*, p. 447.

Thus it is that the content of culture and cultural forms which constitute the history of the race may be said to reflect the experience of self and other in the course of the journey into the unknown. Cultural and religious forms must be read as symbolic projections of "knowledge" of self and other, and aspiration toward such knowledge. And such knowledge is to be conceived in erotic terms, the very terms in which the human psyche had been conceived.

On the face of it, the implications of such a view are utterly anarchic. The suggestion is that culture is wholly the product of the individual psyche. How, one might ask, do the uniformities of psychic experience, making for coherence and consistency within any culture, arise? How are they sustained? How do particular cultures accommodate to the vagaries of individual experience?

Lawrence never addresses himself to such questions. He boldly assumes the existence of coherent national and historical entities and deals with them as though they presented no problems. And indeed, so far is he from an anarchy, that history—in his account of it—comes to seem as rigorously ordered as it does in its schematization within the traditions of nineteenth-century thought. In Lawrence's account, history progressively unfolds the contents of the dynamic psyche. Major historical groups and periods are characterized (and juxtaposed) in such a way as to suggest ordered stages in the progressive unfolding of the human psyche.

Lawrence, to be sure, insists at the time of the Hardy "Study" that the various aspects of psyche and self are perpetually rediscovered by heroic individuals who can explore their deepest potentialities. The actual sequence of the historical unfolding, however, is so rigorously patterned that it suggests both a teleological direction and an ontological end. It is this patterning that points to the real underlying affinities of Lawrence's vision of history: the nineteenth century's visions of order and progress on the one hand, and certain medieval apocalypses on the other. One hears in Lawrence's account the deep echoes of both the nineteenth-century scientism which he strove so hard to put behind him and the Christian optimism that pervaded the chapel culture in which he was reared. His triadic ordering of psychic and historical possibilities is reminiscent, as I have already suggested, of the Hegelian dialectic and the progressivism of the Comtean, Spencerian, and other positivist systems. The apocalyptic element, on the other hand, directly suggests the scheme promulgated in *The Everlasting Gospel,* an apocalyptic tract which has been attributed to a thirteenth-century Cistercian monk named Joachim of Flores. Both tendencies are implied by the categories employed in the discussion—categories employed in the treatment of nature and the psyche as well: those equating femininity, flesh, and Jehovah; masculinity, spirit, and Jesus; and self, consummation, and Holy Ghost.

The Categories

Before turning to the version of history that is sketched in passing in the early works, we must examine the terms that Lawrence employs and the structure of the ideas that frames them. The terms are difficult because they are essentially unhistorical. They are, in fact, the categories that Lawrence employs to describe the life of the psyche and the life of the cosmos and to create the impression, through verbal symmetry, of congruity between them. One suspects that Lawrence chose to employ the same categories here to reinforce the impression that history is a natural phenomenon, or at least an excrescence of nature that can be grasped in the terms appropriate to nature.[12] Yet there are substantial differences in their range of reference.

There is, superficially at least, a similarity to Bachofen here.

[12] See Chap. II for treatment of Lawrence's use of this strategy in his conception of nature.

As in Bachofen's anthropological construct, cultures, religions, or works of art are classified either masculine or feminine. In Lawrence's system, they must be the one or the other because they represent the objectification of the masculine or feminine psychic needs of their creators. As in Bachofen, a wide range of qualities is analyzed in terms of radical masculine or feminine traits. Lawrence differs from Bachofen in that his categories of male and female refer, radically, to aspects of the inner life, not—as in Bachofen—to social structure.[13] The erotic categories are complicated, moreover, by the superimposition of a set of religious categories, involving the Persons of the Trinity. Female-Flesh is paired with the Father (sic!), Male-Spirit with the Son, and Being with the Holy Ghost. Thus, the Mother (Flesh) is equated with the Father, and the Male term, which by strict parallelism with the Female-Mother *should* be the Father, is in fact the Son. The logic of the argument is highly idiosyncratic, but— as with the use of the same erotic and religious categories in the treatment of nature—rationally explicable.

For Lawrence, the female, although it is said to be coeval with the male, would seem to be the more primitive. It is, radically, the maternal element of origins, which are of the flesh and of the blood. As such, it is further associated with darkness—the darkness of the womb and of birth. Hence, by extension to the societal realm, it is associated with dominance by the family and the clan, which are bound by origins and blood, rather than by freely chosen political allegiance. As such, it is further associated with the archaic, hierarchic, hieratic, aristocratic social structures that are rooted in the family. Cosmologically, it is the primordially undifferentiated matter (*materia*)—or, in the vitalist scheme, protoplasm-flesh—out of which differentiated, individuated things emerge.

[13] The best summary of Bachofen in English is to be found in Erich Neumann, *The Origin and History of Consciousness* (New York: Pantheon, 1959).

As the generative principle, the Mother-Flesh is associated with God the Father. This association would seem to arise by virtue of the fact that the god of Genesis creates (generates) the world, chooses his people (a tribe or a clan) Israel, and legislates for it a positive, ritualized order of social relationships grounded in the clan-order of "blood." Along this line of associations, the female-flesh becomes associated with resistant, or limiting, things, primarily the Law, which the Old Testament deity lays down for His people, and, by extension, with any positive social order that limits individual aspiration. By the same logic, it is *physis* as well as *nomos*: the resistant order of inert nature, also formulated in the physical scientists' laws of nature. It may also be applied to the more primitive, but equally rigorous and oppressive, rule of fate.[14]

Within the psyche it is associated with the unconscious, conservative domain of the flesh and of the instincts, where "life springs up at the source." As such, it is not only conservative (the Will-to-Inertia), but also voracious: its mode of aggression is the assimilation of all things into itself. In coping with the world, it swallows rather than extends; as a principle of consciousness, it does not seek out objects but rather absorbs objects, incorporating them into itself.[15]

The masculine element in the psyche is, on the other hand, the aspect of spirit in human life: the volatile, restless, dimension of the personality which aspires toward ends rather than origins. As such, it moves away from the closed, blood-defined world of family and class into a realm of universal relationship. As in the Jungian scheme, it is the organizing, integrating, and generalizing faculty, which posits both ends and universals. Its correlative in the Trinity is the Son—the re-

---

[14] I know of no definite source for these ideas.
[15] Lawrence enunciates this concept in several places, including the Hardy "Study," *Phoenix*, p. 481 and *Twilight in Italy* (New York: The Viking Press, 1958), pp. 28ff.

deemer from flesh and from sin, and the transcender of fleshly and material limits. Jesus, like the individual masculine spirit, lifts both the individual and mankind out of the "givenness" of origins and creates the possibility for self-determination through striving. As a principle of consciousness, it is the mentality which distinguishes among things. As such, if driven too far, it can lead to a loss of particular differentia through subsumption of realities under too-abstract categories.[16]

The dualism of Lawrence's system is a dualism of flesh and spirit, of female and male, of mother and father, of Father and Son. As in the systems of nature and the psyche, moreover, there is a third term, in which the first two terms are mediated, synthesized, or reconciled. This third term is more elusive than the first two. It is, psychically and cosmically, the "being" that emerges between individuals and within individuals at the moment of consummation, when vivid life comes into being by transcending the elements of self or nature. It is the "fourth dimension" of life, that is, what "men once called heaven." It is also the "absolute" which men envision as the end of their erotic consummations, and which is both their fulfilled selves and the ideal condition toward which their selves strive. In Lawrence's trinitarian scheme, it is the "Holy Ghost."

Obviously, the Holy Ghost is a mystic condition; the only analogue with which I am familiar is the Jungian Self, which shares the dubious distinction of being both what the self moves toward in its development and an almost cosmic reality toward which the self develops. Whatever its precise nature, however, it is clear that it has dubious existence even within

[16] *Ibid.*, but also *Twilight in Italy*, pp. 92ff.; *Fantasia of the Unconscious*, pp. 30ff.; the "Democracy" essays, *Phoenix*, pp. 706ff.; and the essay on Whitman in *Studies in Classic American Literature* (New York: Doubleday Anchor Books, 1953), pp. 120ff.

the self, especially since it is not sustainable or constant and would therefore be difficult to objectify in history. If anything, it represents a millennial possibility in history—a kind of heavenly city which might lie at the end of history, or toward which history, personified, might "strive."

The meaning of this third and ultimate term is clearest when it is placed in the context of Joachim of Flores' "Everlasting Gospel," whose substance and influence Lawrence sums up as follows:

> In this book it was said that Judaism was the revelation of the Father; Christianity was the revelation of the Son; now men must prepare for the revelation of the Holy Ghost.
> Wild ideas spread everywhere. Men began to expect the reign of the Holy Ghost. They said that before Jesus was born the Father had reigned: after this, in their own day, the Son had reigned; now the Holy Ghost would reign. In the Everlasting Gospel it was stated that when the Holy Ghost began to reign the papacy and the priesthood would cease to exist. Then there would be no more church to govern the souls of men.[17]

Lawrence's exposition is very brief and stints the proliferation of terms in Joachim's doctrine—a proliferation that, in the formulation of one scholar, is closely reminiscent of Lawrence's alignment of categories. A. C. Turberville writes:

> Joachim had foretold in his "Concordia" that the world would go through three cycles, those of the Father or the Circumcision or the Law; of the Son, Crucifixion, Grace; of the Holy Ghost, Peace and Love. The first had been the era of Judaism, of the Old Testament. It had led to the New Testament and the Christian Church. The second was very shortly to reach its accomplishment. The third and last era, that of "The Everlasting Gospel," was to be inaugurated by a new religious order.[18]

[17] Lawrence, *Movements in European History*, pp. 193–94.
[18] A. C. Turberville, *Medieval Heresy and the Inquisition* (London: Allen & Unwin, n.d.), p. 37.

In its terminology, and in the structure it imposes on history, Lawrence's view is roughly parallel to Joachim's. In *Twilight in Italy*, the "Study of Thomas Hardy," *The Rainbow*, "The Crown" essays, and to a limited degree in *Women in Love*, history is viewed in the following pattern. First there is an Old Testament, "fleshly" Jehovah phase, then a phase dominated by Jesus, of the "spirit" who is the Son, and finally a phase of struggle leading toward the transcendent unity of the Holy Ghost. Each phase of history embodies the term of the Trinity which it unfolds and seems to give rise to the next. The end, however, is substantially erotic—or at least rooted in the erotic—in a way that Joachim's is not. And the actual end toward which history, in Lawrence's vision of it, moves, is, of course, very different: it is chaos and disintegration, with only a remote possibility of renewal.

The Historical Unfolding

Lawrence begins his historical sketch with the ancient Hebrews, rather than with the Greeks. At one level, this can be explained by his love of the Bible's rich sonority and its embodied deity. More fundamental, however, is the readier applicability to the Hebrews of the historical and psychological myth that Lawrence propounds. The Hebrews are an indubitably historical people, but they envision themselves as living near the beginning of time. As Lawrence describes them, the ancient Israelites live in a condition wherein consciousness has just barely distinguished itself from the world. Submerged in the surrounding realm of things, the individual has not yet apprehended either himself or his consciousness as a discrete entity. His feelings are in constant flux within the matrix of nature, so that this flux is virtually continuous with his consciousness. Upon this flux, the light of consciousness must eventually dawn, if man is to become aware of the radical distinction between self-world, between self and other.

There would seem to be some analogy between the historical process which led to the emergence of consciousness from chaos and the emergence of the individual psyche from the state of unconsciousness. Lawrence believes that the mode of consciousness recorded in the works of the ancient Israelites reflects their closeness to the origins in the blood and in the flesh. In this primitive state, they failed to distinguish between self and other. "In the Jewish cycle, David, with his hand stretched forth, cannot recognize the woman, the female. He can only recognize some likeness of himself. For both he and she *have not danced very far from the source.* . . ."[19] As a result, "He hails her Father, Almighty, God, Beloved, Strength, hails her in his own image."[20]

The acknowledgment of woman as Father and as God is comprehensible only in terms of the triangulation I have described above: the deity is always for Lawrence a projection of what is experienced sexually. The flesh, nature, sensuality are identified in Lawrence's mind with God the Father on the one hand and with woman on the other.

Having become subject to his own projection of deity out of experience, the Israelite doomed himself to perpetuating his limitations. In identifying the other with himself, the woman with the man, he symbolizes not only the object of his knowledge and aspiration, but also his own weakness as a male and as a repository of consciousness. Hence, "in the terrible moment when [in the sexual embrace] they should break free again, the male in the Jew was too weak, the female overbore him. He remained in the grip of the female. The force of inertia overpowered him."[21] Consequently, development is arrested. Jews go on knowing God as David knew

---

[19] Lawrence, "Study of Thomas Hardy," *Phoenix*, p. 449. Italics mine.
[20] *Ibid.*, p. 450.   [21] *Ibid.*

him, as "the God of the body, the rudimentary God of physical laws and physical functions. . . . His religion had become
a physical morality, deep and fundamental, but entirely of
one sort. . . . [of] scrupulous physical voluptuousness. . . .
He had become the servant of God, the female, passive."[22]

The relation of the Jew to his God—that of the bride to the
bridegroom—reinforces his original female resistance to the
masculine principle of change and transformation. Hence the
inherent negativity and conservatism of the Old Testament
law and of the social order which is dominated by the Law.
Both are governed by a fossilized ritualism. Such ritualism
inhibits action within the narrow limits of a world-view that
conceives of the world in terms of the hide-bound monism of
the "Father"-flesh. "It were a male conception to see God
with a manifold Being, even though He be One God. For
man is ever keenly aware of the multiplicity of things. . . .
But woman, issuing from the other end of infinity, coming
forth as the flesh, manifest in sensation, is obsessed by the
oneness of things, the One Being, undifferentiated."[23]

Yet, for all this, the Judaic God is not the Fleshly Absolute.
Just as he is not feminine in his form, he is also not feminine
in his essence, since he is the product of a tension between the
poles of individual experience. Hence the victory of the female expressed through him is a relative victory only. The
female core of the experience depends on a balance of masculinity and femininity. The masculine term is not utterly ob-
literated. Judaism remained fixed in the feminine dominance,
but always within it the masculine spirit lived on in bondage.
And it was from the "suppressed male spirit of Judea" that
Christ arose.

Jesus is the Promethean assertion of the suppressed masculine spirit of Judea which had been driven underground by the

[22] *Ibid.*, pp. 450–51.   [23] *Ibid.*, p. 451.

Mosaic tradition. In the most direct terms of Lawrence's dichotomy, Jesus represents the spirit as opposed to the flesh, the soul as distinguished from the body. Ultimately, he represents the demand that the individual renounce the very body which the Mosaic law had sanctified. Metaphysically, moreover, the injunction "Thou shalt love thy neighbor as thyself" negates the "monism" in which one's neighbor was oneself. For Jesus, as Lawrence understands his injunction, one's neighbor is other than oneself and one loves him for his otherness. In love, two disparate rather than identical things are brought together, so that even the communion of Christian love hinges on the reality of otherness.

In sketching the radical difference between Christianity and Judaism, Lawrence points to its obvious reflection in their variant accounts of origins and ends:

> Cunning and according to female suggestion is the story of the Creation: that Eve was born from the single body of Adam, without intervention of sex, both issuing from one flesh, as a child at birth seems to issue from one flesh of its mother. And the birth of Jesus is the retaliation to this: a child is born, not to the flesh, but to the spirit. . . . And the assertion entailed the sacrifice of the Son of Woman. The body of Christ must be destroyed, that of Him which was Woman must be put to death, to testify that He was Spirit. . . .[24]

The central fact of Christianity as Lawrence grasps it is that the Son does not and cannot immediately triumph within it. Hence Lawrence sees the history of Christianity as a struggle between the two principles. Christians continue to affirm the Father while worshiping the Son. As a result, throughout the Middle Ages the force of love as affirmed by the male principle was counterbalanced by the Old Testament, female modes of the Father and the Law, both of which figured in

[24] *Ibid.*, p. 452.

the institutional structure of the Church itself, and in the emergent Cult of the Virgin.

The Cult of the Virgin reflects the survival of the flesh-origin term of the fundamental dichotomy. She is the mother absolutized, and in her man worships the female side of himself and of all reality. The condition of sanctification in the Middle Ages is, however, an almost complete desensualization of the flesh. The Virgin Mother of God is not woman in the flesh; she is an utterly spiritualized being.

During the Middle Ages, Lawrence writes,

The worship of Europe . . . was to the male, to the incorporeal Christ, as a bridegroom, whilst the art produced was the collective stupendous, emotional gesture of the Cathedrals, where a blind, collective impulse rose into concrete form. It was the profound, sensuous desire and gratitude which produced an art of architecture, whose essence is in utter stability . . . that admits . . . no other form, but is conclusive, propounding in its sum, the One Being of All.[25]

Thus, the Middle Ages are only partially able to apprehend the Christ of Revelation, and men aspire toward Him as a remote possibility rather than an embodied actuality. Their immediate experience is in the mode of the woman. Only at the Renaissance does a situation arise where the flesh as projected in the concept of the Father relaxes its iron grip. Suddenly Christian spirituality is at last free to assert itself in relatively pure form, but in perfect balance with fleshliness. "During the medieval times," Lawrence writes,

the God had been Christ on the Cross, the Body Crucified, the flesh destroyed, the Virgin Chastity combating Desire. Such had been the God of the Aspiration. But the God of Knowledge . . . had been the Father, the God of the Ancient Jew.

But now, with the Renaissance, the God of Aspiration became

[25] *Ibid.*, p. 454.

in accord with the God of Knowledge, and there was a great outburst of joy. . . . This was the perfect union of male and female,
in this the hands met, . . . and never was such a manifestation of
Joy.[26]

The "perfect union of male and female," however, was not
the consummation of the Holy Ghost, which is the final goal
of history. At the Renaissance, men welcomed a false consummation, for they celebrated a manifestation of balance, not of
reconciliation-in-tension. The balance, moreover, was precarious, doomed to issue in domination of the female by the male
—that is, in the victory of the Son. The progress of civilization in modern times has led toward the male's absorption of
the female principle, and the subjection of civilization as a
whole to a rigidity and a divorce from nature that threaten to
destroy it completely.

Lawrence analyzes this tendency through a detailed consideration of certain Renaissance painters.[27] In the work of these
painters, he writes, the tendency to subordinate the female
principle to the male

leads on to the whole of modern art, where the male still wrestles
with the female, in unconscious struggle, but where he gains ever
gradually over her, reducing her to nothing. Ever there is more
and more vibration, movement, and less and less stability, centralization. Ever man is more and more occupied with his own . . .
overpowering of resistance, ever less and less aware of any resistance
in the object, . . . less and less aware of anything unknown, more
and more preoccupied with that which he knows, till his knowledge tends to become an abstraction, because it is limited by no
unknown.[28]

[26] Ibid., pp. 454–55.
[27] See Appendix B for a summary of Lawrence's treatment of the
relationship between the supposed erotic experience of a small group
of Renaissance artists and their work.
[28] Lawrence, "Study of Thomas Hardy," Phoenix, p. 456.

The development is rapid and clear. In the history of painting since the Renaissance, "there has been the ever-developing dissolution of form, the dissolving of the solid body within the spirit. . . . It is no longer the Catholic exultation 'God is God,' but the Christian annunciation, 'Light is come into the world.' "[29] This dissolution of the concrete, the sensuous, and experiential finds its first great exponent in Rembrandt. In his treatment of both light and texture, Lawrence finds "the new exposition of the commandment 'Know thyself.' It is more than the 'Hail, holy Light!' of Milton. It is the declaration that light is our medium of existence, that where the light falls upon our darkness, there we are. . . ."[30] Its ultimate expression, however, does not come until the nineteenth century, when Turner and the Impressionists dissolve solid objects in light. They lose the autonomy of space in the dynamism of light, not as it is in nature, but as it is refracted and diffused in a highly intellectualized conception of nature.

What is expressed graphically in painting can be seen in other spheres of culture. The Protestant version of "Know thyself" is the imperative of conscience-ridden introspection, demanding that the individual triumph over the flesh and that he transcend a world governed by the Devil.

Lawrence's discussion of Shelley touches upon the modern adulation of light and all that it symbolizes. Unlike Matthew Arnold, Lawrence does not regard Shelley as a "pale, ineffectual Seraph" futilely beating his wings. In Lawrence's terms, Shelley is the most masculine of the poets.[31] The male, we recall, is the spiritual agent whose entire being is committed to transcendence. Shelley's masculinity is expressed in an adulation of weightlessness and a craving for release from the flesh—qualities that are reflected in his brilliant, substance-

[29] Ibid., pp. 469–70.   [30] Ibid., p. 471.
[31] Ibid., p. 459. Lawrence writes, "The pure male is himself almost an abstraction, almost bodiless, like Shelley or Edmund Spenser."

diffusing, light-aspiring imagery, culminating in the skylark poem. There, as Lawrence understands it, the soul's longing for sublimation out of existence finds its literal expression.

> Hail to thee blithe spirit!
> *Bird thou never wert.*
> In the sky or near it
> Pourest forth thy heart
> In profuse strains of unpremeditated art! [Italics mine.]

Lawrence focuses on the negative: "Bird thou *never* wert." The skylark aspires to a condition of pure spirituality.[32]

Shelley's craving for spiritual transcendence is emblematic of the entire cluster of nonerotic attitudes characterizing post-Renaissance man as Lawrence sees him. These include the idealism of believing in man's perfectability, egalitarianism, and faith in the value of science for ordering the natural world and of democracy for coping with the social one. All these ideals of love in its universal fraternal form find their eloquent exponent in the poet.[33]

In Shelley, or rather in that moment of Western development which is epitomized by Shelley, the movement of spirit toward self-expression is consummated. Renaissance painters had attempted to synthesize the domains of flesh and spirit and had achieved a moment of joy and balance. But this was immediately dissolved in the urgency of the masculine will toward domination. The Reformation represented the extreme form of this compulsion. Here again Lawrence draws on

[32] *Ibid.*, p. 478.

[33] These connections are spelled out more clearly in *Twilight in Italy*, where Lawrence is concerned with the contrast between the cold, industrial north and the warm, agricultural south, as well as with the contrast between Protestant and Catholic, democrat and aristocrat. Lawrence's "polarities" and his sense of history are more dramatically presented in these essays then they are in the Hardy "Study." For example, see *Twilight in Italy*, pp. 92ff.

art rather than religion or philosophy for examples. He cites
Hamlet's suicidal impulse. Hamlet asks whether he is to be or
not to be, and Lawrence interprets the question as referring to
the flesh and to all that the flesh represents in his own system.
As political malcontent and moral agent, Hamlet takes upon
himself the murder of King and Father. Lawrence interprets
Father-King as representing the medieval aristocratic tradition
which exalted the flesh and the passional, self-seeking will.
Significantly for Lawrence, Hamlet is ambivalent. Lawrence
sees what was wish in Hamlet becoming reality in Shelley.
Unconscious conflict becomes conscious desire.[34]

In a sense, Shelley too expresses desire and not realization.
He envies the skylark and conceives of it as not-flesh—"Bird
thou never wert." In doing so, he acknowledges the physical
dimensions of existence. As Lawrence sees it, Shelley's wish is
fulfilled only in the time of Shelley's grandchildren and great-
grandchildren. When this happens, Western civilization itself
reaches the brink of destruction. In Lawrence's view, the
danger consists in a disjunction, or dissociation, of the psychic
elements in the individual. He becomes unable to sustain the
productive life-giving tension between Flesh and Spirit, Father and Son, Male and Female within the self.[35]

Lawrence points to the Hardy novels as evidence of the
realization of Shelley's dream. He reads them as studies in the
fragmentation of the psyche. Sue Bridehead fulfills Shelley's
aspiration. Though Lawrence admires Sue's courage, he sees
her very courage as an aspect of a universal denaturing of
woman and as the subversion of the feminine principle itself.
Sue is so far spiritualized and etherialized that she is no longer
able to yield herself to the archetypal self-generating journey
into the unknown. She is therefore unable to come into being.
In Lawrence's view, all of Hardy's characters are beset by

[34] Lawrence, *Twilight in Italy*, pp. 87ff.
[35] *Ibid.*, pp. 93ff.

Sue's problem. Where they have not been driven to crave complete transcendence, like Angel Clare, they are trapped in a debased sensuality, like Alec D'Urberville.[36]

There is a sense in which the Hardy characters represent the end of the historical journey which Lawrence traces in the "Study." As present beings who grow out of the past and are shaped by it, they serve as the culmination of history. At the same time, they represent the possibility of terminating history. The very mode of being which they incarnate is a life-negating mode. Cut off from the fertile hinterland of the flesh by their spirituality, they cannot regenerate themselves or their societies.

What has happened in the nineteenth century is that the individual has lost the ability to experience himself autonomously in the realm of sexuality. Civilization has come to dominate the individual entirely. Man has been cut off from the natural sources of his individuality. This is the condition which Lawrence renders in the image of society as a stony encampment posed against the wilderness. Others of Lawrence's writings render this in a variety of related images that dramatize the sequestration of man within the civilization. In the Hardy "Study" the stony walls are said to represent a constant condition. The actual treatment of the historical sequence, however, suggests that the condition depicted in the "Study" is a historical condition: one that reflects all that has preceded it and that, owing to man's perversity in history, is against nature. What has happened is that man, in fulfilling his nature, has gone against his nature and created a diabolical world of death and destruction instead of a paradisal world of fulfillment.

The psyche, in other words, does not fulfill itself in history. Rather, it destroys itself. In the formulation I have suggested earlier, it has *denatured* itself and trapped itself within the

[36] Lawrence, "Study of Thomas Hardy," *Phoenix*, pp. 488ff.

limits of the historical world—the world it has itself created. And this world is both nightmarishly limited and hellishly morbid, utterly cut off from all the sources of vitality with which psyche, cosmos, and civilization are—ideally—informed.

Such a view is enunciated most freshly and dramatically in the works that immediately follow the Hardy "Study." The "Study" was written in the first months of the Great War and is marked by a fervor that is part faith and part hope— hope that was sustained, one imagines, in the face of deepening despair. Indeed, by the time the war had entered its second year, the horizons of Lawrence's vision had darkened; while he continued to call for action, such action was conceived as a means of averting imminent disaster. "The Crown" essays (1915), the letters of 1915 and 1916, the latter portions of *The Rainbow* (1915), and all of *Women in Love* are marked by a pervasive sense of disaster, compounded by a sense of betrayal: the betrayal of nature by history, of the human present by the human past, of human possibilities by human institutions.

Altogether, Lawrence's work between 1915 and 1926 pivots on his sense of betrayal in and by a world that has lapsed from its best possibilities. It is this sense of a lapsed world, and the imagery in which it is presented, that I wish to examine in the following chapter, before going on to examine Lawrence's efforts to explain the fall and to deal with its consequences.

IV

The Fallen World

The Lawrence who holds that history has reached an impasse is the familiar Lawrence, whose disenchantment with civilization is so deep as to lead him at moments to consider discarding civilization together with its discontents. Lawrence was to remain fundamentally antagonistic to modern civilization from 1915, when he wrote "The Crown" essays, until his death in 1930. After 1915, he no longer views civilization as an unfolding of human and natural possibilities. Instead, he sees it as a wasteland cut off from the sources of life in the greater world of nature and the deeper strata of the self. The historical world comes to be seen as a fallen world, reflecting in all its aspects the radical and necessary corruption of the human psyche.

In "The Crown" essays (1915) this condition tends to be rendered in the apocalyptic image of birth, or rather of failure to bring things to birth. Time is conceived as bearing events in its womb. As the medium of change, time gives birth to emergent newness in each historical epoch. Yet, since man and his needs are the source of history, the womb which bears newness is not so much time as the psychic life out of which possibilities spring in the medium of time. At every crisis in history the enwombing stock of images and attitudes through

which man apprehends himself and his world begins to con-
strain the individual—even as at the time of birth the uterus
constrains the child that is about to be born. At that point,
healthy civilizations, like healthy babies, burst out of the
womb.

A civilization that fails to bring new possibilities to birth is
envisaged as a sterile civilization that encysts its people within
the terms of consciousness it has imposed. Working with the
metaphor of time and consciousness as a womb, we might say
that in such a civilization the walls of the womb have grown
hard and resistant, so that life potentialities cannot emerge
into the clear air of history. In that condition, the walls of the
womb then become analogous to what Lawrence, in the
Hardy "Study," had termed the stony walls of the social
encampment, which prevent individuals from venturing out
onto the heath. In terms of still another image, the life that is
trapped within the hard walls of the womb-encampment is
akin to the life of the "fat cabbages, going rotten at the core"
of which Lawrence speaks both in the Hardy "Study" and in
"The Crown" essays. It constitutes a sort of noxious organic
matter, releasing poisons as it rots.

This is the condition of modern man as Lawrence describes
it in "The Crown" essays. "Within the womb of the established past," Lawrence writes in the fourth of "The Crown"
essays,

the light has entered the darkness, the future is conceived. It is
conceived, the beginning of the end has taken place. Light is
within the grip of darkness, darkness within the embrace of light,
the Beginning and the End are closed upon one another

They come nearer and nearer, till the oneness is full grown
within the womb of the past, within the belly of Time, it must
move out, must be brought forth, into timelessness.

But something withholds it. The pregnancy is accomplished, the
hour of labour has come. Yet the labour does not begin. The loins
of the past are withered, the young unborn is shut in. . . . the dry

walls of the womb . . . cannot relax. . . . [A]t this moment when
the birth pangs should begin, when the great opposition between
the old and the young should take place, when the young should
beat back the old body that surrounds it, and the old womb and
loins should expel the young body, there is a deadlock. The two
cannot fight apart. The walls of the old body are inflexible and insensible, the unborn does not know that there can be any travelling
forth.[1]

The "unborn" is the ego, the artificial, self-conscious self.
Lawrence was later to call this the "social self," which is
"ideal" and which consists of "all that we *conceive* ourselves to
be." Within the womb of time, when birth cannot take place,

there is a struggle. . . . the darkness, having overcome the light,
reaching the dead null wall of the womb, reacts into self-consciousness, and recoils upon itself. At the same time the light has sur-
passed its limit, become conscious, and starts in reflex to recoil
upon itself. *Thus the false I comes into being, the I which thinks
itself supreme and infinite, and which is, in fact, a sick foetus
shut up in the walls of an unrelaxed womb.*[2]

In this unnatural state, the self, or ego, instead of opening
out to the world or inward to the self that is consanguineous
with the world, turns inward upon itself and devotes its energies to the work of disintegration. Shifting to a related metaphor, one may say the metabolism, or life-process, becomes
catabolism, or death process.[3] History, instead of moving
forward, stands still, and men, instead of dedicating their
energies to the work of creation, destroy.

At first, their debility takes the form of illusory omnipo-
tence, a sense of finality which makes of the self as it now is

[1] Lawrence, *Reflections on the Death of a Porcupine*, pp. 49–50.
[2] *Ibid.*, pp. 49–50. Italics mine.
[3] D. H. Lawrence, "A Propos of Lady Chatterley's Lover," *Sex,
Literature and Censorship*, ed. Moore (New York: Compass, 1959),
p. 103.

the end of history. The self conceives of itself in terms of a perfection that is deathly. In this state, the ego loses its organic life quality and becomes a glazed essence that is impervious to change and therefore incapable of development. This is the state into which modern man has fallen. "That which we *are*," Lawrence writes in "The Crown" essays, "is absolute. There is no adding to it, no superseding this accomplished self. It is final and universal. All that remains is thoroughly to explore it."[4]

Exploration, in this instance, means analysis. Echoing both Wordsworth and D'Annunzio, Lawrence writes that "Analysis presupposes a corpse"—it murders to dissect.[5]

So circumscribed within the outer nullity [of the ego], we give ourselves up to the flux of death, to analysis, to introspection, to mechanical war and destruction, to humanitarian absorption in the body politic, the poor, the birth rate, the mortality of infants, like a man absorbed in his own flesh and members, looking for ever at himself. It is the continued activity of disintegration—disintegration, separating, setting apart, investigation, research, the resolution back to the original void.

All this goes on within the glassy, insentient, insensible envelope of nullity. And within this envelope, like glassy insects within their rind, we imagine we hold the whole cosmos, that we contain within ourselves the whole of time, which shall tick forth from us as from a clock, now everlastingly.[6]

What modern man seeks, according to Lawrence in "The Crown" essays, is the death that lies in the disintegration (analysis, catabolism) of all things into their component parts. He is exhilarated by the experience of releasing the "static data of consciousness" Such data are not primarily intellectual, but they are reduced in the crucible of self-conscious intellect. In the last analysis, all that man can seek

[4] Lawrence, *Reflections on the Death of a Porcupine*, p. 52.
[5] *Ibid.*, p. 52. [6] *Ibid.*, pp. 53–54.

when he enters into this state is what Rupert Birkin, in *Women in Love*, calls "acute reduction in sensation."

Women in Love, which was drafted in 1914 but revised in the later war years and published in 1920, renders novelistically the condition which Lawrence had written of in "The Crown" essays. Lawrence writes in his own voice of the "womb of time" and the "glassy envelope" of the self-conscious ego; Rupert Birkin, who is pretty much the *raisonneur* of *Women in Love*, says that civilization is trapped in the "tight skin of consciousness." Mankind, he tells Ursula, has grown deathly; men have become "Sodom apples on the tree of life."[7] The human world has exhausted its creative possibilities and finds itself "part of the inverse process, the blood of destructive creation."

Like Lawrence, Birkin believes that dissolution is the opposite equivalent of life. "We always consider," he tells Ursula,

> "the silver river of life, rolling on and quickening all the world to a brightness, on and on to heaven, flowing into a bright eternal sea, a heaven of angels thronging. But the other is our real reality—"
>
> "But what other? I don't see any other," said Ursula.
>
> "It is your reality, nevertheless," he said; "that dark river of dissolution. You see it rolls in us just as the other rolls. . . . our sea-born Aphrodite, all our white phosphorescent flowers of sensuous perfection, all our reality, nowadays."[8]

Indeed, Birkin suggests the destructive process may have gone too far. He regards himself, Ursula, and everyone else in the novel, as "*fleurs du mal*," decadent products of internal corruption. This corruption is so radical that Birkin believes mankind may have reached the end of its history. "Man is a mistake," he tells Ursula, and he is a mistake because of his failure to evolve creatively:

[7] Lawrence, *Women in Love*, p. 112.
[8] *Ibid.*, p. 179.

If only man was swept off the face of the earth, creation would go on so marvelously, with a new start, non-human. Man is one of the mistakes of creation—like the ichthyosauri. If only he were gone again, think what lovely things would come out of the liberated days;—things straight out of the fire. . . .

Humanity never gets beyond the caterpillar stage—it rots in the chrysalis, it never will have wings. *It is anti-creation, like monkeys and baboons.*[9]

At another point, Birkin tells Gerald Crich that the human race is "just one expression of the incomprehensible. . . . if mankind passes away, it will only mean that this particular expression is completed and done. . . . Humanity doesn't embody the utterance of the incomprehensible any more. Humanity is a dead letter."[10]

Birkin's vision of the end of the days is rooted in splenetic hatred of the modern world, a hatred close to Lawrence's own. And Birkin conceptualizes the difficulties of modern life in terms close to those Lawrence had employed in the Hardy "Study" and "The Crown" essays. Birkin holds that the impasse of history stems at least in part from man's failure to leap into the unknown and to unfold his deepest energies there. He believes that modern men may have lost the capacity for vital relation to each other and for bringing the dual aspects of their psyches into integral, reciprocal relation with each other.

Contemplating a West African statuette which epitomizes what he takes to be the essential decadence of West African culture, Birkin wonders whether the African races have not "lapsed" out of "the desire for creation and productive happiness . . . leaving the single impulse for knowledge in one sort, mindless progressive knowledge through the senses, . . . mystic knowledge in disintegration and dissolution. . . ."[11] And it

[9] *Ibid.*, p. 132. Italics mine.   [10] *Ibid.*, p. 60.
[11] *Ibid.*, pp. 265–66.

occurs to him that "the white races" may be in the grip of an analogous process: "Having the arctic north behind them, the vast abstraction of ice and snow, [they] would fulfill a mystery of ice-destructive knowledge, snow-abstract annihilation,"[12] diametrically opposed to the "sun-sensuous" African "knowledge."

Birkin's categories of mind and sensuality, of sun and snow, are closely akin to categories already encountered in Lawrence. Indeed, they are lurid extensions of the categories of flesh and spirit Lawrence had employed in his discursive writings. We recall that Lawrence's ideal is a productive tension between the elements of the self. The creative self, as opposed to the destructive ego, is made up of polar opposites existing in dynamic tension with each other. The "Holy Ghost" of the personality emerges from the tension and conflict of flesh (Father) and spirit (Son); it is the total pattern of selfhood that arises spontaneously within experience. Throughout history man has enjoyed the dynamic imbalance of the relationship between the elements. At all times, however, the relationship has been one of complementarity as well as conflict.

What Birkin envisions is an end of the creative tension between the two. The balance-in-tension of flesh and spirit has become the utter hostility of blood and mind. Mindless sensuality is opposed to senseless intellectuality and torrid lust seems to be posed against frigid ratiocination. In the vision that is enunciated through Birkin, we see how one of Lawrence's nightmares has come true. The novel shows how "the ideal mind, the brain, has become the vampire of modern life, sucking up the blood and the life."[13] Mind and blood, or intellect and sensuality, are the cross on which mankind is crucified.[14] Society itself is identified with the life-destroying

[12] *Ibid.*, p. 266.
[13] Lawrence, *Fantasia*, p. 106.
[14] Lawrence, *Studies in Classic American Literature*, pp. 94–95.

intellect; society controls the individual through the "ideal," "mental" consciousness. The ego is the "sum total of what we *conceive* ourselves to be," and the conception of self is obtained from the world of men—from society. To exacerbate this difficulty, the social, mental, ideal self enters into an unholy alliance with the will and through it attempts to tyrannize over the "living unconscious"—that is, over the integral self.[15]

The optimal relationship between the aspects of the self is enunciated in works which precede and follow *Women in Love*. In nature, Lawrence insists in the "Study," in "Education of the People" (1918), and in the treatises on the unconscious, the will is treated as an agency of "sensitive life adjustment." It is a pure instrumentality of the living unconscious on its way to self-expression and self-realization in history. Consciousness has a similar status. It is a derivative function of life and exists at various levels, of which mental consciousness is merely a partial and terminal mode: "the whole sum of the mental [consciousness] . . . is never . . . more than a mere tithe of the vast surging primal consciousness, the affective consciousness."[16] Man is given intelligence "in order that he may effect quick changes, . . . preserving himself alive and integral through a myriad environments . . . which would exterminate a non-adaptable animal."[17] So with the will; it is "a . . . spontaneous control factor, . . . a great balancing faculty . . . whereby automatization is *prevented* in the . . . psyche."[18]

What ails modern man is not the introduction of a new faculty into his psychic system, but rather the emergence of a pair of subordinate functions as dominant ones and the conse-

[15] See Chap. V.
[16] Lawrence, "Education of the People," *Phoenix*, p. 629.
[17] *Ibid.*, pp. 614–15.
[18] Lawrence, *Psychoanalysis and the Unconscious*, p. 47.

quent derangement of an organism not meant to be under their domination. This is the condition that Birkin contemplates in *Women in Love*—the condition to which all its people are subject. All the important characters are coerced by the need to undergo an "acute reduction in sensation." They are driven in this direction by the nearly demonic possession of their sensual being by their intellectual faculties and volition. The mind and the will drive them to perverse excesses that are destructive of self and society. Thus, they enact the disintegration Lawrence attributed to all modern men in "The Crown" essays.

What the novel adds to the conception of the essays is the urgent reality of hatred and violence as an element in the process. A deep and generally unconscious compulsion governs much of Gerald Crich's behavior, as well as—in varying degrees—that of Gudrun, Loerke, Halliday, the Pussum, Hermione, and even Birkin. Their compulsive commitment to intellectualized sensual indulgence, or to the "plausible ethics of productivity," is seen to be grounded in hatred and violence of a deeply personal order. The vampirism of the mind is a vampirism of the self; the icy frost of knowledge, which is death by perfect cold, is the concomitant of a passionate fear and hatred of life. Gerald, the central figure in the novel's *danse macabre* of consciousness and sensuality, is laid low by the hate and fear generated in the quest for love within a self unable to yield itself to the urgings of vital desire.

Gerald is the crucial case in point because he embodies a variety of evils: the narrowness of the social self, the conventions within which the social self moves, and the compulsions which drive it to create the kind of constraining world that Gerald organizes and affirms. Like Thomas Buddenbrooks, Gerald is a man who hides behind conventions to hold together a crumbling self and conceal the chaos that informs it. Buddenbrooks changes his shirts several times a day; Gerald

dresses for dinner and insists that the rules of a formal deco-
rum be observed in his household. His rationalization is that
the household would fall apart did he not demand observ-
ance. All the potential violence and disorder of the Crich
household is contained within Gerald himself.

Lawrence uses a telling image to render the tension between order and chaos. Gerald's father is dying, and Gerald is
in attendance, "seeing it through."

[I]n the stress of this ordeal, Gerald too lost his hold on the outer,
daily life. . . . Work, pleasure—it was all left behind. . . . The
real activity was this ghastly wrestling for death in his own soul.
And his own will should triumph. Come what might, he would
not bow down or submit or acknowledge a master. He had no
master in death.
But as the fight went on, and all that had been and was continued to be destroyed, so that *life was a hollow shell all round
him,* roaring and clattering like the sound of the sea, a noise in
which he participated externally, and *inside this hollow shell was
all the darkness and fearful space of death,* he knew he would have
to find reinforcements, otherwise he would collapse inwards upon
the *great dark void* which circled at the center of his soul. His will
held his outer life, his outer mind, his outer being unbroken and
unchanged. But the pressure was too great. He would have to find
something to make good the equilibrium. *Something must come
with him into the hollow void of death* in his soul, fill it up, and
so equalise the pressure within to the pressure without. For day by
day *he felt more and more like a bubble filled with darkness,* round
which whirled the iridiscence of his consciousness, and upon which
the pressure of the outer world, the outer life, roared vastly.[19]

The inner chaos contains violence, against himself and
against the world. It includes the wish to destroy and the wish
to be destroyed. Everything else—work, productivity, manners, morality, intellectual conversation, the arts, politics—all
these are means of deflecting the violence at the core of his

---

[19] Lawrence, *Women in Love,* p. 340. Italics mine.

being. What Lawrence says of Hermione, who is a female counterpart of Gerald, is true of Gerald as well. "Her long, pale face," Lawrence writes, ". . . seemed almost drugged, *as if a strange mass of thoughts coiled in the darkness within her*, and she was never allowed to escape."[20] Birkin says that Hermione, who is farther gone in consciousness and decadence than Gerald, lives with the light of consciousness turned on.[21] Even sensuality cannot turn off the lights or allay the glaring consciousness which seeks surcease in sensation. Both Gerald and Hermione are, in a sense, committed to consciousness and the conscious life. Both are unconscious of the real motives that coerce them, motives of hate and destruction leading each of them into murderous assaults on his lover and forcing them to seek orgastic pleasure in the extremity of violence itself.

Gerald's violence is in part rooted in "reaction against his father's principles of Christian Charity."[22] The elder Crich, having negated aggression and the will to power, has sent these impulses underground, only to have them surface in his son. Hence Gerald's radical will-to-destruction; we hear of him that "he had all his life been tortured by a furious and destructive demon, which possessed him sometimes like an insanity."[23]

Lawrence suggests that Gerald's demonic fury is what drives him in the work of bureaucratizing and rationalizing his father's coal mines. "This temper," he says, "now entered like a virus into the firm, and there were cruel eruptions."[24] Gerald attempts to reduce everything to pure instrumentality, pure mechanism. We are told that Gerald, in his travels, "had come to the conclusion that the essential secret of life was harmony. . . . And he proceeded to put his philosophy into practice by forcing order into the established world, translat-

[20] *Ibid.*, p. 16. Italics mine.   [21] *Ibid.*, p. 45.   [22] *Ibid.*, p. 229.
[23] *Ibid.*, p. 240.   [24] *Ibid.*, p. 240.

ing the mystic word harmony into the practical word organisation."[25] The imposition of his will upon the world around him causes the disintegration of the organic form of that world. He creates an efficient machine that deforms the natural shape of men and subjects nature itself to a chaos-creating order. The very physical environment of the world created by his nature-subjugating will is seen as chaos by the sensitive heroines of the novel. The industrial order has reduced nature to an essential formlessness.

Lawrence suggests that the entire social-industrial world over which Gerald rules is an emanation of his imperious will and his corruption, just as earlier cultures had emanated from the spontaneous, creative aspects of the psyche in life-loving men. Gerald, the miners who submit to the "theology" of pure instrumentality, and all those who are caught in the ambience of the industrial world seem to emit a green-hornet-like radiation of "mystic hatred." They have a mystic fear and hatred of "organic life" and of human feeling. The very passion for equality which governs their political aspirations is destructive: in reducing the natural hierarchic forms of social relationships, they destroy life. Men, in their social roles, became ciphers and noughts, the equivalent of matter in man's struggle with objective nature: "He, the man, could interpose a perfect, changeless, god-like medium between himself and the Matter he had to subjugate. There were two opposites, his will and the resistant Matter of the earth. And between these he could establish the very expression of his will, the incarnation of his power, a great and perfect machine, a system, an activity of pure order, pure mechanical repetition. . . ."[26]

Man's effort to subjugate external nature has as its correlative the effort to restrain his own nature both in its violent

---

[25] *Ibid.*, p. 238.   [26] *Ibid.*, p. 239.

and its affectionate aspects. Gerald denies his feelings. What Lawrence often terms the feminine, fleshly aspect of human nature is denied in the name of efficiency, productivity, and the common good. The novel describes the breakdown of this effort and the enactment, in his life and in his death, of his real feelings, denied because of fear. His restraint collapses because his father is dying, but also because he has finally completed the organization and modernization of the mines. He has, in short, accomplished the instrumental task he has set for himself. As a result, he must turn in on himself and consider what he really wants from life. He can no longer pretend, as he had pretended in an early conversation with Birkin, that he lives in order to make it possible for others to eat. In other words, he can no longer live in accordance with the "plausible ethics of productivity."[27] He must ask where he wants to go. "[N]ow he had succeeded," we learn.

And once or twice lately, when he was alone in the evening and had nothing to do, he had suddenly stood up in terror, not know-ing what he was. And he went to the mirror and looked long and closely at his own face, at his own eyes, seeking for something. He was afraid, in mortal dry fear, but he knew not what of. He looked at his own face. There it was, shapely and healthy and the same as ever, yet somehow, it was not real, it was a mask. He dared not touch it, for fear it should prove to be only a composition mask. His eyes were blue and keen as ever, and as firm in their sockets. Yet he was not sure that they were not blue false bubbles that would burst in a moment and leave clear annihilation. He could see the darkness in them, as if they were only bubbles of darkness. He was afraid that one day he would break down and be a purely meaningless bubble lapping round a darkness.

But his will yet held good, he was able to go away and read, and think about things. He liked to read books about the primitive man, books of anthropology, and also works of speculative phi-losophy. His mind was very active. But it was like a bubble float-

[27] See Chap. I, pp. 7ff.

ing in the darkness. At any moment it might burst and leave him
in chaos. He would not die. He knew that. He would go on living,
but the meaning would have collapsed out of him, his divine
reason would be gone. In a strangely indifferent, sterile way, he
was frightened. But he could not react even to the fear. *It was as
if his centres of feeling were drying up.* He remained calm, calculative and healthy, and quite freely deliberate, even whilst he felt,
with faint, small but final sterile horror, that his mystic reason was
breaking, giving way now, at this crisis.[28]

Gerald seeks relief through love. He has an affair with a
woman whose will is stronger than his and whose detachment
is greater. Instead of bringing him into being, his love destroys
him. In the ensuing struggle for power, all the hate and
destructiveness that have filled the "black bubble" of chaos
within him are released, first on Gudrun and then on himself.
In the end, he seeks icy death among the snow-covered mountains of the Tyrol, destroying himself partly because he lacks
further objects for his destructive will. Gerald, who in childhood had "accidentally" killed his brother, now deliberately
kills himself, though only after he has died "mystically" in the
spirit.

In structuring the action of this novel, Lawrence in effect
reverses the traditional relationship between love and work,
especially as it figures in the Protestant bourgeois conception
—that is, of work as the opposite of pleasure, and of achievement in the world of work as purchased through renunciation
of pleasure. This view pervades late nineteenth-century literature and thought. It is ultimately symbolized in the Wagnerian *Ring*, where the plot hinges on the necessity of renouncing love to forge the ring that gives power over the
material world. The Ibsenian hero must make a similar
choice. For him, too, the condition for achievement is sacri-

[28] Lawrence, *Women in Love*, pp. 243–44. Italics mine.

fice, and love and passion threaten to undermine the respecta-
bility and productivity that sacrifice makes possible.[29]

Freud also falls within this tradition. His notions of delay,
renunciation, and sublimation as the basis of civilization
translate into subtle, psychological terms much the same
scheme that Wagner had dramatized in his operas and Ibsen
in his plays.[30] Man, according to Freud, seeks happiness in
union with a woman. To earn the love of woman and to
create the conditions for their life together, he renounces a
modicum of the pleasure which he most deeply desires and
invests his energy in those socially useful tasks. It is only in
the later formulations of his metapsychology that Freud radically revises this view, stressing the fact that man does not
choose to renounce but is rather forced to renounce owing to
the peculiar psychic configuration imposed upon him by life
in a human family. This configuration necessarily involves
repression of instinctual desires. All of man's later life is a
struggle—a neurotic struggle—to reconstitute the structure of
infantile satisfaction through circuitously reached substitute
objects in the arena of socially approved activity. This, as
Norman O. Brown points out, in the Freudian view, is the
source of movement and change in history.[31]

This last point is just what Lawrence is asserting in his
treatment of Gerald. Hence the dramatic force of the substantive statement with regard to modern civilization and, by
extension, to civilization in general. Gerald is sick, a specimen
of the neurotic animal. The entire social, intellectual, and
technological civilization with which he is identified is the
product of the sickness that holds him in its power. The

[29] See especially *Peer Gynt, Brand,* and *John Gabriel Borkmann.*
Shaw regards this as the central dialectic in Ibsen.

[30] Freud held this view as late as *Civilization and Its Discontents.*

[31] Norman O. Brown, *Life Against Death* (New York: The Modern
Library, n.d.), pp. 15ff.

industrial civilization over which Gerald reigns is shown to be
the objectification in act and in artifact of his innermost
corruption. He does not renounce pleasure or love in order to
achieve ends which his conscience affirms, but rather must
strive toward the appearance of mastery and the simulacra of
achievement because he cannot experience himself in any
other way. He does not, in other words, renounce love in order
to gain power, but rather, he seeks power because he cannot
love. In the absence of redeeming and binding love, his entire
being is overwhelmed by the tide of aggression that wells up
within him.

In the language of the Hardy "Study," Gerald cannot abandon himself to the drift of the "unknown" because of the
dreadful realities contained in his own psyche—namely, death
and the related wish to inflict death on himself and on others.
Having in childhood killed his brother, he lives—according to
Birkin—in terror of having his aggression turned on himself,
owing in part to the wish to be destroyed. Hence the entire
structure of Gerald's conscious personality must be committed to remaining within the conscious, daylight, social-produc-
tive world, from which psychic horror has apparently been
banished. Ironically, to be sure, his conscious personality becomes the vehicle for the very horrors it seeks to avoid just as
the daylight world becomes the mirror or extension of those
horrors.

In Gerald, Lawrence diagnoses the ills of civilization in his
time. Gerald is the civilization-hero of the early twentieth
century· soldier, explorer, engineer, administrator, potential
politician. It is suggested that, in spirit, he rules not only the
mines and streets of blighted Beldover, but the entire scope of
industrial England, indeed, of any analogous industrial society. Beyond that, as the "snow-demon from the north," he
symbolizes all the "white races" with the "arctic behind
them." As Cain-like fratricide, moreover, he is symbolically

identified with cities in general; we recall that Cain is the founder of the first city and the father of sons who instituted the civilized arts, specifically the arts of music and metallurgy. When Gerald expires in the distant, ice-bound mountains, it is suggested that the entire civilization with which he is identified dies with him. And it would seem to go under for the very reason that *he* goes under: because of the demonic fury and aggression that drive him, and it.

In the perspective of Gerald and his psychic life, consciousness itself becomes the vehicle for the destructive impulses within the "unknown" of the self. Intellectuality, knowledge, science, and control all become means for directing at the world the aggression that inhabits the self. That aggression would shatter the entire structure of the self were it allowed to infiltrate consciousness and be experienced for what it really is. Intellectual knowledge, like social convention, is one means of depersonalizing and anesthetizing those areas of relationship that might activate feelings which must be avoided at all costs.

The will serves the same functions in Gerald as in Hermione. It is the psyche's means of controlling itself and the ego's means of controlling others. The will seeks to regulate the movement and pattern of relationships in such a way as to afford the self a sense of itself and of its integrity. In characters like Gerald and Hermione, whose lives are organized with the unconscious aim of circumventing the great, dark void within themselves, the will, with its rigid commitment to limited goals, is the only means of experiencing the self. Without the rigid forms of control and dominance, one of two things would happen: either the sense of self would collapse, leaving only the void, or the void would take over and unleash all its potentiality for destruction.

As in the speculation as to the origins of society with which Lawrence opens the Hardy "Study," anxiety is seen here as

the cause of man's outward-thrusting, reality-dominating, na-
ture-denying, and sensuality-repressing compulsions. Here,
however, the anxiety is not about survival, but about pleasure
and contact and irrational dependency—as well as about the
death-dealing aggression that inhabits the innermost reaches
of the terrorized self. The will that governs the lives of Gerald
and Hermione is fixed because it is governed by anxiety. It is
fixed in resistance to the feelings that threaten to overwhelm
the disintegrating self.

The entire novel, in short, dramatizes the process of corruptive distintegration within the "shell," as described in "The
Crown" essays. It dramatizes the psychological correlative of
the metaphysical process described in the essays. But it shifts
the emphasis as well. In the essays, death seems to be a
metaphor, a way of making a radical judgment of the reduc-
tive quality of consciousness in the modern world. In *Women
in Love*, death has concrete psychological sources and correla-
tives as well. These are structured to suggest that death is not
merely the result of the process of psychic disintegration, but
also its source. Just as the vitality of earlier periods in history
reflects the life of the psyche, so the deadliness of Lawrence's
times is seen as a projection into history of the death, the
distintegration, and the unintegrated aggression that are at
the heart of man's inner life. Evil in the world is the externalization of evil in the psyche. Nitroglycerine, Lawrence was to
write in *Fantasia of the Unconscious*, is the product of the
hate that permeates man's soul, just as slums are the outcome
of the hatred of beauty and the fear of sexuality that afflict
him in his everyday life.

The crystallization of a sense of evil explains one of the
more radical shifts in the tone of Lawrence's work. Any reader
must be struck by a qualitative difference between *Women in
Love* and the work that precedes it. *Sons and Lovers* and *The
Rainbow* are full of conflict, failure, and frustration. Both

thrust into the modern world of minds and machines. Both, and especially *The Rainbow*, engage with the vexing problems of the democratic-utilitarian ideologies. Yet the sense of evil that pervades *Women in Love* is almost completely absent from their worlds. Men are thwarted, fail to realize their potentialities, succumb to their own limitations, and torment each other. But there is a kind of innocence in their failure. They cannot be other than they are, since they are in the grip of forces greater than themselves.

Women in Love is very different in this regard. Its characters are self-conscious in the extreme, and Lawrence implies that they choose to be corrupt because they lack the courage to be human. One should perhaps say that they refuse to be natural, to realize the resources of their deeper selves. Yet the oppressive atmosphere of the novel suggests that even if they should wish to reach down to their natures, their wills are not adequate to the task. The will itself, with the mind, is corrupt. There is no escape from the nightmares that are unconsciously engendered.

The world of *Women in Love* is, in other words, a fallen world, almost a demonic world, where evil is a necessary concomitant of experience, and where salvation is possible only for those who are willing to renounce that world completely. We have here the vision Lawrence had enunciated in the Hardy "Study": a vision of man entrapped within the social encampment, peering out into a wilderness, which is nature. But in Lawrence's harsh vision, the encampment is an industrial concentration camp where men "reduce" each other with noxious radiation emitted by their decomposing selves. And the wilderness, while it is accessible to a transcendent individual like Birkin, is less a concrete emotional reality within the self than an abstruse metaphysical principle toward which he gropes.

History, as I have already indicated, has turned on itself,

negating its own possibilities. More accurately, the psyche, from which history stems, has turned on itself, trapping itself in a womb of its own conception. The psyche, which began as the source of life, becomes the source of death. The unconscious, where life in principle "springs up at the source," becomes, in Blake's image, a cistern, a place of standing water where pestilence is bred.

The question, of course, is how this has come about, and how, within the terms of Lawrence's conception, it could have come about. To this question—finally unanswerable in Lawrence's terms—I turn in the following chapter, where I deal with Lawrence's conception of the psyche and with his views of the modern world.

V

How the Psyche Fell

The world of *Women in Love* is in a sense a familiar world; it is Lawrence's version of the wasteland of modern life. The novel's interest, however, lies not so much in the image it presents of the world as in the relation it establishes between the outer world and the personalities of those who make and inhabit it. "The system," Lawrence had written elsewhere, ". . . is only the outcome of the human psyche, the human desires."[1] The world created by Gerald Crich is the expression of his deepest fears and desires; it is a disintegrated world because he is a disintegrated personality. The fallen world is the objective expression of man's fallen inner state, the outward manifestation of his inward spiritual malaise.

The problem, in terms of Lawrence's vision of history, is how the psyche came to fall from its integrity. How, one must ask, can civilization, which is an outgrowth of nature, turn against nature? And how can the psyche, which is in its essence a natural rather than an historical configuration, fall out of its integrity? How can it produce a disintegrative civili-

---

[1] "Education of the People" (1917), *Phoenix*, p. 590.

zation?[2] How can the dialectical play of flesh and spirit become the dualistic antagonism of mind and blood? In the language of Lawrence's Christ imagery, how can the complementary realities of Father and Son become the cross of blood and mind on which the Holy Ghost of the Self is crucified? In more psychologically concrete terms, how can the subordinate, instrumental faculties of mind and will come to dominate the psyche which, in nature, they were designed to serve?

In the last analysis, Lawrence cannot really deal with these questions. He merely presents a forceful account of what has happened, as he perceives it. Then he juggles fragments of his various "systems" in an effort to make sense of what has happened and to spell out its implications more clearly.

The gaps in logic are so considerable as to render a wholly systematic exposition pointless. The problem of how the world came to fall is an important one, however, since a great number of the "connections" within Lawrence's thought are expounded in the course of his attempt to understand it. His theory of the unconscious, for example, seems to have been worked out in its most highly developed form in the effort to render the fallen world intelligible. The greatest logical leap in Lawrence's thought also figures here. I refer to the terminological leap that almost unintelligibly identifies "love" and the "love"-mode with the self-consciousness and the scientific intellectuality of the modern mind.

The leaps in question cannot be justified in strictly logical terms, but they have their relatively rigorous imagic logic. Lawrence's system is, as we have already seen, organized in terms of images, whose associative logic weighs heavily in the total pattern of values and judgments he wishes to convey. If we are to achieve any discursive understanding of his notions of the psyche and how it fell—as of how the world fell with

[2] See Chap. III.

it—we must examine the associative logic of such governing images. It is the structure of such images, and the more discursive constructs with which they are linked, that I wish to examine in this chapter.

The Imagery

We recall that Lawrence negates the social agencies of control and repression and affirms the passional reality of the self. He tries to negate the traditional dichotomy of flesh and spirit altogether, striving to proclaim the seamless unity of the radical self.

Yet Lawrence, even while urging a revaluation of the traditional opposition, actually recapitulates in his imagery the dualistic traditions of East and West. He links spirit with light and flesh with darkness. Spirit strives upward toward the light; eventually it is conceived as light itself. Flesh, on the other hand, is heavy and downward-tugging. Light springs from the darkness of flesh. Yet light struggles to overcome darkness, even as darkness struggles to quench the light.[3]

The imagery is familiar insofar as it emphasizes the struggle of light for supremacy. In the old mystery religions, and in Christianity as well, the initiate "sees the *light*." Dante, for example, is drawn into the dazzling light which, revealed to him, is God.[4] In the Platonic tradition, the light which is the object of the soul's striving is the light of reason. It is the intellect which illuminates the dark places of life, even as the dawning light of the sun clears away the shadows of darkness and night.

Light is associated with *Logos* in both the Platonic and the Christian-Hellenistic traditions.[5] This leads Lawrence to the

---

[3] I refer to the "systems" of the "Study of Thomas Hardy" and "The Crown" essays, which I discuss in Chaps. I, II, and III.

[4] Dante, *Paradise*, Canto XXXIII, 11.40ff.

[5] John I: 1–6.

further identification of the light-of-reason with repression. This too follows directly from the imagery of the Socratic realm of discourse.[6] Socrates' light-strewing intellect is aggressive. It is a flesh-, matter-, and nature-subjugating entity. But Socrates had conceived of the intellect as vastly superior to the flesh. The flesh is a prison to the soul: "Every seeker after wisdom knows," says Socrates, "that up to the time when philosophy takes it over his soul is a helpless prisoner, chained hand and foot in the body, compelled to view reality not directly but only through its prison bars. . . ."[7] In order to free itself, the mind seeks to unite with the idea of the Good, which is fixed, changeless, and eternal. Mind achieves this by subjugating the "lower" faculties.

In the *Phaedrus*, reason is imagined as a charioteer who drives the horses of the soul toward the heavenly fields of light, where truth, goodness, and beauty exist. To reach those fields, the charioteer must utterly subjugate the ugly steed of passion which, instead of straining upward toward the good, struggles downward toward sensual gratification. Only through effective control of the steed of unreason, or passion, can the soul reach its destination.[8]

[6] Herbert Marcuse generalizes effectively on this point in *Eros and Civilization: A Philosophical Inquiry into Freud* (Boston: The Beacon Press, 1955), pp. 120 and 124ff. Two of his subtitles suggest the drift of his argument: "Logos and logic of domination" and "Ego as aggressive and transcending subject."

[7] Plato, *Phaedo*, trans. Hugh Tredennick (Baltimore: Penguin Books, 1959), p. 135. I should note that the *Phaedo* represents only one tendency in Plato's thought—the ascetic tendency that is elaborated in Christianity. Another strain is to be found in *The Symposium*, where Socrates affirms the body and the erotic interest in the body as vehicles for apprehension of higher things and as participators in the reality of higher things. See Plato, *The Symposium*, trans. W. Hamilton (Baltimore: Penguin Books, 1951), pp. 92ff.

[8] Plato, *Phaedrus*, in *Phaedrus, Ion, Gorgias and Symposium, with Passages from Republic and Laws*, trans. Lane Cooper (Oxford: Oxford University Press, 1938), pp. 24–41, especially 38f.

There are substantive as well as imagic links between the
Socratic tradition and Lawrence's identification of the intellect and its objects with death. Socrates, considering the immortality of the soul, maintains that the philosopher's life is a
perpetual dying because he must always struggle to subjugate
the flesh. He must do this because the flesh involves one in
actions and passions which are in themselves impure, or de-
grading, and also because real knowledge cannot be obtained
through the senses, which communicate only with the world
of change and death.

> When the soul uses the instrumentality of the body for any in-
> quiry, whether through sight or hearing or any other sense . . . it
> is drawn away by the body into the realm of the variable, and
> loses its way and becomes confused and dizzy. . . . But when it
> investigates by itself, it passes into the realm of the pure and ever-
> lasting and immortal and changeless; and being of a kindred na-
> ture, when it is once independent and free from interference, con-
> sorts with it always and strays no longer, but remains, in that realm
> of the absolute, constant and invariable, through contact with
> beings of a similar nature.[9]

In a sense, some such valuation colors the Romantic conception of the relationship between life and knowledge.
Wordsworth's criticism of the meddling intellect which
"murders to dissect," and D'Annunzio's assertion that anatomy presupposes a corpse, both assume that the living organism cannot be known. In Lawrence's formulation: "To know
is to lose. When I have a finished mental concept of a beloved, or a friend, then the love and the friendship is dead."[10]

[9] Plato, *Phaedo*, p. 131.
[10] Lawrence, *Fantasia of the Unconscious*, p. 108. The idea is more
forcefully expressed elsewhere: "To *know* a living thing is to kill it.
You have to kill a thing to know it satisfactorily. For this reason the
desirous consciousness, the SPIRIT [*sic*], is a vampire." *Studies in
Classic American Literature*, p. 79.

Indeed, from Lawrence's point of view, all *a priori* certainties are "dead." The Kantian thought-forms, through which reality is known, are as dead as the Platonic forms. Mosaic morality, too, is fixed and immutable. Engraved in stone—the Tablets of the Law—it imposes its petrified ideals on both individual consciousness and communal behavior. For Lawrence, the idea, the thought form, and the moral absolute are evil in their deadness and their fixity. They are also evil because they mechanically impose an unjustified uniformity on man's image of the world, on the forms of his personality, and on his behavior.[11]

It is understandable, then, that Lawrence ultimately focuses on the machine to symbolize the tyranny of mind, morality, and the code of "love" which governs the psychic life. For Lawrence, the machine is the instrument of civilization that best symbolizes the qualities and achievements of modern man. It is the natural product of all the modes of consciousness, value, and social organization that govern the modern world as Lawrence sees it. The machine is created when man applies scientific knowledge to the pragmatic needs of society; it is, moreover, the instrument through which man harnesses the power of nature.

The machine has two values for Lawrence. In concrete terms, it symbolizes the impersonality and the cold efficiency of industrial capitalism. In more abstract terms, mechanism is opposed to organism, as it had been in the Romantic reaction against eighteenth-century rationalism. To the Romanticists, as to Lawrence, the living organism is an evolving entity, full of unknown potentialities, and vivid with the life that inheres in those possibilities. This antithesis of mechanism and organism can be applied, metaphorically, to societies (e.g., Burke's

[11] See "Him with His Tail in His Mouth," *Reflections on the Death of a Porcupine*, pp. 127–45 and *Kangaroo* (London: Martin Secker, 1923), p. 122.

and aggressive in a way that no machine can be. In Lawrence's own imagery, when the mind rides herd on the soul, it does so in passionate fixity, functioning in relation to the "body of life" as master to slave, or as rider to rebellious steed.[15] It is, moreover, a mad master and a mad rider: a demonic "God-in-the-machine," power-obsessed and compulsive, driven by its "mystic hatred" to try to reduce all things to ultimate *thing*hood.[16] In another, more occult image, the mind is a vampire that sucks the life-blood of the organism: "The ideal mind, the brain, has become the vampire of modern life, sucking up the blood and the life."[17]

The imagery of Edgar Allan Poe's "The Fall of the House of Usher," regarded from an allegorizing viewpoint akin to Lawrence's own, illuminates Lawrence's image of the mind as a vampire, as well as his sense of the dangers that inhere in the mind. It also casts further light upon Lawrence's entire conception of the internecine struggle between the mind and the blood, and upon the images—especially the images of light— that he employed in conveying it.[18]

In the Poe tale, we have twins, male and female, who exist in a reciprocal relation of love; an incestuous identification is implicit. At the same time, they may be taken allegorically to

---

[15] The image of rider and steed is central to *Women in Love*, where Gerald is seen tormenting a sensitive Arabian mare by forcing her to stand firm as a locomotive thunders by. See *Women in Love*, pp. 124–27. There is a comic parody of this image in *Fantasia of the Unconscious*, p. 95, where Lawrence writes: "Well, then, our human body is the bicycle. And our individual and incomprehensible self is the rider thereof."

[16] Gerald is described as "the God of the Machine, Deus ex Machina" in *Women in Love*, p. 239. Here Lawrence is concerned more with will than with intellect, but the two are closely intertwined in his presentation of the modern malaise.

[17] Lawrence, *Fantasia of the Unconscious*, p. 106.

[18] The reading of the tale is my own, but my reading takes off from essays by Lawrence and Allen Tate. See Lawrence, "Edgar Allan Poe," *Studies in Classic American Literature*, pp. 85ff.

represent the dual aspects of the soul. Roderick is both an
intellectual and an artistic type. He writes hymns to reason,
though he really keens the toppling of the monarch reason
from his throne. Roderick is dying of the atrophy, through
oversensitization, of his sensory mechanisms. Madeleine, the
female counterpart of Roderick, is identified with the flesh.
She dies of a mysterious disease and is laid out in an ancient,
corroded powder-storage vault deep underground. Because she
will not be denied in this way, she returns to destroy Roderick
in a final ghostly confrontation.

Poe, it seems to me, is suggesting the return of the repressed
—the repressed fleshly desire, the repressed incestuous wish,
and the repressed murderous impulse, now recoiling on the
repressor through the agency of an overstimulated imagination. This element within the fable is reinforced by the imagery of a painting by Roderick which is described in detail—
a painting that shows a mysterious underground vault, bathed
in relentless, incandescent light coming from no visible
source.

There is a curious congruity between the imagery of light in
the Poe tale and Lawrence's imagery. The similarity, it seems
to me, does not reveal direct influence, or borrowing on Lawrence's part. Rather, it stems from the use by both writers of
an image within a tradition. The light in both instances is the
light of consciousness waxed destructive. This is the connota-
tion Birkin gives to the electric lights which, he tells Hermione, are turned on when modern man makes love. He says:
" 'There's the whole difference in the world . . . between the
actual sensual being, and the vicious mental-deliberate profli-
gacy our lot goes in for. In our night-time, there's always
the electricity switched on, we watch ourselves, we get it all in
the head.' "[19] The light has become the vehicle of the deepest
unconscious destructive energies, as in the case of Gerald

[19] Lawrence, Women in Love, p. 45.

Crich, who is associated with radium, with electrification, and with the uncanny: "like sunshine refracted through crystals of ice."[20]

Lawrence contrasts the corrosive, disintegrative consciousness of the compulsive characters with the natural, creative consciousness by means of an alternative image of light. We see in point of contrast the warm, golden, just barely dawning, fleshly "dangerous" light that lies "meshed" in Ursula. This light is natural just as certain landscapes in *Women in Love* are natural and suggestive of the potentialities of the spontaneous or natural self.[21]

That Ursula, a woman, should embody such light is consistent with the overall Lawrencean view. Women, for him, symbolize the flesh and the feelings, which must absorb and integrate the light without negating it. Much later in his career he was to make the resurrected Jesus the symbol of the re-embodiment of spirit in flesh.[22] In *Women in Love*, he uses

[20] *Ibid.*, p. 15.

[21] Light is brilliantly handled throughout the "Class-Room" scene in which Birkin speaks of consciousness as electrical, and throughout the novel. One example must suffice. At the beginning of the classroom scene "A heavy copper-coloured beam of light came in at the west window. . . . Ursula . . . was scarcely conscious of it. . . . [Then] she heard . . . the click of the door. . . . She saw, in the shaft of ruddy, copper-coloured light . . . the face of a man." Then Birkin switches on the electric light. "The class-room was distinct and hard, a strange place after the soft dim magic that filled it before he came. . . . Ursula . . . looked like one who is suddenly wakened. There was a living, tender beauty, like a tender light of dawn shining from her face." The image may be said to be consummated when their love affair is consummated: "He stood on the hearth-rug looking at her, at her face that was upturned exactly like a flower, a fresh, luminous flower, glinting faintly golden with the dew of the first light. . . . Her face was now one dazzle of released, golden light."— *Women in Love*, pp. 36–37 and 329–30.

[22] I am thinking of the novella *The Man Who Died* and of the essays "Resurrection," *Phoenix*, pp. 737–39 and "The Risen Lord," *Assorted Articles* (London: Martin Secker, 1930), pp. 105–17.

the image of natural light shining within the female-flesh as a way of suggesting the potentialities of the natural, harmonious self. In both instances, the vision is one of harmony (or harmony-in-conflict) within man, as it is of harmony (or harmony-in-conflict) between man and nature. This vision is implicit in Lawrence's more abstruse attempts to render the dynamism of the psyche, even as it is in the imagery through which he renders his metaphysic.

The Structure of the Psyche

The natural psyche is essentially the unconscious psyche which is immanent in the flesh. Like Jung, Lawrence does not distinguish clearly between the conscious and unconscious portions of the psyche, even though he likes to rant and rave about the distinction.[23] One measure of this failure is the difference between Lawrence's concept of the unconscious and Freud's. "The Freudian unconscious," Lawrence wrote, "is the cellar in which the mind keeps its own bastard spawn."[24] Again, Lawrence mocks the Freudian concept by writing that it contains "nothing but a huge slimy serpent of sex, and heaps of excrement, and a myriad repulsive little horrors spawned between sex and excrement."[25]

Lawrence's image is pejoratively distorting, but it highlights an important element in Freud, who thought of the personality in terms of geological and archeological stratification, with

[23] Edward Glover, Freud or Jung? (Cleveland and New York: The World Publishing Company, 1963), Chap. I, esp. pp. 24–28. Glover holds that Jung subverts the Freudian distinction between the conscious and unconscious minds and in effect reverts to the faulty psychology that Freud superseded. The same may be said of Lawrence; his is essentially a faculty psychology.

[24] Lawrence, Psychoanalysis and the Unconscious, p. 9.

[25] Ibid., p. 5.

earlier layers beneath later ones.[26] The past lives on in the present as ruins underlie contemporary construction. Freud thinks that past experience lives on in the unconscious, which abuts on the body of the organism and is contained within it, but which is a mental entity.

For Lawrence, as for Freud, the unconscious is something that lies below the surface of ordinary consciousness. It is not a cellar, however, or a heap of ruins whose configurations bespeak the history of the individual. Rather, "the true unconscious is the well-head, the fountain of real motivity."[27] Experience does shape the individual, but the unconscious is not the repository of experience so much as a source of energy, "where life springs up at the source." As I have already indicated in the treatment of Lawrence's concepts of nature and personality, the essential self is regarded as an out-growth of nature. Just as nature in its vivid existence contains "the fourth dimension, what men used to call heaven," so the essential self is in the "unconscious," which "men used to call the soul."

By the unconscious we wish to indicate that essential unique nature of every individual creature, which is, by its very nature, unanalysable, undefinable, inconceivable. . . . And, being inconceivable, we will call it the unconscious. As a matter of fact, *soul* would be a better word. By the unconscious we do mean the soul. But the word *soul* has been vitiated by the idealistic use, until nowadays it means only that which a man conceives himself to be.[28]

Lawrence makes grand claims for the unconscious. "It is the active, self-evolving soul, bringing forth its own incarnation

---

[26] For treatment of Freud's imagery, in this connection, see Edgar Stanley Hyman, *The Tangled Bank* (New York: Atheneum, 1962), pp. 304ff.

[27] Lawrence, *Psychoanalysis and the Unconscious*, p. 9.

[28] *Ibid.*, p. 15.

and self-manifestation." The "unconscious brings forth not only consciousness, but tissue and organs also."[29]

In formulating his concept of the unconscious in this way, Lawrence echoes not only the mystic tradition but also the Romantic poets, who sought, like him, to free man from the determinism of environmental-associationalist psychologies. Blake, in *There Is No Natural Religion*, insists that the senses are organs of the soul; Keats, in one of his letters, writes that Milton's *Paradise Lost* represents the essential truth of the imagination: Adam dreamed, and Eve was real. Lawrence differs from the Romantics, however, in mistrusting imagination and dream as part of the mental-intellectual apparatus. Lawrence tends to reject, or at least to mock, writers like Blake and Keats because of the central place they give to fancy and imagination. Through exercise of imagination, Lawrence points out, man attempts to impose his will on nature.[30] Often as not, as Lawrence sees it, fantasy becomes detached from the real emotional needs of the individual and isolates (or insulates) him within the closed circle of the self.

This does not mean that Lawrence rejects fantasy; he merely rejects the excesses to which certain writers have carried their exaltation of the life of dream and fantasy, and he dramatizes the dangers implicit in this. In fact, within his concept of the unconscious, Lawrence implicitly promulgates the ideal which he was later to enunciate in the "Autobiographical Fragment." The "Fragment" indulges a Wellsian fantasy of people who are like "roseberries . . . a whole fruit,

[29] *Ibid.*, p. 42.
[30] See, for example, the story "None of That," *The Tales of D. H. Lawrence* (London: William Heinemann Ltd., 1934), pp. 898–917. "The Man Who Loved Islands," *ibid.*, pp. 917–40, explodes another Romantic cliche: the value of solitude. The story actually recapitulates the theme of Shelley's *Alastor*, showing how the wish to commune with nature is a death wish and also a flight from life and life-involvements.

body and mind and spirit, without split."[31] The treatises on the unconscious which, with "Education of the People," are Lawrence's most concerted attempt to work out a psychology, try to formulate a basis for such wholeness. In accordance with Lawrence's vision of the naturalness of civilization, he strives in all three works to naturalize all the civilized and civilizing faculties by making them a direct outgrowth of the spontaneous soul.

Reading the treatises, one is struck in this connection by Lawrence's essential conservatism. At his most radical he refuses to relinquish any one of the faculties or achievements of Western man, past or present. He merely wants to renaturalize them, to redeem them from their perversity within the present mode of civilization. I have already suggested this in the preceding chapter. Lawrence affirms the naturalness of all the faculties.[32] Mind, imagination, conscience, spirit—all of them are rooted in the unconscious. "This is indeed the main point of all full knowledge," he writes, "that it is contained mainly within the unconscious, its mental and conscious reference being only a sort of extract or shadow."[33] The mind, as I have noted, is not in principle opposed to the blood. It is rather the organ in which apprehension through "blood-consciousness" is "terminated."

Even its terminality of mind is equivocal, however. Viewed in the perspective of evolution, mind plays a heroic role. "Man is given mental intelligence in order that he may effect quick changes, . . . preserving himself alive and integral through a myriad environments and adverse circumstances which would exterminate a non-adaptable animal."[34] Yet

[31] Lawrence, "Autobiographical Fragment," *Phoenix*, p. 830.
[32] See Chap. III.
[33] Lawrence, *Psychoanalysis and the Unconscious*, p. 15.
[34] Lawrence, "Education of the People," *Phoenix*, p. 614–15. See, too, *Fantasia of the Unconscious*, p. 165, and *Kangaroo*, p. 279.

mind, which is meant to mediate between man and the world, can become the end of man's experience of the world. In the world that Lawrence knows, "the brain is . . . the terminal instrument of the dynamic consciousness. It transmutes what is a creative flux into a certain fixed cipher. It prints off, like a telegraph instrument the glyphs . . . which we call percepts, concepts, ideas."[35] The terminal mind is the "ideal" mind. And that mind has a will-to-power which is benign only when the self remains dynamically responsive to the promptings of the unconscious. Then the mind's will-to-power is curbed by the natural will. For, optimally, the will "is the faculty of self-determination in every living creature." The will, we recall, is "originally . . . a purely spontaneous control factor or the living unconscious. It seems as if, primarily, the will and the conscience were identical, in the premental state . . .[:] a great balancing faculty whereby automatization is *prevented* in the evolving psyche. The *spontaneous* will reacts at once against . . . exaggeration."[36]

Lawrence here uses the word "will" in a way that conflates several disparate meanings. It still bears something of the Elizabethan meaning of "inclination," "disposition," "appetite," and "lust"—that is, it suggests the instinctual aspects of man's nature. In this usage, it feeds into the concept of the will in Schopenhauer, who thinks of will as a cosmic force which drives living beings in ways completely concealed from them.

At the same time, the word is not completely purged of the opposite meaning, in which it refers to the agency, allied to reason, through which man's instinctual nature is controlled. In Socrates' imagery to which I have alluded, the will is allied with the charioteer who controls the steeds of the soul. Hence its association with conscience and with all the values and

[35] Lawrence, *Psychoanalysis and the Unconscious*, p. 4.
[36] *Ibid.*, p. 47.

strictures which the conscience of civilized man enforces upon him.

The identity of the spontaneous will and conscience in the premental state points to another element in Lawrence's vision of the seamless self. The conscience is as natural as the will or the mind. Furthermore, the very virtues which have generally been associated with civilization and with the formation of conscience are conceived as a "spontaneous adjustment of the living unconscious." "Honour is an instinct. . . . Pure morality is . . . an instinctive adjustment which the soul makes in every circumstance."[37]

In this regard Lawrence's ideal vision of the self is akin to the form of Blake's and Nietzsche's, even though he differs seriously with Blake on the question of imagination and with Nietzsche as to intellect. "Without contraries," Blake had written, "there is no progression": real civilization is beyond good and evil, the product of energy, thrust, and tension.[38] Nietzsche had held that morality within the Judeo-Christian tradition is the product of resentment and fear. For Nietzsche, true morality should be based on the free conflict of the instincts, without any effort on the part of a separate faculty of reason to subdue any one of the conflicting instincts. Nietzsche, like Lawrence, had protested the notion that the instincts or passions were opposed to reason and intimated that reason is a sort of "spontaneous control factor" in the free play of the passions. Nietzsche protests against "the whole conception of the rank of the *passions*: as if it were right and normal to be led by *reason*, while the passions are considered abnormal. . . . and nothing but *desire for pleasure*. Thus passion is degraded (1) as if it were only in *un*seemly cases, and not necessarily and always, that which activates; (2) insofar as it is taken to aim at something which

---

[37] Lawrence, *Fantasia of the Unconscious*, p. 116.
[38] William Blake, *The Marriage of Heaven and Hell*.

has no great value, namely mere amusement."[39] He also emphasizes "the misunderstanding of passion and *reason*, as if the latter existed as an entity by itself, and not rather as a state of the relations between different passions and desires; and as if every passion did not contain in itself its own quantum of reason."[40]

As I have suggested in my opening chapter, moreover, the Lawrencean self is also akin to the Dionysian ego of which Norman O. Brown speaks in *Life Against Death*.[41] Brown holds that Freud's late metapsychological speculations imply the possibility of freeing man from repression. Brown admits that Freud usually thinks in terms of the necessary conflict between nature (instinct) and civilization and therefore affirms the need to repress instinct. He maintains, however, that Freud's conception of the instincts admits the possibility of lifting repression. Brown terms the self that will be capable of self-regulation without self-repression the "Dionysian ego," alluding to Nietzsche's distinction between the Dionysian and Apollonian modes of dealing with experience. The Dionysian ego is an ego whose coherence does not depend on repression.

It seems to me that Brown errs in his reading of Freud. Freud sees the world tragically as a place of unremitting tension between nature and civilization and thinks of the human personality as a battleground where the two necessarily clash. It is Brown's error with reference to Freud, however, that makes his concept the more applicable to Lawrence. Lawrence, unlike Freud, conceives of civilization as the natural outgrowth of nature. His vision is based on the notion of a condition in which the self is not rent by devastating conflict, but can ride out the terms of its conflicts without endangering

[39] Cited in Walter Kaufmann, *Nietzsche*, p. 203.
[40] *Ibid.*, p. 203.
[41] Goodheart, *The Utopian Vision of D. H. Lawrence*, p. 105.

either itself or civilization. This is possible because civilization is the natural outgrowth of the realized self—if we wish, the Holy Ghost of the Self—and its natural medium of existence.[42]

Lawrence posits the existence of such a self almost from the outset and insists that it has existed throughout history. At this point the problem for us is not that he believes this, or the grounds on which he affirms it, but rather the fact that he came to conceive of modern man as living in a *fallen* state, within which the natural harmony between self and civilization no longer prevails. In the modern, fallen world, the spontaneous Holy Ghost of the Self can no longer spring into being out of the interplay of faculties and impulses. It cannot come into existence owing to the agencies of repression and oppression generated outside the self—agencies that constitute a kind of alter ego, or alternative self, at odds with the spontaneous self.

Lawrence thinks of this second self as the "social self," the "ego," or the "self-conscious ego." These are linked to the agencies of social control on the one hand and the forces of "ideal" reason as conceived within the Western tradition on the other. The social self is the "ideal" self—the self, again, that serves as charioteer of Socrates' chariot of the soul. The identification is enunciated as follows. The ego is "the sum total of what we *conceive* ourselves to be."[43] Moreover, it is "a sort of second self" made up of "[the] body of accepted consciousness, . . . inherited more or less ready-made. . . ."[44]

Criticizing the "second" or superimposed self, Lawrence writes:

Nothing in the world is more pernicious than the *ego* or spurious self, the conscious entity with which every individual is saddled.

[42] See Chap. I. Goodheart makes this point very effectively. See *The Utopian Vision*, pp. 170ff.

[43] Lawrence, *Psychoanalysis and the Unconscious*, p. 28.

[44] Lawrence, "Democracy," *Phoenix*, p. 710.

He receives it almost *en bloc* from the preceding generation, and spends the rest of his life trying to drag his spontaneous self from beneath the horrible incubus. And the most fatal part of the incubus, by far, is the dead, leaden weight of handed-on ideals. . . . A finely or fantastically decorated mill-stone is called a personality.[45]

In its various aspects—and especially as it is depicted in the experience of the major characters in *Women in Love*—the social self is akin to the Freudian superego ("ego-ideal") and the Jungian *persona*.

Freud defines the superego as a psychic "institution" that "performs the activities of self-observation, conscience and the holding up of ideals."[46] Obviously, he is speaking of what men have traditionally called the conscience. The chief role of the superego in the Freudian system is the imposition of its judgments on the impulsive life of the organism, an impulsive life that is grounded in instinct.

What makes the Freudian conception of the superego seem especially relevant to the Lawrencean social and mental self is the fact that the superego is as thoroughly submerged in the Freudian unconscious as the instinctual wishes which it must combat. The superego is conceived as a tyrannical force that rages against the rebellious self and that punishes it for wishes as well as deeds. As a result, it is not subject to rational control and, in its destructiveness, wreaks havoc without the possibility of control or intervention from the conscious mind. Just this, we recall, had been one of the main emphases of *Women in Love*: that the agencies and institutions of consciousness, order, and social control can become, in morbid people like Gerald Crich or Hermione Roddice, the vehicle for the violence and chaos that they seek to subdue or avert.

[45] *Ibid.*, pp. 710–11.
[46] Sigmund Freud, *New Introductory Lectures on Psychoanalysis*, p. 90.

The snowballing violence of both the political and the private life of modern man is one of Lawrence's main themes in the postwar years. The compulsive, aggressive, self-destructive energy of the characters in *Women in Love* would seem to stem from the compulsions of the mind in its aggressive, hate-filled state. Civilization, as in Gerald Crich's experience, turns the human faculties on themselves and decomposes them, to the detriment of the individual and of all civilization. Freud was to analyze an analogous process, rooted in the instincts themselves, in his *Civilization and Its Discontents* (1930).

In a more obvious way, there is an affinity between Lawrence's concept of the self and the Jungian *persona*. The Jungian *persona* is defined as "personality reaction to the world of objects"[47] or "the habitual external attitude of the personality."[48] It is the mask-like, type-cast surface of the personality that takes the shape of the "face" that a man must assume in performing his stereotypical social tasks. This is virtually Lawrence's definition: "And now for Personality. What meaning . . . ? *Persona*, in Latin, is a player's mask, or a character in a play: and perhaps the word is cognate with *sonare*, to sound. . . . The old meaning lingers in *person*, and is almost obvious in *personality*. A person is a human being *as he appears to others*, and personality is that which is transmitted from the person to his audience."[49]

In effect, if we leave out the complications introduced by the idea of the unconscious aggressiveness of the mental and social self, the imagery of the personality employed here suggests the formulation of the Hardy "Study." In the "Study," we recall, society is conceived as a walled encampment de-

[47] Glover, *Freud or Jung?*, p. 30.
[48] Frieda Fordham, *Introduction to Jung's Psychology* (Baltimore: Penguin Books, 1953), p. 47.
[49] Lawrence, "Democracy," *Phoenix*, p. 710.

signed to shut out the wild heath, where "the instinctive life heaves up." Human life within the encampment is conceived as a petty "morality play" wherein men play roles that do not embody the greater part of their instinctive life.[50] These roles are the *personae* of the social self, which is "analytical, critical, constructive but not creative, sensational but not passionate, emotional but without true feeling."[51] It is, again in the language of the "Study," like the society whose laws cannot "put into being something which did not before exist."[52]

The social or *persona* self is conceived as a created rather than a creative entity, and one that enters into tension with the integral, unconscious self which is the "well-head" of human creativity. Each individual, in Lawrence's conception, is faced with the challenge of establishing a viable relationship between the social and mental self and the somatic self, which is the seat of individuality as well as creativity.

Despite Lawrence's rage against the constraining *persona*, he assumes that the individual cannot exist without one. Man must, in virtually all of Lawrence's accounts of the personality, develop a *persona*. Man, after all, "comes into being in the middle of life" and not at birth. Although his self is "uncreated" and the magical creature of the unknown, the unknown itself is *within* life and emerges out of it—even as being emerges out of the clash of the waves that constitute life and that, in the formulation of "The Crown" essays, emerge from the rival psychic and metaphysical eternities. And human life, though it is always potentially in touch with the unknown, is generally mediated through social forms.

Lawrence's essay on education touches on the necessity for adaptation to social environments—and the need to maintain

[50] See Chap. I.
[51] Lawrence, "[The Individual Consciousness v. the Social Consciousness]," *Phoenix*, p. 763.
[52] Lawrence, "Study of Thomas Hardy," *Phoenix*, p. 405.

autonomy within them. Lawrence writes that "education and growing up is supposed to be a process of learning to escape the automatism of ideas, to live direct from the spontaneous, vital centre of oneself."[53] Every society must therefore strive to condition its young "to that point where at last there will be a perfect correspondence between the spontaneous, yearning impulsive-desirous soul and the automatic *mind* which runs on little wheels of ideas."[54]

As to the ideational, self-conscious constellation of the social self, Lawrence suggests that it is imposed in the course of education. "The human being, more than any other living thing, is subject to falsification. We alone have mental consciousness, speech, and thought. And this mental consciousness is our greatest peril."[55] The modern world has fallen victim to this peril:

our process of universal education is today so uncouth, so psychologically barbaric, that it is the most terrible menace to the existence of our race. We seize hold of our children, and by parrot-compulsion we force into them a set of mental tricks. . . . And then, after a few years, with a certain number of windmills in their heads, we turn them loose, like so many inferior Don Quixotes, to make a mess of life. All that they have learnt in their heads has no reference at all to their dynamic souls. . . .
. . . ideas are the most dangerous germs mankind has ever been injected with. They are introduced into the brain by injection, in schools and by means of newspapers, and then we are done for.[56]

It would seem that by this process the higher faculty of mind—that is, the "ideal mind" comes to dominate the rest of the psyche. Mind comes to control the lower faculties and also comes to dominate the social and historical worlds.

[53] Lawrence, "Education of the People," *Phoenix*, p. 604.
[54] *Ibid.*, p. 605.   [55] *Ibid.*, p. 604.
[56] Lawrence, *Fantasia of the Unconscious*, p. 118.

How the Psyche Fell

Quite obviously, if this were the only way Lawrence had of explaining the fall of self and world, there would be little to be said for it. If the Lawrencean psychology simply held that the "social self" and the "ideal self" are created by "injecting" dangerous ideas by means of school, books, and newspapers, it would be patently fatuous. He would, in effect, be saying that the oppressive, automatistic, mechanistic mental-social-conscious self is wholly a fabrication of self-conscious social and ideological agencies. The inorganic, superimposed self would literally be impressed upon the personality from the outside, and it would be impressed without clear reference to the needs of the being upon whom it is impressed. This is a radically problematic position in any circumstance, but especially from within Lawrence's own system, which holds that history and society are rooted in the psyche and that the workings of society necessarily express or satisfy prior psychic needs.

Actually, Lawrence generally leaves himself open to no such drastic difficulty. The static unnatural ideals which are injected into the modern child's head are in his view the outgrowth of its parents' unconscious needs. These are passed on to him, in the form of emotional predispositions, of learned affective responses, inculcated long before he comes to hear of school or learns that there is such a thing as an alphabet.[57] The problems of modern man, as Lawrence ex-

---

[57] Lawrence expresses this in several peculiar and interesting forms: (1) he occasionally writes that "we are such stuff as our grandmothers' dreams are made on," implying that the wishes of the parents are directly inflicted on their children; (2) he sometimes speaks of the souls of the dead inhabiting the places in which they have lived and thus shaping the spiritual (or "spirit") environment of their descendents. See "Making Love to Music," *Assorted Articles*, p. 163; "Introduction," *Fantasia of the Unconscious*, p. 64; and "Spirit of Place," *Studies in Classic American Literature*, pp. 16ff.

pounds them in the treatises on the unconscious and in "Education of the People," stem from an affective as well as an intellectual ailment, from a somatic-unconscious as well as a mental-conscious distortion of the human being.

As with so many other things in Lawrence's work, the process is best exemplified in the characterizations of *Women in Love*. Gerald and Hermione are addicted to their intellectuality, just as they are compulsively in quest of self-aggrandizing power, not because they are oversocialized, but because they are psychologically and spiritually sick. Their sickness takes the form of fierce aggression against others and against nature. As I have already pointed out, they have a compulsive need to dominate, at any price, in order to strengthen their flagging sense of self; they must compensate for some flaw (or void) at the center of their being.[58] Their aggression is, as Lawrence conceives of it, inseparable from their intellectuality and their technological and political interests, but it is not identical with them. Though the precise source of the disease ultimately eludes precise definition, it is related to certain clearly defined emotional and ideological circumstances.

These are spelled out in the characterization of Gerald, whose difficulties are shown to spring from his immediate family circumstances. Specifically, the death and hatred that Gerald embodies are conceived as a reaction against the charity that has governed his father's life and that has poisoned his entire environment. This charity is ultimately a manifestation of "love" in the Hardy "Study" sense of "spirit" and the aspiration toward transcendence. In Gerald, the victory of "mind," and its sadistic tyranny, is derivative. It stems from the alliance between destructiveness (or aggressiveness) and mentality, as these manifest themselves both in the objective world of social values and in the subjective world of affects and relationships. The latter, however, is primary.

[58] See Chap. IV.

The etiology of Gerald's condition is given. His father hated his mother and her fierce aristocratic independence. "With unbroken will, [however,] he had substituted pity for all his hostility,—pity had been his shield and his safeguard, and his infallible weapon."[59] Pity is related, in old Mr. Circh, to charity—to Christian charity, which demands that he respond with love and sympathetic self-abnegation toward others:

He had been so constant to his lights, so constant to charity, and to his love for his neighbor. Perhaps he had loved his neighbor even better than himself—which is going one further than the commandment. Always, this flame had burned in his heart, sustaining him through everything, the welfare of the people. He was a large employer of labor, he was a great mine-owner. And he had never lost this from his heart, that in Christ he was one with his workmen. Nay, he had felt inferior to them, as if they through poverty and labor were nearer to God than he. He had always the unacknowledged belief that it was his workmen, the miners, who held in their hands the means of salvation. To move nearer to God, he must move towards his miners, his life must gravitate towards theirs. They were, unconsciously, his idol, his God made manifest. In them he worshipped the highest, the great, sympathetic, mindless Godhead of humanity.[60]

We are told the suppression of hatred and the resort to charity in the father's marriage had rendered him "more and more hollow in his vitality, the vitality was bled from within him, as by some haemorrhage."[61] He dies of the cancerous corruption that is felt to inhere in repressed violence. As for Gerald, "He was in reaction against Charity, and yet he was dominated by it; it assumed supremacy in the inner life, and he could not confute it."[62]

Significantly, Gerald's death upon the frosty Alpine heights of ice and snow takes place under a crucifix. The God who, in

[59] Lawrence, *Women in Love*, p. 245.   [60] *Ibid.*
[61] *Ibid.*, p. 248.   [62] *Ibid.*, p. 249.

one of Lawrence's formulations, gave his life for the "great unsympathetic mindless Godhead of humanity" is the being under whose gaze Gerald dies. The irony, is, in its way, magnificent. The deity who, in Dante's vision, had been at the opposite pole to the abysmal lake of ice that symbolizes the infernal Satanic negation of His own warmth and love has come to preside over the mountain-heights of freezing cold.

The inversion is obviously significent. Jesus, who brought mankind the gift of a warm and saving love, has, in Lawrence's judgment, been instrumental in evolving the icy mode of damning intellect; the God who had sought to unite men in a community of healing love has helped to create a world that is consumed by hate from within and torn by a narrow egotism that destroys any possibility of individual or communal contact and warmth. Gerald, who consciously denies all the values Jesus had affirmed, is nonetheless the spiritual creature of Christianity, a Christianity that, in Lawrence's view, did not begin to fulfill its ultimate possibilities until the beginning of the modern period.[63]

It will be noted that even as one interprets Lawrence's concrete exposition of the causes of the Gerald-malaise, one is confronted with the problem that we started out to solve, though it figures here in a variant form. On the one hand, Gerald's disease is emotional, the product of an overstimulation of the love-aspect of his psyche. On the other, that overstimulation is related to ideological or intellectual attitudes.

This may, in the final analysis, be Lawrence's point: that one cannot properly dissociate the two. The *ideas* that Jesus

[63] One should note here that the novel suggests a simple and even "total" psychological derivation for Gerald's difficulty: an Oedipal fixation on the one level, and an enraged craving for return to passive symbiotic relation to the mother on the other. Neither derivation contributes substantially to the problem of how Gerald's world came to be as destruction-ridden and disintegrated as it in fact is.

represents imply feelings and these feelings in turn give rise to ideas. The order of causality becomes irrelevant in such a scheme; the wish to ascertain causes in itself becomes perverse —and Lawrence in fact renounces the quest for causes in history. History becomes, for him, the open-ended entity he had described in the "Preface" to Movements in European History.[64] Yet civilization, however fragmented and perverse its content, is to be conceived as of a piece: each moment in history is utterly coherent, representing a total relationship of parts that hang together because they all stem from impulses or compulsion that springs up in man, either out of his sick dissociation from nature, or, through him, out of the heart of nature itself.

Such a sense of the total coherence of a civilization and the interrelatedness of all its parts is reflected in Lawrence's treatment of the actual process of deterioration in the West. If he fails to formulate an adequate theory of why things have gone the way they have gone—that is, if he cannot explain how the "love"-mode has come to dominate and to generate hatred and disease—he deals extensively and often convincingly with a wide range of phenomena that he regards as symptomatic of the modern malaise, and that together define both the problem and the grounds on which it might be tackled.

Lawrence tries, moreover, to relate them all to what he considers the central phenomenon of his culture: the dominance of the "love"-mode in all phases of experience and its pervasive influence both in the inner emotional life and the social and ideological domains. He sees the two areas, in fact, as inextricably bound up with each other. The emotional predispositions which individuals bring to experience and the experience in which they are expected to participate conspire to produce the result that is, for Lawrence, the modern world. This is the case in the great world just as it is in Gerald's

[64] Lawrence, Movements in European History, pp. ix-x.

family. If Mr. Crich's insensitivity and latent brutality are cloaked in high-flown Christian morality, so are those of other men. If his weakness and lack of self-confidence are nurtured by the Christian values, so are those of other men. Ideology is both the source and the product of human frailty—or strength.

In the following pages I shall deal with Lawrence's sketch of the operation of the "love"-mode in both realms: in the subjective dimension of feeling, and in the objective realm of social, political, economic, and ideological life. I shall also attempt to show how the meaning of the term "love" ramifies so as to come to mean not only *eros* or *agape*, but also "consciousness," "self-consciousness," and even "thought" and "scientific speculation"—a shift of meaning that must be understood if one is to grasp the full scope of Lawrence's indictment of the modern world.

a. *The subjective dimension*

As I have indicated earlier in this section, susceptibility to the devastations of the "love"-mode is the organic outgrowth of the individual's life history.

Even the early Lawrence had acknowledged that the self is to some extent shaped by the circumstances of birth and breeding, although he insisted that the individual could free himself from these restrictions through the erotic foray into the unknown. The Lawrence of *Women in Love* and of the postwar treatises on the unconscious is increasingly aware of the extent to which men are unable to break out of the given modes of experience and consciousness. In the language of the Hardy "Study," love is no longer the via media to being; men can no longer be reborn through love.

In "Education of the People" and in the treatises on the unconscious, Lawrence probes, discursively, the process of psychological corruption within the family. In all three works, but especially in *Fantasia of the Unconscious*, he insists that modern man's subjection, from the moment of birth, to an exaggerated dependency has resulted in the dominance of the "love"-mode. This dependency involves premature stimulation of the sentiment of love in the child and hence the premature birth of self-consciousness.

Every individual must have warm, life-giving relationships with others, but he must also preserve his separateness. Healthy individual development hinges on maintenance of a polarity of attraction and repulsion, of love and hate. In the normal process,

the child cleaves back to the old source. . . . With joy and peace it returns to the breast, almost as to the womb.
But not quite. Even in sucking it discovers its new identity and *power*. . . . it draws itself back suddenly; it waits. . . . [It utters] the scream of revolt from connection. . . . The child is screaming itself rid of the old womb, kicking itself in a blind paroxysm into freedom, into separate, negative independence.[65]

This desire for disjunction and independence is rooted in the soma, below the threshold of consciousness. Writing in the opaque idiom of his physiological theories, Lawrence insists that "the two [nerve] centres beneath the diaphragm are centres of dark subjectivity, centripetal, assimilative."[66] Lawrence holds that this polarity of attraction and repulsion is actuated along sets of nerve centers, classified as "higher" and "lower." This ranking has no reference to value; it merely designates the position of nerve centers in the body.

The first set of centers to awaken in the infant is the "subjective" set, which is the lower and is located in the solar plexus. This set, identified with the sensual will, corresponds

---

[65] Lawrence, *Psychoanalysis and the Unconscious*, pp. 22–23.
[66] *Ibid.*, p. 29.

to the "flesh" in Lawrence's earlier dichotomy. The "objective," "higher" set, located in and around the chest, is made up of a complex of nerves that serve the love-function. In Lawrence's earlier system, this is the "spirit." Although contrasted with radical sensuality, it is of the flesh and the senses.

Yet, even though these upper centers (the objective ones) are of the flesh, or the "blood," they function much as the mind does. They are concerned with apprehension of objects in an objective mode. The tender feelings directed toward such objects are quite clearly associated with "mother love" (or love of mother) as opposed to sensual love.

Lawrence's eloquence in rendering the quality of this feeling reflects the great importance he attaches to society's deterioration under the "love"-mode, which is also—incongruously —the mode of mentation. This link is forged as follows:

The great sympathetic plexus of the breast is the heart's mind. . . . From the sympathetic centre of the breast as from a window the unconscious goes forth seeking its object, to dwell upon it. . . . [F]rom the cardiac plexus goes forth that strange effluence of the self which seeks and dwells upon the beloved, lovingly roving like the fingers of an infant or a blind man over the face of the treasured object, gathering her mould into itself and transferring her mould forever into its own deep unconscious psyche. This is the first acquiring of objective knowledge, sightless, unspeakably direct. *It is a dwelling of the child's unconscious within the form of the mother. . . .*[67]

Clearly this is the "love" treated earlier as the "love"-mode of Shelley—a mode which now dominates mankind. In our era "the great plexus of the breast . . . is the great planet of our psychic universe. In the previous sympathetic era the flower of the universal blossomed in the navel. But since Egypt the sun of creative activity beams from the breast, the heart of the

[67] *Ibid.*, p. 31. Italics mine.

supreme Man. This is to us the source of light—the loving heart, the Sacred Heart."[68]

Lawrence attributes man's present psychic state to the dominance of one aspect of the cardiac plexus, the aspect that involves "the devotional, self-outpouring of love, love which gives its all to the beloved." "It is really self-devoting love, not self-less," because its negative aspect "searches and explores the beloved, *bringing back* pure objective apprehension. . . . This is the other half of devotional love—perfect *knowledge* of the beloved."[69]

[T]he outgoing, the sheer and unspeakable bliss of the sense of union, communion, at-oneness with the beloved –and then the complementary objective *realization* of the beloved, the realization of that which is apart, different. This realization is like riches to the objective consciousness. It is, as it were, the adding of another self to the own self, through the mode of apprehension. Through the mode of dynamic objective apprehension, which in our day we have gradually come to call *imagination*, a man may in his time add on to himself the whole of the universe, by increasing pristine realization of the universal. This in mysticism is called the progress to infinity."[70]

The danger is that the self may lose the ability to return and distinguish itself from those objects:

Primal is the blissful sense of ineffable transfusion with the beloved, which we call love. . . . It is a mode of creative consciousness. . . . It is a great objective flux, a streaming forth of the self in blissful departure, like sunbeams streaming.

If this activity alone worked, then the self would utterly depart from its own integrity, it would pass out and merge with the beloved."[71]

Thus, the "love"-mode leads directly to the corruption of mentality and abstraction, which, in principle, are alien to it.

[68] *Ibid.*, p. 36.   [69] *Ibid.*, p. 37. Italics mine.   [70] *Ibid.*, p. 40.
[71] *Ibid.*, p. 38. Italics mine.

This corruption is the result of corrupted maternal function. The mother is no longer able to allow the infant simply to *be* in terms of its dynamic needs. "A child has *no* mental consciousness and *no* self, and ten times less than no mental consciousness of self until that fiend, its mother, followed by a string of personally affected females, [that is, schoolmarms] proceeds to provoke this mental consciousness in the small psyche. . . . How can we help being neurotic when our mothers provoked self-consciousness in us at the breast: provoked . . . ideal lust for communion in self-consciousness?"[72]

Lawrence explores this betrayal of the natural maternal function in *Fantasia of the Unconscious*. He feels that modern women cannot fulfill themselves in marriage. They lack faith in their husbands, who have lost faith in themselves and in their masculine role in the world. Hence, as wives, they cannot give themselves up to sexual fulfillment. Instead, despairing of their own lives and satisfactions, they turn to their children for love, comfort, and fulfillment:

Seeking, seeking the fulfillment in the deep passional self; diseased with self-consciousness and sex in the head, foiled by the very loving weakness of the husband who has not the courage to withdraw into his own stillness and singleness, and put the wife under the spell of his fulfilled decision; the unhappy woman beats about for her insatiable satisfaction, seeking whom she may devour. And usually, she turns to her child. Here she provokes what she wants. Here, in her own son who belongs to her, she seems to find the last perfect response for which she is craving. He is a medium to her, she provokes from him her own answer. So she throws herself into a last great love for her son, a final and fatal devotion, that which would have been the richness and strength of her husband and is poison to her boy.[73]

In doing so, mothers stimulate their children, especially their sons, in the upper, objective centers, so that the sons

[72] Lawrence, "Education of the People," *Phoenix*, p. 622.
[73] Lawrence, *Fantasia of the Unconscious*, p. 157.

remain crippled by the "ideal," "ineffable transfusion" of self
in the beloved. The result is a weak, dependent male, unable
to fulfill himself in the flesh because he is unable to bring the
full force of his affection to bear on his mate; he is therefore
inhibited in the lower, specifically sexual centers.[74]

By adopting this theory of polarized nerve centers, Lawrence has linked love to knowledge through the "objective"
knowing of the upper or "love" centers of the organism. He
believes this love to be stimulated early in life within the
relation between child and parents, at a nonsexual level, provoked by a prior lack of personal and sexual fulfillment in
women. It is noteworthy that this last point is one of the
major motifs in Lawrence's very early work. Even in The
White Peacock he had urgently remarked the way in which
women shirked "responsibility" for themselves by throwing
themselves into motherhood. He shows this to be especially
strong when a marriage has failed to satisfy the "integral"
selves of the partners.[75]

Lawrence clearly thinks of the psychological process he is
rendering—here, the emergence of the "love"-mode—as
rooted in social reality. Women are unfulfilled because their
husbands have not been able to demand or to confer the
ultimate erotic fulfillments. Men cannot make sexual demands in part because they lack dignity as men. Such dignity
is in part rooted in work and in the male work-world, and the
conditions of modern industrial labor obviate its existence.
But the plight of modern men and modern marriages is also
the result of the grinding moralism of middle-class values,

[74] It will be noted that here Lawrence is rendering much the same
process that had been rendered in Sons and Lovers. In formulating his
system, Lawrence clearly drew on insights explored and elucidated in
the writing of his novels—even as, in his novels, he drew on speculative
notions evolved in the discursive writings—as Daleski has shown con-
clusively in his splendidly balanced study, The Forked Flame.

[75] Lawrence, The White Peacock, p. 280.

values that have come to pervade the life of the working class as well.

Pursuing the social and historical concomitants of this unmanning, one must note Lawrence's treatment of the Victorian cult of sexual purity and its necessary desexualization of the mother. Lawrence often shows how woman becomes the "Great Mother" in relation to her husband as well as her children. Although idealized and officially desexualized, woman has been given a great deal of power. From it, she draws the courage to assert her sexuality in an independent and unmanning way. One of the bitterest complaints of the men in *Aaron's Rod*, for example, is that women no longer wait for the erotic "call" from men. They refuse even to answer the "call" because they wish to have men answer to *their* needs.[76] At the same time women are seen as craving release from the need to initiate and sustain relationships. They want—ambivalently, to be sure—to submit and succumb to the strong male. Virtually all the novellas of the postwar years are about this: "The Captain's Doll," "The Woman Who Rode Away," "The Princess," and *St. Mawr*. This is also a major theme in *The Plumed Serpent*, as it is in *Lady Chatterley's Lover*.

It is characteristic of Lawrence not to emphasize the obvious historical causes of the difficulty. His fiction often implies such causes, and his discursive writings from time to time touch on them. For the most part, however, he fulminates about the ideational and ideological effects of those causes. One might say that he is concerned almost exclusively with "superstructure" and the purely psychological sources of the elements that constitute that superstructure. Only rarely is he directly interested in the mediating social circumstances that might cast light on the subjective feelings which predis-

[76] Lawrence, *Aaron's Rod* (London: William Heinemann Ltd., 1922), pp. 258ff.

pose the individual to espouse certain ideals, or on the ideals themselves. Though he rants about the pernicious effects of ideation and calls for rebellion against the tyranny of ideas, he gives ideas a remarkably central place in his account.

The major consideration here, therefore, must be the ideological manifestations of the "love"-mode to which modern men are subject.

b. *The objective dimension*

The overstimulation of children by parents explains the predisposition to the "love"-mode. It also explains the susceptibility of modern men to the "love values" that characterize the modern world. The fact is, however, that even the elaborate psychological and neurological predispositions hinge in some way on the mental-ideological affirmation of love and sympathy. As Lawrence sees her, the mother who turns to her son because her husband has failed her is afflicted by the "love ideal." She seeks, with her husband, not passional fulfillment, but rather a pal —an ideal mate who is gentle and human and in sympathetic harmony with her. Thus, she reflects not only her own emotional predispositions, but also the prevailing creed. "Now the good old creed we have been suckled in," Lawrence writes in "Education of the People," "teaches us that man is *essentially* and *finally* an ideal being: essentially and finally a pure spirit . . . a term of abstract consciousness. As such he has his immortality and his identity with the infinite. This identity with the infinite is the goal of life. And it is reached through love, self-abandoning love. All that is truly love is good and holy; all that is not truly love is evil."[77]

This love ideal in the objective world of modern culture has much in common with the "love"-mode as it had been conceived in the Hardy "Study."[78] In the post-war writings, how-

[77] Lawrence, "Education of the People," *Phoenix*, p. 615.
[78] See Chap. III.

ever, the social, political, economic, technological, and psychological concomitants of the mode are more clearly enunciated. They are, moreover, enunciated in such a way as to include everything Lawrence finds objectionable about the modern world and to dramatize the complete "disembodiment" of that world.

The scope of the phenomena that Lawrence subsumed under the "love"-mode is astonishing, and—as I shall attempt to show—very oddly assorted. The manifestations of the mode, however, do fall into several simple and meaningful categories. Essentially, Lawrence links to the "love"-mode three ideological aspects of modern life: the democratic ideal, the scientific-intellectual ideal, and the Protestant theological ideal.

1. *The democratic ideal*, which has prevailed since the eighteenth century, has inculcated both altruistic benevolism (the modern form of Christian charity) and atomistic, self-interested individualism. In this sphere, identity with the infinite —the characteristic aim of the "upper centers" in Lawrence's psychological system—takes the form of identification with the mass of citizens in the commonwealth. This is the great Whitman's great failing: the will to merge with the cosmic and the political "all." This ideal is defined as the ideal of "Love, Self-Sacrifice, Humanity, united in love, in brotherhood, in peace."[79] Lawrence holds that psychic need normally draws one apart from others, but at the same time he holds that the democratic ideology (and ideals) neutralizes the impulse to isolation and self-integrity and even comes to preclude it.

2. *The scientific-intellectual ideal*, which came into being a century earlier, has exalted consciousness and self-consciousness. Here "identity with the infinite" would seem to involve the effort to "add the world onto the self" through an act of

[79] Lawrence, *Kangaroo*, p. 296.

conscious awareness, akin to the mimesis of natural process implied by Lawrence's conception of thought itself. Related to this ideal is the technology that makes industrialism possible, the "conquest" of nature through formulation of its "static" laws and utilization of its resources. Scientific intellectuality ties in with democratic humanitarianism through the leveling, abstractive tendency of mathematics. In democracy, men are reduced to the abstract symmetry, or conformity, of hands, feet, mouths, stomachs, votes. *L'esprit géométrique* governs both spheres.

3. *The Protestant-theological ideal,* which further antedates the preceding pair, demands negation of the world and the flesh. In this view, the world is the work of the devil, and the individual must struggle toward uncontaminate, virtually disincarnate spirituality. Puritanism not only questions pleasure and hence the entire domain of the flesh but also isolates the individual from the community, throwing him back on himself and his conscience. Though Lawrence does not state this specifically, one presumes that he is aware of the role of Protestant individualism in the creation of the kind of intense self-consciousness to which he is so direly opposed. Protestantism tends to atomize society, directly by opposing the Mother Church and its institutions and, indirectly, by sanctioning the bourgeois entrepreneur. Lawrence must also have been aware of the impetus that the Calvinist determinism gave to the Faustian subjugation of nature through its encouragement of the "Spirit of Capitalism." "Identity with Infinite" here would take the form of union of the self with the abstractions through which it apprehends the world of its God, but also of limitless appropriation-through-subjugation, material or spiritual.

Even so schematic an exposition of the elements that Lawrence seems to subsume under the "love"-mode does not obviate the difficulties that such subsumption presents. Obviously, there is no necessary connection between the three dominant constituents of the "love"-mode, though it is possible to see some historical relation between them. All three are post-Renaissance phenomena. All three have been linked in various ways with the rise of the middle class. All three can be related to the breakdown of traditional feudal structures and the emergence of modern individualism. All three are associated with a certain kind of aggressive rationality, the kind of rationality which has made for the progressive demythologization of the universe. Most of all, when regarded from Lawrence's special point of view, all three are marked by an element of abstraction from immediate, self- and sense-oriented experience. And all three share a tendency to subordinate elements, values, and faculties that are opposed to them; like the soul in the Socratic mythos, they exert pressure on some aspect of self or civilization.

There is, moreover, a tradition, long antedating Lawrence, that has tended to link them with each other. That tradition is made up of loosely related postures and positions, generally formulated within the ambience of Romanticism and generally adopted by thinkers who have been critical of the modern world. I refer to (a) the tendency among Romantic poets and idealist philosophers to identify love as spirituality with "mentality," and thence with "self-consciousness," generally; (b) the tendency to identify love with social consciousness, or the awareness of others and of otherness within a community; (c) the further identification of social- and self-consciousness with the modes of scientific induction, which reason from sense data to the laws of nature and its inflexible mechanisms; and (d) the harnessing of both social and scientific "reason" or "consciousness" to middle-class "rationality," which is the rationality of calculative thrift or self-interested prudence. Max Weber calls this last the rationality of the Protestant Ethic and links it to the rationalized bureaucratic structure of business and social organization in capitalist societies. Weber holds that all of Western society since the Renaissance has moved in this direction.

These "connections" are more or less familiar; they have the weight of the entire Romantic and post-Romantic tradition behind them. Yet, both in Lawrence and the writers he echoes, they are full of obvious gaps and contradictions. Certainly, there is nothing necessarily mechanical about the scientific mind or the merchant's mentality. To calculate profits is to be engaged in strenuous, aggressively competitive activity —as the imagery of social Darwinism, for example, indicates. Nor is it easy to equate the self-abnegation implicit in the "democratic" ideal of brotherly love with the selfish aggressiveness of the profit motive. Lawrence insists that both are aspects of the "love"-mode and, by his lights, they may very well be. Regarded with undialectical innocence, however, they seem to be radically antithetical qualities.

Yet, if we suspend the criticism for a moment, and sympathetically consider Lawrence's constellation of terms and concepts, certain congruities among the oddly disparate materials in the various categories are evident. All the elements involve some abstruse notion of reason, and all of them involve, in varying degrees, control and delay, as well as what I have already noted: a measure of abstraction and a considerable distance from the immediate experience of either the world or the impulsive-passional self. In sum, they all tend to stress instrumentality and the mediate use of men and faculties, rather than ultimate ends, in the experience of men.

Science, which we ordinarily think of as amoral, has this in common with ethics—especially with the utilitarian calculus of pleasure. Accounting and the "rational" choice of political officers in a democracy also share this quality. In a sense, this may also be said to be true of self-abnegating social service and its apparent antithesis, the pursuit of one's immediate self-interest. The social servant gives of himself to others, renouncing, in the course of doing so, his immediate, passional interests. The self-interested entrepreneur takes from others instead of giving to them, but what he takes is dictated by his rational calculative self, and not, as Lawrence might say, by his deeply desirous self. Even where avarice or manipulation becomes a passion, it may be regarded as a derivative and instrumental passion. It may be said to represent, moreover, desire for dead instrumentalities rather than for living relationships. Similarly, Gerald Crich's passion for organization and for domination is a real passion, but one which stems from a sense of deadness and powerlessness within himself; when it finds suitable objects it deadens and destroys the world within which they exist.

The ultimate instrumentality, and the ultimate vehicle for the mediate as opposed to the immediate in human relationships, is the instrumentality of money. This instrumentality represents for Lawrence not only the ultimate materialism, but the ultimate idealism as well. Money is the *medium* of exchange, the abstract, symbolic nothing which can serve as the pragmatic equivalent of *any*thing while in no way participating in the reality of the primary things which men desire, and which can be exchanged and interchanged through it.

In the Hardy "Study" Lawrence had insisted that men worry about the pragmatic, organizational elements of society because of their excessive dread of hunger and their need to propitiate the Unknown God who controls death and the sources of nourishment.[80] In his later work he was to insist that the material system, with its emphasis on material things, and especially on Mammon, stemmed not so much from a fear of death as from a fear of life.[81] Men seek to amass wealth in the hope of obscuring not only their mortality but also

[80] See Chap. I; Lawrence, "Study of Thomas Hardy," *Phoenix*, p. 398.   [81] Lawrence, "John Galsworthy," *Phoenix*, p. 543.

their vacuity, i.e., their inability to undergo the immediate stresses of life. The mechanism of the dollar system—of the cash nexus—is the mechanism of evasion: the distancing of the true passions and impulses of men, and substitution for them of the ideal system. It does not matter whether that system is the "ideal love" of Whitmanian democracy, with its contempt for merely material things, or the materialism of the industrial system, which is committed to the "plausible ethics of productivity" without regard for its ends.

It is essentially through money and the machine that the ultimate idealism can become the ultimate materialism. Lawrence observes in the *Studies in Classic American Literature* that the two are opposite aspects of the same phenomenon.[82] As indicated earlier in my analysis of the images of transcendence and of mechanism within the traditions to which Lawrence may be referred, abstraction and domination are both part of the struggle against nature and, at the same time, against the substantial quiddity of things in their natural state. Through them reality is "unfleshed," disembodied, disincarnated, desubstantialized within all the "love"-modes of ideality. So, indeed, is man—though the vicious circle begins in him.

It may be well at this point to indicate two constructs that constitute interesting parallels to Lawrence's insistence on the pervasive abstraction of modern man from life. One is formulated by Jung, in *Symbols of Transformation,* and the other by Ernest G. Schachtel in an essay, "On Memory and Childhood Amnesia."

Jung holds that scientific thought involves directed thought almost exclusively: man, contemplating the world objectively, shuts out the affects that normally constitute the bulk of experience. He writes:

[82] This is one of the major themes of the *Studies in Classic American Literature;* see p. 93.

directed or logical thinking is a reality thinking, . . . a thinking
which adjusts itself to actual conditions, where we . . . imitate the
succession of objectively real things, so that the images in our mind
follow after each other in the same strictly causal succession as the
historical events outside of our mind.

We call this thinking, thinking with directed attention.[83]

Jung believes that modern man's achievements in the realms
of scientific and social engineering stems from an unprecedented adjustment of the human mind, an adjustment
achieved through education. These occur

for absolutely the first time in the history of the world. . . . The
ancients almost entirely, with the exception of a few extraordinary
minds, lacked the capacity to allow their interest to follow the
transformations of inanimate matter to the extent necessary for
them to be able to reproduce the process of nature, creatively and
through their own art, by means of which alone they could have
succeeded in putting themselves in possession of the force of
nature.[84]

Jung holds that the overdirection of attention and of psychic
energy is responsible for the atrophy of certain vital life functions in the psychic life of modern man.

Schachtel is not concerned with science so much as with
the universal fact of childhood amnesia and the problem of
why men repress the rich, sensory, affective experience of
childhood. He suggests that such repression is rendered necessary by the exigencies of modern society. Memory of childhood experience is difficult because "the categories (or sche-
mata) of adult memory are not suitable for early childhood
experience and therefore not fit to preserve those experiences
and enable their recall." He goes on: "The world of modern
Western civilization has no use for [childhood] experience.
. . . It cannot permit the memory of it because such memory,

[83] C. G. Jung, *Psychology of the Unconscious* (New York: Dodd,
Mead & Company, 1949), p. 14.   [84] *Ibid.*, p. 20.

if universal, would explode the restrictive social order of this civilization."[85]

Culture, as Schachtel conceives of it, shapes consciousness and limits the range of experience; it constitutes a procrustean bed for the experience of the child.[86] Its goal is the substitution of "the conventional cliche for the actual experience. . . . Memory . . . is even more governed by the conventional patterns than perception and experience are."[87] What causes the limitation on memory and experience as well is a long process of conditioning that involves not only the jamming of impressions into limiting categories, but also a radical limitation upon the utilization of the senses themselves. The course of socialization, says Schachtel, involves a change in emphasis from the proximity-senses (smell, taste, touch) to the distance-senses (sight and hearing).[88] As a result, the sensuous but also the affective content of experience is limited in the service of efficient social function.

Schachtel does not deal with the question of why modern man is more heavily subject to repression of sensory and affective responses than men of earlier times, who were surely more thoroughly enslaved by the rigors of labor and servitude.[89] Jung, who is more historical in his orientation, does not really come to grips with the question of why the

[85] Ernest G. Schachtel, "On Memory and Childhood Amnesia," *Interpersonal Relations,* ed. Mullahy (New York: Hermitage Press, 1949), p. 9.   [86] *Ibid.,* p. 22.   [87] *Ibid.,* pp. 15–16.

[88] *Ibid.,* pp. 25–26. Schachtel's formulations with regard to discrimination among the senses is reminiscent of Wordsworth's complaints about the "tyranny of the eye," and of Lawrence's similar dicta, e.g., see *Fantasia of the Unconscious,* p. 102.

[89] Only Freud, whom Schachtel claims to follow, seems to offer an adequate and consistent theory to explain the modern malaise, and he does this by making only quantitative distinctions between modern and premodern man. Freud assumes that modern society demands ever-greater instinctual renunciation, and in one essay he even writes of the danger of atrophy of the sexual function. But such changes, or limits, do not represent the radical qualitative jolt that they imply in Lawrence's view, or that of Jung.

sensory-affective content of experience is thinned out in modern man. Like Lawrence, he tends for the most part to speak only of the exhaustion of the old modes of channeling and discharging energy, and of the need to escape the rationalistic-scientistic way.

Neither Schachtel nor Jung ultimately comes to grips with the problem of the historical causes of the modern state of mind (or soul). In dealing with the severance of abstractive and analytic consciousness from the affective and sensory life, however, both of them touch on the factor which was crucial to Lawrence in explaining the phenomenon. Both of them are concerned with the problem of *abstraction* from the sense world and the partial anesthetization of subjective responses to the sense world.[90] In pointing to this factor, their formulations illuminate this most opaque, though also most familiar and even conventional of Lawrence's ideas.[91] It is to this factor, in its most radical formulation, that I turn in the following section.

A Solitary (Historical) Cause

The neat schematism of Lawrence's view of modernity, and the elusive logic of his intertwined terminologies often gives one a sense of being trapped in a tower of babble. At times one feels he is riding a conveyor belt that goes nowhere, but that carries one round a neatly landscaped circuit designed to create the illusion of world and of substance. The difficulty of Lawrence's terminology, however one tackles it, lies in a willful vagueness and in a consistent lack of clear referents within

[90] In an unpsychological sense, this is a commonplace of the Romantic period. We have only to think of Keats's complaint that Newton has unstrung the rainbow of its colors.

[91] Jung's views, as the next chapter will suggest, also illuminate Lawrence's conception of myth and symbol as a way of overcoming the disjunction of sense from sensibility.

the known and definable world. All his formulations add up
to the assertion that modern man, for all his energetic "go," is
engaged in a mad flight from life, and that this flight from life
is caused by a radical alienation from the flesh. The flesh, as in
the Hardy "Study" formulations, remains the center and medium of life, and all the goods that Lawrence can affirm are
associated with the flesh, or with unself-conscious passions
that seem to be in and of the flesh. The question with which I
opened this chapter—the question of how the historical world
could have fallen in the first place—can, within the framework of Lawrence's scheme, be answered only in these
terms. Man, at some point in his history, has become alien-
ated from the flesh; he has been trapped in a terminal mode
of consciousness that can drive him to exploit the flesh in the
quest for "acute reduction in sensation" but cannot put him
back in touch with its life-giving qualities.

Lawrence himself seems fully aware of the problem. Rather
late in his career he even came to offer a concrete historical
cause for it. In "Introduction to These Paintings" (1928), he
inquires as to the source of the puritanism of modern culture,
the reason for the desexualization of women in the English
novel since Jane Austen, and the tendency to abstraction and
intellectualization in late-nineteenth-century painting. Tentatively, he advances an answer: fear of the body and its sexuality. "What appeared to take full grip on the northern consciousness at the end of the sixteenth century was a terror,
almost a horror of sexual life. The Elizabethans, grand as we
think them, started it. The real 'mortal coil' in Hamlet is all
sexual; the young man's horror of his mother's incest, sex
carrying with it a wild and nameless terror which, it seems to
me, it had never carried before."[92] He continues: "This, no
doubt, is all in the course of the growth of the 'spiritual-men-

[92] D. H. Lawrence, "Introduction to These Paintings," *Phoenix*, p.
551.

tal' consciousness, at the expense of the instinctive-intuitive consciousness. Man came to have his own body in horror, especially in its sexual implications: and so he began to suppress with all his might his instinctive-intuitive consciousness, which is so radical, so physical, so sexual."[93] This "grand rupture . . . in the human consciousness" had started with the Elizabethans, and its cause can be specified: "in England . . . the physical self was not just fig-leafed over. . . . In England it excited a strange horror and terror. And this extra morbidity came, I believe, from the great shock of syphilis and the realization of the consequences of the disease."[94]

The English joked about the pox, but they didn't think it funny.

Even poor Elizabeth's lack of eyebrows and her rotten teeth were not funny. And they all knew it. They may not have known it was the direct result of pox: though probably they did. This fact remains, that no man can contract syphilis, or any deadly sexual disease, without feeling the most shattering and profound terror go through him, through the very roots of his being. And no man can look without a sort of horror on the effects of a sexual disease on another person. . . .[95]

The consequences of this horror are dire:

The appearance of syphilis in our midst gave a fearful blow to our sexual life. The real natural innocence of Chaucer was impossible after that. The very sexual act of procreation might bring as one of its consequences a foul disease. . . . The terror-horror element which had entered the imagination with regard to the sexual and procreative act was at least partly responsible for the rise of Puritanism, the beheading of the king-father Charles, and the establishment of the New England colonies. . . .

[93] *Ibid.*, p. 552. One may note that "hatred of the body" surely does not begin with the Elizabethans. We have only to think of the medieval literature on women to realize that Lawrence was simplifying the historical picture considerably. [94] *Ibid.* [95] *Ibid.*, p. 554.

*But deeper even than this, the terror-horror element led to the
crippling of the consciousness of man. . . .* The terror-horror element struck a blow at our feeling of physical communion. In fact,
it almost killed it. *We have become ideal beings, creatures that
exist in idea, to one another, rather than flesh-and-blood kin. And
with the collapse of the feeling of physical . . . kinship, and the
substitution of our ideal, social or political oneness, came the falling of our intuitive awareness.* . . . We are *afraid* of the instincts.
We are *afraid* of the intuition within us. . . . We suppress the
instincts, and we cut off our intuitional awareness from one
another and from the world. *The reason being some great shock
to the procreative self.*[96]

The "cause" of the "recoil" is concrete. Man lives with a
pervasive consciousness of the death that the flesh can bring.
In a sense, the metaphysical center of death and darkness
which governs—say—the life of old Mr. Crich and of Gerald
Crich in *Women in Love* is thus given a literal, historical, and
even scientific derivation. What in *Women in Love* had been
a mysterious malaise compounded of repressed aggression,
will-to-power, and the castrating flesh of the woman here has
its ultimate root in the imagination of death through venereal
disease.

The result is much the same in both instances, however.
The modern negation of the flesh and the modern ideology of
production are part and parcel of the same phenomenon—recoil from full experience in and of the flesh. Thus the great
wealth resulting from the ideology of production and the
entire system of values and attitudes ratifying that ideology
are all part of the recoil from the dangers felt to be inherent
in the flesh. Through fear, man has erected structure on
structure of defense against experience of his own true needs
and qualities, as well as the needs and qualities of others.

The recoil is so great as to constitute a sort of rebellion and

[96] *Ibid.*, pp. 555–56. Italics mine.

denial of all those things which for Lawrence are the substance of life.

Yet—need one say?—the specific cause that Lawrence adduces is not convincing. It comes at the end of his career and fails to take into account the full range of phenomena that Lawrence had included in his account of the fallen world. One measure of the difficulty in assigning a cause is his inability even to assign a clear time and place for the fall. In most of his early work, as I have indicated in the course of my discussion, the fall occurs at the Renaissance or the Reformation. The post-Renaissance world declares that "light is given to the world," and light alone. Even this fall is completed only in the nineteenth century, and even then only with the full emergence of industrialism.

Elsewhere, however, and without any indication of systematic inquiry, he will date the fall with:

1. The sinking of Atlantis into the sea—that is, with the loss of the ancient "life-wisdom" and its dispersion within the myths and religions of various peoples.[97]

2. Socrates, who is said to have instituted the rationalistic-moralistic tradition of transcendence through consciousness and intellectual apprehension of the world; as in Nietzsche, the "charge" against Socrates is the de-mythicization of the world and of man, and the substitution of the rational demon for the passional-Dionysiac demon. This would seem to be related to the corrosion of myth by the Ionian philosophers.[98]

[97] Lawrence, *Fantasia of the Unconscious*, p. 55. In the passage to which I refer, one hears echoes of Frobenius as well as of Blavatsky.

[98] Lawrence, *Apocalypse*, p. 125. Here, Lawrence echoes Nietzsche's view of Socrates and of Socratic rationalism. See Friedrich Nietzsche, *The Birth of Tragedy*, trans. Clifton Fadiman (New York: The Modern Library, n.d.), sections 13–16, pp. 251ff, esp. p. 259. Like Nietzsche, Lawrence suggests that there was some necessity for Socratism—just as he says that there was an urgent necessity for the doctrines of Jesus at the moment of his appearance in history.

3. The Romans, when they supplanted the "life-wisdom" of the Etruscans with their coercive sense of order, discipline, and social morality.[99]

4. Jesus or perhaps Paul, i.e., Christianity as it has come down to us, with its emphasis on spirit as opposed to flesh.[100]

5. Implicitly, the Hebrews, with their repressive morality.

Linked to all these, but not so specifically historical, is the moment of the "fall into consciousness" itself—a moment that Lawrence tends to represent in the imagery of the Christian Fall and its action of "eating the apple of consciousness." In the essay "[The Individual Consciousness v. the Social Consciousness]," Lawrence goes so far as to suggest that man fell from his naturalness the moment he began to arrive at consciousness of himself as a discrete being, with a discrete existence and discrete goals that set him apart from the continuum of the nature within which he had once dwelt as part of an unconscious whole.[101] If this is so, all of what we ordinarily term history—whatever its temporal moment of origin—constitutes a fallen state, since man could not have had a history before the inception of some sort of consciousness of his discrete existence.

This quite obviously contradicts the entire construct with regard to history which I sketched in Chapter III, and which

[99] D. H. Lawrence, *Etruscan Places* (New York: The Viking Press, 1957), pp. 10 and 125ff.

[100] This is one of the main themes of *Apocalypse*. In an unhistorical form—that is, in a form which identifies Jesus with the Word and the Spirit, without reference to the historical Jesus—this notion is to be found as early as the "Study of Thomas Hardy" and the *Twilight in Italy* essays. It is only in the New Mexico phase, and especially in the last years, that the historical Jesus seems to have engaged Lawrence's imagination

[101] Lawrence, *Phoenix*, pp. 761ff. Birkin rants extensively about eating the fruit of the tree of knowledge, and, speaking in his own voice, Lawrence employs the same imagery in the *Fantasia of the Unconscious*.

has served as the basis of discussion so far in this chapter. In the earlier construct, history is natural and is an outgrowth of the natural, spontaneous self. In the construct which seems to govern much of Lawrence's later work, most of recorded history is unnatural, or antinatural, and the problem would seem to be one of how to restore man to a natural condition, the condition of existence before history itself: the very problem that emerges in Western thought with the final secularization by Rousseau of the Judeo-Christian vision of history as involving a fall and a final redemption—that is, the vision that Lawrence, at the end of his life, anatomized in *Apocalypse* (1930).

The answers that Lawrence proposes are interesting, not because they solve the problem, but because they imply a reversal in the pattern and direction of his thought. After 1916–1917, Lawrence no longer lays massive emphasis on the resources of individual men. The Hardy "Study" had called upon men to venture away from civilization and to bring their unapprehended, unimagined selves into being. In a sense this remains central to Lawrence's picture of things: the individual necessarily remains the crucial element in the "re-sourcing" of life. But the goal of individual effort changes, as does the individual's relation to community.

Once he perceives the cul-de-sac into which man, from his point of view has entered, Lawrence comes to insist on the impossibility of re-sourcing civilization through the "mere" journey into the unknown of individual consciousness. In doing so, he renounces the ideal of ever-greater individuation through negation (or, more accurately, circumvention) of socially and culturally determined forms of consciousness. Indeed, Lawrence comes to hold that it is virtually impossible directly to apprehend the primordial stuff of experience that underlies the social self. Independent individuals must strive, not to realize themselves, but to restore the "organic," communal consciousness. Lawrence now seeks a positive form of integral community that will work through the forms of a symbolic, mythic mode of shared consciousness.

This mode of consciousness, in turn, will not cut man off from the cosmos and from the primordial elements of his own experience. Rather, it will put him back in touch with it. "Mythic consciousness," of which Lawrence makes so much in his later years, is a mode of affective consciousness that is not mental and is beyond the influence of the ego-centered will. It is, moreover, incapable of the goal-directed instrumentalization of the self to which the self-conscious mentality of modern, or Christian, or fallen man is subject.

The groping toward definition—or imagination—of such a mode is inextricably bound up in Lawrence's work with the quest for community. Lawrence's quest reverses its direction: from search for a higher degree of independence and individuality, it turns into a search for a higher degree of communality. This, in essence, is the theme of the "political" novels of Lawrence's middle period. The heroes of these novels are faced with the problem formulated by Birkin at the end of *Women in Love*—the one which Lawrence himself obviously experienced in his own life. This is the problem of the necessary limits to satisfaction in the relationship between an individual and his mate. The heroes of the "political" novels all commit themselves to the exploration, not of the self and its unique possibilities, but of the various worlds within which they must seek satisfactory connections with others. In the course of rendering their search for satisfaction of their societal needs, Lawrence again and again throws himself at the question of the nature and consequences of the "love"-mode at the communal rather than the individual level, and at the problem of the "ideal" forms of consciousness entailed by the "love"-mode.

It is to this question that I turn in the next chapter.

VI

The Communalist Phase

Sons and Lovers (1913), *The Rainbow* (1915), and *Women in Love* (1920) had depicted the struggle of individuals to free themselves from the encumbrance of their "communal adhesion"; *Aaron's Rod* (1922), *Kangaroo* (1923), and *The Plumed Serpent* (1926) render a countermovement: the quest of the free individual for some sort of viable community. This does not mean that Lawrence has changed his mind about modern society: "Nowadays society is evil," he wrote in *Studies in Classic American Literature* (1921), and he proceeded to castigate society as vigorously as ever.[1] Yet the evil of modern society is no measure of society's value.

On the contrary, even as he freed himself from his own communal adhesion, Lawrence seems to have discovered the radical need for community. If the natural aristocrat of the Hardy "Study" (1914) was to cut all ties and seek a place in the wilderness with only a mate, the individual, aristocratic or plebeian, of "Education of the People" (1918) is called upon to derive actual sense-nourishment from contact and communion with his fellows: "Life consists in the interaction between a man and his fellows, from the individual, integral

[1] Lawrence, *Studies in Classic American Literature*, p. 91.

love in each."[2] Much later, in 1927, he wrote Trigant Burrows: "What ails me is the absolute frustration of my primeval societal instinct. . . . I think societal instinct much deeper than sex instinct—and societal repression much more devastating. There is no repression of the sexual individual comparable to the repression of the societal man in me. . . ."[3]

Aaron's Rod, Kangaroo, and *The Plumed Serpent,* often termed the leadership novels, are concerned with the fulfillment of the societal (or political) as opposed to the merely erotic man. The heroes of these novels seek vital connections with others outside the limiting scope of erotic or marital relationships. All of them have found that marriage alone is not a satisfactory solution to the quest for meaning, identity, and experience. So has Lawrence. If sex, passion, and marriage had once seemed to him the via media to human naturalness and creativity, they now seem to him a great source of sterility and death, at least when pursued as the chief means of individual fulfillment.

Lawrence makes this point again and again in his essays and treatises. Nineteenth-century novelists, he writes, had tried to protest against societal coercion and repression by making love the be-all and end-all of human life. The result, he says, has been catastrophic. "Assert sex as the predominant fulfillment, and you get the collapse of living purpose in man. You get anarchy."[4] "Sex as an end in itself is a disaster: a vice."[5] If sex "is the starting point and the goal as well: then sex becomes like the bottomless pit, insatiable."[6] This, he says, is the subject of modern tragedy—of the tragic dissolution of Anna Karenina, of Emma Bovary, and of Cathy Earnshaw in *Wuthering Heights:* "Ecstacies and agonies of love, and final passion of death."[7]

[2] Lawrence, "Education of the People," *Phoenix,* p. 614.
[3] Lawrence, *Letters,* p. 685.
[4] Lawrence, *Fantasia of the Unconscious,* p. 145.
[5] *Ibid.,* p. 214.   [6] *Ibid.,* p. 220.   [7] *Ibid.*

Aaron Sisson and Richard Lovatt Somers, the protagonists of *Aaron's Rod* and *Kangaroo*, find that love and marriage as ends-in-themselves are dead ends. They must seek further connections with men in what Lawrence calls the "power"-mode, a mode that is antithetical to the "love"-mode. Kate Forrester, protagonist of *The Plumed Serpent*, experiences the same need, as does Don Cipriano. Kate and Cipriano glimpse the possibility of such connections, and they are said to be able to do this in part because they live in a revitalized community which has begun to achieve an optimal relation to the greater cosmic whole. Ramon and Teresa, more deeply immersed in the communal vision, go still further in this direction.

The marital difficulties of Sisson, Somers, and Kate Forrester are, to be sure, not grounded in the exclusively passional nature of their relationships. None of them is, by any stretch of the imagination, an Anna Karenina or an Emma Bovary who gives all for love. Quite the contrary, all of them are people who have grounded their marriages in a variety of less subjective and passional functions, or have at least set them within broader purposive contexts. Aaron, a musician, a teacher, and a coal-miner, has reared a family with Lottie, his wife. Somers is a writer whose life with Harriet, his wife, is intimately, if frictionally, bound up with his intellectual, literary, and political concerns. And Kate Forrester has been through two highly functional marriages: one bourgeois and heavily familial, which has ended in divorce, and one radical and political, ending in the early death of her husband. The problem of these marriages lay not in their privacy, exclusiveness, and complete dedication to passion, but rather in a universal societal, cultural, and psychological condition which has rendered satisfaction in either the private realm of marriage or the public world of culture and politics impossible.[8]

[8] Goodheart cites Denis de Rougement in confirmation of the idea that the postwar period was a period of unrest in which writers

That this should be the case is integral to Lawrence's concerns in these novels. By the end of World War I, Lawrence was no longer centrally interested in marriage or the relations between the sexes as the chief means of individuation—as the "*via media* to being." Even earlier, in *The Rainbow* and in *Women in Love*, he had sketched the problem of social rootlessness and the atrophy of social function in the vital life of the individual. Now this problem comes to the fore, not in the experience of individuals like Will Brangwen, who would rather "fuse out" into the subjective ecstacy of his own response to Lincoln Cathedral than think about the creeping industrialism engulfing his community, but rather in the experience of men and women whose lives have been oriented to escaping the suffocation of an exclusively personal life. What interests Lawrence in the leadership novels is the way that society at large has been affected by the "love"-mode, and affected in such a way as to render satisfaction of the "societal instinct" impossible within the individuals who actively seek to satisfy it.

The three novels, along with the discursive writings of the years 1918–1930, diagnose the societal disease in some detail, spelling out the manifestation of the "love"-ideal in the objective political realm, as opposed to subjective-psychological and objective-ideological realms which I have discussed in the preceding chapter. At the same time, the novels, together with the related discursive writings, prescribe answers to the

___

throughout the West were expressing dissatisfaction with marriage as an institution. Lawrence, Goodheart insists, reflected a general trend, and hence his discontent is not to be reduced to personal terms—i.e., to be interpreted exclusively as an expression of Lawrence's own unhappiness. (See *The Utopian Vision*, pp. 138ff.) Goodheart's formulation presents the problem of perceiving the necessary connection between the prevalent discontent and the cultural climate of the time, especially since Lawrence presents the condition in question as inevitable, and as typical of the modern world in general.

difficulties that present themselves at both the political and the personal levels. In the course of doing so, they revise the earlier formulations with reference to consciousness, individuality, and convention and explore the radical communalism of the late speculative works.

It is these three steps—(a) the spelling out of the "love"-mode and of its operation at the political and societal levels, (b) the proposed solutions, and (c) the implied changes in Lawrence's overall conception of man, nature, and society—that I wish to explore in the sections that follow.

The Manifestation of Love at the Communal Level

A. Lawrence observes that those who stress sexual and familial love destroy the public world—they deny both politics and art and cause anarchy.[9] In *Fantasia of the Unconscious* (1922), he parodies the impulse to retreat into a completely private world of *eros* in the refrain "to build a world for you, Dear," obviously referring to the sentimental ideal of the male who labors in the great world only in order to create a love-nest (or familial burrow) for his dearly beloved. He observes that in Tolstoy's *Anna Karenina* and in Mérimée's *Carmen*, the male renounces the world ("gives all") for love and is destroyed as a man because he has renounced his specifically masculine function in the public realm of purposive male activity.[10]

Lawrence is quite concrete in making this point, and particularly in the *Fantasia*. His indictment is interesting because he recognizes certain ambiguities in explaining the causes of this difficulty, not in the specialized experience of a Vronsky or a Don Jose, but in the universal experience of modern man. Women would seem, in Lawrence's account, to be in part

---

[9] Lawrence, *Fantasia of the Unconscious*, p. 145.   [10] *Ibid.*

responsible in that they seek to confine the energies of the male within the narrow scope of the familial *eros*.

Lawrence's formulation of the conflict between civilization and woman's desire for love is quite like the one that Freud makes in *Civilization and Its Discontents*. In that essay, Freud speaks of the antagonism between women and advanced forms of civilization. He writes: . . . "discord is caused by women, who soon become antithetical to cultural trends and spread around them their conservative influence —women who at the beginning laid the foundations of culture by the appeal of their love."[11] He goes on:

Women represent the interests of the family and sexual life; the work of civilization has become more and more men's business; it confronts them with ever harder tasks, compels them to sublimations of instinct which women are not easily able to achieve. Since man has not an unlimited amount of mental energy at his disposal, he must accomplish his tasks by distributing his libido to the best advantage. What he employs for cultural purposes, he withdraws to a great extent from women and his sexual life. . . . Woman finds herself thus forced into the background by the claims of culture and she adopts an inimical attitude towards it.[12]

Freud, to be sure, differs from Lawrence in that he sees such conflict as universal, whereas Lawrence sees it as characteristic of modernity alone. Only in modern times, according to Lawrence, has man lost his will "to make a world" and found that he must choose between woman and culture, between the family and art or politics. And this is not woman's fault. It is a man's responsibility, Lawrence held, to be rooted in what he termed the "religious" aim of "making a world"—that is, of creating and participating in a commu-

[11] Sigmund Freud, *Civilization and Its Discontents* (New York: Doubleday Anchor Books, n.d.), pp. 50–51. The essay was originally published in 1930.   [12] *Ibid.*

nity.[13] To a degree, however, society itself is responsible, since it denies the individual a man's work and a man's legitimate pride in his work.

Because it is impossible to find meaningful work and meaningful social purposes, man is willing to withdraw into the circle of woman and family. The result is atomization. Couples live in a state of what Birkin calls *"egoisme à deux"*—a matter of "hunting in couples."[14] They enjoy neither the satisfaction of communal *eros* nor the fulfillment of real passion. The absence of the latter, as well as of real love, is one of the main points, as it happens, of *Aaron's Rod*. Aaron and Lottie are locked in a battle of wills, their entire relationship defined by intransigent mutual resentment; the Marchese delle Torre and his wife live in much the same condition. Both Aaron and the Marchese feel that man has lost his erotic dignity and autonomy: it is no longer his prerogative, even with young girls, to "call" so that the woman must "answer." Man has lost his male prerogatives, psychologically as well as sociologically, and therefore his very maleness is rendered problematical.[15] Within the all-encompassing and all-defining family, it is the woman who is dominant: man serves her, the Queen Bee, the Great Mother.[16]

B. The second meaning of the term "love" is political and psychological, and is diametrically opposed to the first. Love and marriage draw one into the private world and out of the public domain—that is, out of the realm of "pure, purposive activity." Yet purposive dedication within the realm of communal experience—that is, "love" in this meaning of the word —cuts one off from the substantial life of the flesh and of the

---

[13] Lawrence, *Fantasia of the Unconscious*, p. 60.

[14] Lawrence, *Women in Love*, p. 372.

[15] Lawrence, *Aaron's Rod*, pp. 252ff.

[16] This theme is already central in *The Rainbow*, though there Lawrence stresses man's wish to worship woman and mother, rather than woman's insistence that he do so.

senses. "Assert sex as the predominant fulfillment, and you get the collapse of living purpose in man. You get anarchy. Assert *purposiveness* as the one supreme and pure activity of life, and you drift into barren sterility, like our business life of today, and our political life. You become sterile, you make anarchy inevitable."[17]

"Purposive activity" is not the chief manifestation of the "love"-mode at the societal level, however. It is, at one level, merely the productive activity that Lawrence had criticized in the Hardy "Study," where he insisted that man no more lives to produce than he lives to eat. In the leadership novels, however, purposiveness and social adhesion are not thought of as entailing anything so pragmatic as productivity. Rather, they are thought of as dedication to humanitarian ideals: "love" in this context means "brotherly love" and refers to the ideals of liberty, equality, and fraternity.[18]

The dangers of these ideals are the direct outcome of psychological difficulties discussed in the preceding chapter.[19] They stem from the fact that egalitarian fraternity coalesces all too easily with the Christian injunction to love one's neighbor. Both lead to a dissipation of the substantial, passional, independent self. One is likely, in Lawrence's view, to diffuse one's essence in waves and fumes of sympathy toward others in the world, in a way that resembles the abstraction of "maleness," or the Son, in the Hardy "Study" formulation. This can, in Lawrence's conception of things, lead to an emptying of the self's integral contents and its resistant will, and hence to a collapse of the vital personality.

The danger of "love" as "brotherly love" is somewhat analogous to the problems of "other-direction" in David Reisman's vision of the "lonely crowd." Instead of being oriented to a center of feeling and consciousness within himself, the

---

[17] Lawrence, *Fantasia of the Unconscious*, p. 145.
[18] See above, pp. 153ff.   [19] *Ibid.*

individual is oriented to and governed by signals that come from without.[20] In Lawrence, the issue is not one of control (conscience vs. signals from the peer-group), but rather of the orientation of the self to others, and the emphasis given to the values of self and others in the individual's process of self-direction. The ultimate danger—exemplified for Lawrence in Whitman—is the achievement of so heightened an empathetic and sympathetic sense that one stands in danger of literally merging with the objects of one's consciousness.[21]

The process is in a sense double and involves two stages. One is the imaginative process, described in Lawrence's rendering of the dynamics of the upper centers of consciousness: the process of sending the self out toward objects, the "mode of dynamic objective apprehension, which in our day we have gradually come to call *imagination*."[22] This mode involves "self-destroying" but not selfless love. It involves momentary identification with the object of consciousness, but also a return to the solid center of the self. The second step, "the goal of enthusiasts," is a "passing out and merging" with the beloved—this being the aim of "male mysticism."[23] At a less esoteric level, it involves altruism, selflessness achieved by utterly subordinating the self to an object which has been apprehended through empathy. Excessive striving in this direction leads to chaotic, disintegrating personalities.

Lawrence believed that mobs and mob-violence were one of the more dangerous phenomena of modern life. He seems to have believed that at least a part of the chaotic aggression that characterizes the life of the mob stems from the disintegration of the personality within the "love"-mode.[24] Mobs are made

[20] David Reisman, *The Lonely Crowd* (New York: Doubleday Anchor Books, 1955), pp. 32ff and pp. 105ff.
[21] Lawrence, *Studies in Classic American Literature*, pp. 186ff.
[22] Lawrence, *Psychoanalysis and the Unconscious*, p. 40.
[23] *Ibid.*, p. 32.   [24] See Lawrence, *Kangaroo*, pp. 307ff.

up of agglomerations of self-disintegrate individuals who huddle together in fear, seeking to discharge the pent-up violence which has resulted from the dissolution of the integral forms of selfhood.

One must note a difficulty here. Lawrence conflates a psychological mechanism (the process whereby one imaginatively, through "objective dynamic apprehension," adds the world on to the self) with a pathological state (the dominance of that mechanism within the entire personality). When Keats, for example, speaks of negative capability and of the fact that the poet has no identity or self but rather passes into and around the objects that he experiences, one assumes that he is speaking of his "poetic" identity, or lack of one.[25] This is a necessary inference, since the "real," social, letter-writing Keats is very substantially "there." One is reminded in this connection of the psychoanalytical concept of controlled regression as the mechanism of artistic creation. This view holds that the artist regresses emotionally and expresses in his art the feelings and fantasies which he can reach only in the state of regression.[26] Yet, as artist, he returns to a present, nonregressive self which is able to control and embody the experience undergone in the state of regression.

Lawrence, in speaking of the disintegrative, anarchic effect of the "love"-mode, suggests that the entire self is possessed by the mechanisms of this mode. But it is not clear how this comes about. Perhaps the clearest evidence of Lawrence's failure to have conceived this state in psychologically concrete terms is the fact that he never renders it directly in his fiction. He often speaks of characters who have gone soft, or disinte-

[25] John Keats, The Letters of John Keats, ed. M. Buxton-Forman (Oxford and New York: Oxford University Press, 1952), pp. 71, 226–27.
[26] This notion is formulated by Ernst Kris. See his Psychoanalytic Explorations in Art (New York: International Universities Press, 1952), pp. 61–63, 197, 317–18.

grated. In Clifford Chatterley, for example, he attempts an extended portrait of a man whose springs of vitality have dried up and whose personality is essentially formless. But the fact is that this is asserted, rather than shown, of Chatterley, as of other characters. Lawrence easily manages the fictive rendering of moments of "enthusiasm," when the self "flows out," but he never renders a personality totally given to love or sympathy.[27] Nor is he able to render convincingly the operation of the phenomenon on a mass scale. Whenever he attempts to deal with it, he must resort either to symbolism or to abstract construct-making, as when, in *Women in Love*, he describes rather than renders the psychic collapse of the miners of Beldover in the state of "mystic equality." Elsewhere— as in *Kangaroo*—he lapses into spirited autobiographical digression rather than direct novelistic portrayal of the phenomenon.

C. Lawrence fails to concretize the psychological mechanism of that love which leads the soul first to flow out toward the objects of its concern and then to merge with them to the detriment of its own integral being. This is not the case with the next manifestation of love in modern society: the love that manifests itself as love of woman and as love of one's fellow citizen. This love is grasped in terms of its dialectical opposite—hate. Lawrence "shows" how conformity, submissiveness, dependency, and social altruism all stem from the repression of hate; modern man pays only lip-service to the ideal of universal love. It is Lawrence's view that modern society has an unprecedented potentiality for brute violence because it sends aggression underground, providing no civilized, socially sanctioned forms for its expression. And he renders that violence with gross immediacy.

Brutal, mechanized war, the hideous mechanical assault on nature, and the nastiness of mob violence are the objective

[27] See Chap. II, pp. 30–34, for communion scenes.

social expression of the emphasis on love in the family. Modern mothers, we recall, initiate their children into the "love"-mode by demanding a self-conscious acquiescence in their demands and by repressing the normal violent expression of their children's "sensual will."[28] The "love"-ideal, in this sense, operates in the public as well as in the private domain. In addition to the relationships between parents and children and husbands and wives, it shapes the relationships between men as social creatures, implementing the ideals of ". . . Love, Self-sacrifice, Humanity united in love, in brotherhood, in peace. . . ."[29]

Lawrence believes that these ideals are dead, but that there was a time when they were very much alive and very effective in repressing and intensifying the hatred and violence that are latent in each individual. The process, as I have indicated in the preceding chapter, had been depicted at the individual level in the characterization of Gerald Crich and his father. Old Mr. Crich is eaten away by a cancerous disease that is associated with the hostility he had suppressed in the name of compassion. In Gerald, compassion and charity no longer prevail; all that remains is the aggressive drive to subjugate nature. At the broad, societal level, the phenomenon manifests itself, not in a will-to-achieve, which has its objects in nature and society, but rather in a smoldering resentment always in danger of erupting. This danger is intensified by two factors: the breakdown of individual identity—"B" above—which makes possible mob-reactions, and the exhaustion of the ideal itself, with the consequent generation of hatred for its deadly oppressiveness.

This theme is explored most thoroughly in *Kangaroo* (1923), where Somers, Lawrence's protagonist, confronts it in the Diggers movement, an active, parafascist organization in

[28] Lawrence, "Education of the People," *Phoenix*, pp. 638ff.
[29] Lawrence, *Kangaroo*, p. 296.

Australia. When open violence breaks out between the Diggers and their socialist antagonists who, like the Kangaroo, preach love as the source of social salvation, Somers remembers the "nightmare" of his experience during the war hysteria in England in the years 1914–1915. It was at that time that he had realized that the ideals of ". . . Love, Self-sacrifice, Humanity united in love, in brotherhood, in peace" were dead, and that as a result of their life and subsequent death, society had fallen subject to the "accumulating forces of social violence."[30] Lawrence writes of Somers' experience in the war years: "One thing he realised, however. . . . If the fire had suddenly erupted in his own belly, it would erupt one day in the bellies of all men. Because there it had accumulated, like a great horrible lava pool, deep in the unconscious bowels of all men. All who were not dead."[31] The cause is the compulsion of the dead ideal of love and the "post-mortem" effects of its demise: "When a man follows the true inspiration of a new, living idea, he then is the willing man whom the Fates lead onwards. . . . But when the idea is really dead, and *still* man persists in following it, then he is the unwilling man whom the Fates destroy, like Kaiser Wilhelm or President Wilson or, to-day, the world at large."[32]

Lawrence describes the society that is dominated by the dead "love"-ideal as an anthill where men and women live without love, and where their relationships are full of a cold, hate-filled energy.

"Man that is born of woman is sick of himself. . . .

"But the men that are born . . . out of the cold interval, and are womanless, they are not sick of themselves. They are full of cold energy, and they seethe with cold fire in the anthill . . . they alone know what for. And they have cold, formic-acid females, as restless as themselves, and as active about the anthill, and as identi-

[30] *Ibid.*, pp. 292 and 297.   [31] *Ibid.*, p. 293.   [32] *Ibid.*, p. 296.

cal with the dried clay of the building, . . . the cold, barren corridors of the anthill."[33]

D. As I have indicated at length in the preceding chapter, the immediate expression of the "love"-ideal in political life is democracy, and the ideological and practical assumptions on which it rests.

Lawrence's treatment of the problems of democracy involves three elements:

1. He challenges the imposition of mentation and self-consciousness on the entire population through the political responsibilities of modern democracy. Everyone must learn to read and write and must, at least formally, be informed of all sorts of things that are not only irrelevant to life itself but even destructive of it.[34]

2. He also condemns the breakdown of social forms through which a viable social structure should maintain itself, and through which men can find their essential social satisfactions. Specifically, Lawrence seems to think of aristocracy as the natural form of social organization, basing the notion of such naturalness on the biological fact of differentiation within species and of superiority of some individuals in point of function, survival, and the like.[35]

3. This directly leads to his attack on the leveling force of democracy: the assumption that all men are equal, and therefore the same. In "Education of the People," for example, he speaks of the ravages of the assumption that every John and every Jane is a Shelley or a Newton, that all men must be educated in order to redeem them from the muteness of the

[33] *Ibid.*, pp. 130–31.
[34] Lawrence, "Democracy," *Phoenix*, p. 703; *Fantasia of the Unconscious*, pp. 117ff.
[35] Lawrence, "Aristocracy," *Reflections on the Death of a Porcupine*, pp. 223–40.

unsinging Milton in them.[36] Such leveling blurs distinctions and reduces all things to a least common denominator. It also entails a refusal to acknowledge manifest excellence. This had already been a theme in *The Rainbow*, and it recurs in several important conversations between the Brangwen sisters in *Women in Love*.[37]

Lawrence elaborates the problems presented by the leveling aspect of democracy. In "Education of the People," for example, he writes:

The true democracy is that in which a people gradually cumulate, from the vast base of the populace upwards through the zones of life and understanding to the summit where the great man, or the most perfect utterer, is alone. The false democracy is that wherein every issue . . . is dragged down to the lowest issue . . . today, the wage. . . . In its living periods mankind accumulates upwards, through the zones of life-expression and passionate consciousness, upwards to the supreme utterer, or utterers. In its disintegrating periods the reverse is the case. Man accumulates downwards. . . .[38]

Employing a telling metaphor, Lawrence continues: "The people is an organic whole, rising from the roots, through trunk and branch and leaf, to the perfect blossom. . . . The populace partakes of the flower of life: but it can never *be* the supreme, lofty flower of life: only leaves of grass."[39]

In *Apocalypse*, Lawrence stresses the depressing effect of democratic leveling not only on the repressed aristocrats but on the common, "leaves of grass" types as well. He insists that man's sense of his own value and dignity can and must be enhanced through identification with the "lords of power"— the aristocrats.

Any rule of saints must be horrible. Why? Because the nature of man is not saintly. The primal need, the old-Adamic need in a man's soul is to be, in his own sphere and as far as he can attain

---

[36] Lawrence, "Education of the People," *Phoenix*, pp. 595f.
[37] Lawrence, *The Rainbow*, pp. 308ff; *Women in Love*, p. 56.
[38] Lawrence, *Phoenix*, p. 609.   [39] *Ibid.*, p. 610.

it, master, lord and splendid one. Every cock can crow on his own muck-heap, and ruffle gleaming feathers; every peasant could be a glorious little tzar in his own hut, and when he got a bit drunk. *And every peasant was consumated in the old dash and gorgeousness of the nobles, and in the supreme splendour of the Tzar.* The supreme master and lord and splendid one: their own, their splendid one: they might see him with their own eyes, the Tzar! And this fulfilled one of the deepest, greatest and most powerful needs of the human heart. The human heart needs, needs, needs, splendour, gorgeousness, pride, assumption, glory and lordship. Perhaps it needs these things even more than it needs love: at least more than it needs bread. And *every great king makes every man a little lord in his own tiny sphere, fills the imagination with lordship and splendour, satisfies the soul.* The most dangerous thing in the world is to show man his own paltriness as hedged-in male. It depresses him and makes him paltry.[40]

The integrity of the self has been destroyed by the debilitation of the self through imaginative overextension, but also by the lack of the vicarious satisfactions to enhance one's self-respect.

There seems to be a further evil in the loss of objects of superior identification in the modern, democratic world. Lawrence is never completely explicit about this, and he always complicates his formulations with idiosyncratic notions about leadership, power, and the role of leaders in transmitting cosmic energy. But he clearly holds that much of the aimless mob-experience of modern man comes from the loss of cohesion-producing identification with leaders, or with elites. He seems throughout the leadership novels to lean toward a thesis not very different from one which Freud suggests in *Civilization and Its Discontents.* In that essay, Freud holds that

over and above the obligations of putting restrictions upon our instincts . . . we are imminently threatened with the dangers of a state one may call "*la misère psychologique*" of groups. *This*

[40] Lawrence, *Apocalypse*, p. 30.

danger is most menacing where the social forces of cohesion con-
sist predominantly of identifications of the individuals in the
group with one another, whilst leading personalities fail to acquire
the significance that should fall to them in the process of group-
formation.[41]

E. Closely related to *la misère psychologique* of groups is
the frustration of what Lawrence calls the "societal instinct."
Lawrence's view seems to be that modern life dissolves individual identity in the whole even as it denies the individual so
immersed in the whole all the satisfactions it once afforded
him. Modernity not only presents contradictory values and
ideologies (e.g., the notion of "self-interest" and the democratic version of "Love thy neighbor") but it also subjects the
individual to radically contradictory experiences. He experiences total, irrevocable belonging, belonging so strong that he
loses the sense of his own quiddity as an individual, at the
same time as he feels he does not belong to any sustained or
sustaining group.

Obviously, we are dealing here with an insight that is, in
appearance at least, quite paradoxical. Yet Lawrence's apparently paradoxical meaning can be rather simply elucidated in
terms of later developments in social theory. David Reisman,
for one, propounds a similar position in his study of contemporary American society.[42] In *The Lonely Crowd*, Reisman
holds that the mid-twentieth-century American has lost the
ruggedly individualistic autonomy of judgment and action
which characterized the nineteenth-century American. Instead, he has become dependent on a vast, amorphous, impersonal entity which is identified in his consciousness as the peer
group. The peer group, however, is really no more than a
vague constellation of images and ideas that are projected by
society through the mass media of communications. This
lonely individual seeks the security of the group (the

---

[41] Freud, *Civilization and Its Discontents*, pp. 66–67. Italics mine.
[42] Reisman, *The Lonely Crowd*, p. 105.

"crowd"), but the group gives him neither security nor strength. Essentially he stands alone, and yet he cannot renounce the "togetherness" within which he seeks approval and security.

This, it seems to me, is essentially what is involved in the dialectic that Lawrence is describing. He seems to posit the existence of something akin to what sociologists might call oversocialization and observes that the concomitant of an excessive dependency on society is an excessive dissociation from it. Like some contemporary analysts of our mass society, he sees a correlation between the loss of the communal dæmon and the loss of a strong sense of independent selfhood.

Lawrence treats this dialectic rather elaborately, insisting that modern society is characterized at one and the same time by the atomization of communities and the *Schmelzung* of individuals within the group. The "world" of modern group-life is, paradoxically, an amorphous realm that, for all its chaos, is absolute (totalitarian) in its demands. It is this pair of paradoxes that seems to govern Lawrence's apparently contradictory expectations. Men must have, at one and the same time, both the ability to stand absolutely alone and the capacity to subordinate the self within the community.

In this respect, it seems to me, he is recapitulating in a peculiar form the eighteenth-century liberal ideal of the relation between self and society. The liberal eighteenth-century vision was in part, at least, rooted in a conception of property as the ground of selfhood. The bourgeois emerged from the substantial propertied domain, where he was anchored in things, to the public world of politics, where he functioned as a member of the body politic, without relinquishing the sense of his substantial independence. Lawrence makes the same demand for the extra-social substance of the self. He makes it, however, not in terms of property, but in terms of the irreducible, presocial, nonmaterial essence of that self.

This demand is made in the early, individualist works and

it remains in the communalist works. It is, however, distinguished in the leadership novels by the assertion that the quiddity of the self stems from the natural entities that Lawrence calls "dark" and "demonic" and that hold selves centered in their own, extra-social integrity. These "dark gods," who preserve individual identity, are integrally related to the societal instinct. Together, and, in a manner of speaking, dialectically, they counteract the effect of socialization—or of participation mystique—which draws the individual into the community by shattering his individual integrity, yet which nonetheless fails to satisfy his dark, "somatic," societal needs.

Lawrence formulates the problem and its solution in *Kangaroo*, where he writes that "when human love starts out to lock individuals together, it is just courting disaster. . . . Without the polarized God-passion to hold them stable at the centre, break down they would. With no deep God who is source of all passion . . . to hold them separate and yet sustained in accord, the loving comrades would smash one another. . . ."[43]

The societal instinct, which Lawrence does not treat directly in the novels, seems, conceptually, to be rather closely related to the dark gods and demons of *Kangaroo*. It seems to involve a deeply felt experience of contact with others. This experience is somatic—that is, in and of the body. To derive satisfaction from communal contacts, men must have the possibility of entering into immediate, unreflecting relationships with others. Such relationships take place within a dense emotional medium that is charged with the peculiar Lawrencean experience of the "blood," thereby implicating the somatic self—the physical person, sensory and intuitive, inviolably separate and "beyond knowledge."

Lawrence renders the dense, energic immediacy of such contact, together with the religious and communal experi-

[43] Lawrence, *Kangaroo*, pp. 222–23.

ences that are inseparable from it, in *The Plumed Serpent*. He defines it in more abstract, and perhaps more familiar, terms in a passage, already cited, from "Introduction to These Paintings." Speaking in that essay of the horror of the body that was engendered in the English at the Renaissance, he says:

> deeper even than this, the terror-horror element led to the crippling of the consciousness of man. Very elementary in man is his sexual and procreative being, and on his sexual and procreative being depend many of his deepest instincts and the flow of his intuition. *A deep instinct of kinship joins men together, and the kinship of flesh and-blood keeps the warm flow of intuitional awareness streaming between human beings.* Our true awareness of one another is intuitional, not mental. Attraction between people is really instinctive and intuitional, not an affair of judgment. And in mutual attraction lies perhaps the deepest pleasure in life. . . .
>
> The terror horror element struck a blow at our feeling of physical communion. In fact, it almost killed it. We have become ideal beings, creatures that exist in idea, to one another, rather than flesh-and-blood kin. And *with the collapse of the feeling of physical, flesh-and-blood kinship, and the substitution of our ideal, social or political oneness, came the failing of our intuitive awareness,* and the great uncase, the *nervousness* of mankind. We are *afraid* of the instincts. We are *afraid* of the intuition within us. We suppress the instincts, and we cut off our intuitional awareness from one another and from the world.[44]

F. Last of all, Lawrence dramatizes the unhappiness and unhealthiness ("nervousness") that are brought about by the "love"-mode, or rather, by the conjunction within it of individualistic atomism and its characteristic intellectual, abstractive attitudes. Modern man has lost the immediate intuitive flesh-and-blood communion with other men which is vital to

[44] Lawrence, "Introduction to These Paintings," *Phoenix*, p. 556. Italics mine.

his life. At the same time, he has lost his immediate, vital contact with the cosmos.

In the leadership novels, Lawrence dramatizes as he never had before, his conviction that life exists in some other-than-social dimension, where the radical self relates to the life of nature. Still more than in the earlier works, he speaks in explicitly religious terms of the divine life, of "the dragon of power" of *Apocalypse*, that pervades the cosmos, and of the need to contact and absorb the power that is generated by that life. With emphasis on the vitalistic-deific nature of nature (the cosmos), Lawrence comes to emphasize the need for organized religious institutions which can put men in touch with that deific quality.

Such institutions are most often discussed in the course of examining the culture of ancient or primitive peoples. Lawrence singled out for admiration those peoples he believed were able to contact the life of the cosmos through communal rituals. These rituals accomplish the same goals of communion and invigoration that mark the end at Birkin's or Paul Morel's sexo-spiritual exercises. Their advantage, from Lawrence's point of view, lies in the fact that even while absorbing the power of the cosmos, those who performed them were experiencing the invigorating reality of community, and of leadership.

The chief value, however, was the absorption of power—religious-communal-cosmic power. Lawrence writes: "Behind all the Etruscan liveliness was a religion of life. . . . To the Etruscan all was alive; the whole universe lived; and the business of man was himself to live amid it all. He had to draw life into himself, out of the wandering huge vitalities of the world."[45] The same, he finds, was true of the old American peoples. From them he generalizes to all of humanity: "For the whole life-effort of man was to get his life into direct

[45] Lawrence, *Etruscan Places*, pp. 82–83.

contact with the elemental life of the cosmos, mountain-life, cloud-life, thunder-life, air-life, earth-life, sun-life. To come into immediate *felt* contact, and so derive energy, power, and a dark sort of joy *This effort into sheer naked contact, without an intermediary or mediator, is the root meaning of religion.*"[46] The "naked" contact is experienced, however, within the framework of the Indian religious rituals.

Having lost the capacity for such religious experience, modern man has lost the power that men once drew from the cosmos. He has lost the religious faculty of contact because the "love"-mode entails both the loss of community and the fragmentation of consciousness. Lawrence lays particular emphasis on the latter point. Man is cut off from the cosmos owing to the way he has come to conceive of it. The scientific way formulates laws of nature and denies the reality of the "dragon of power" that lies coiled at the center of the cosmos.

The dead world of modern science is a world that man projects into nature. "*When we describe the moon as dead,*" Lawrence was to write in "Dragon of the Apocalypse," "*we are describing the deadness in ourselves.* We know everything in terms of our own deadness. . . ."[47] Elsewhere he writes: "The eye of man photographs the chimera of nature as well as the so called scientific vision. We are at the phase of scientific vision. This phase will pass, and this vision will seem as chimerical to our descendents as the medieval vision seems to us."[48] He continues: "The upshot of it all is that we are pot-bound in our consciousness. . . . We are prisoners inside our conception of life and the universe. We have exhausted the possibilities of the universe, as we know it."[49]

Lawrence insists, as I shall show in detail, that for all the

[46] Lawrence, "New Mexico," *Phoenix*, p. 147. Italics mine.
[47] Anthony Beal, *Selected Literary Criticism of D. H. Lawrence* (London: William Heinemann, 1955), pp. 163–64. Italics mine.
[48] *Ibid.*, p. 95.   [49] *Ibid.*, p. 96.

urgency of "sheer, naked contact" with the cosmos, man always apprehends the cosmos through some form of consciousness. Such forms are communal in essence. The trouble with the scientific consciousness of modern man is not only that it is mechanistic; the trouble with it is also that it has exhausted its own possibilities, even as it has begun to exhaust the life energies of those who live in terms of it. As a result, "We are starved to death, fed on the eternal Sodom-apples of thought-forms. What we want is *complete* imaginative experience, which goes through the whole body and soul."[50]

In the variant of this notion that is presented in *The Plumed Serpent* (1926), it is not the scientific world-view that is exhausted, but rather the Christian vision of love. Since love is associated with railroad stations, socialism, and electrification, as well as with Jesus Christ—as it had been since *The Rainbow* and *Women in Love*—the distance between the two formulations is not very great. The "love"-mode that is promulgated by Christianity is at once radically isolative and fiercely intellectualistic or scientistic. The two outgrowths of the mode are linked by the fact that intellectual consciousness is a purely subjective phenomenon. The scientist is alone, cut off from others and cut off from his own experience. Lawrence obviously regards the isolation from other men and the isolation from the dragon of power that lies coiled at the heart of the cosmos as two aspects of the same phenomenon. To break through the scientistic forms of consciousness that "kill" the universe, it is necessary to reconstitute communal modes of consciousness and to weld man to man even while seeking to weld him to the universe.

I wish to examine next the measures that Lawrence proposed in solution of these problems, first sketching them in broad outline, then probing their presuppositions with a view to demonstrating how—in Lawrence's terms, of course—they

[50] *Ibid.*, p. 160.

might serve to solve the problems that Lawrence had posed in the leadership novels.

The Proposed Solution

Once Lawrence comes to assume that man is driven by a societal instinct, the nature of the solution he was seeking is fairly clear. What man needs is restoration of the organic, intuitive, flesh-and-blood kinship of the closely knit community. This can be achieved only if he is relieved of the burdens of love and of mentality and allowed to experience his dynamic selfhood within a framework which makes possible vital relationships with men on the one hand and with the cosmos on the other.

A living relation to the living cosmos will, moreover, restore the lost sources of power that were available to the ancients and thus reinvigorate all of civilization. Such revitalization hinges on premental, intuitive modes of consciousness. Its achievement waits upon the establishment of a new religion to replace the exhausted Christian religion of love and its modern political consequences. The new religion must be more than a religion in the modern sense. It must provide a hierocracy to replace the democratic machinery of modern government, and it must establish an all-encompassing mythic frame of reference through which consciousness can be defined, and within which men can secure their relation to each other and to the cosmos.

Lawrence propounded plans for such a system more than once, and in all his plans, priest-rulers stand at the head of a clearly structured, hierarchic community. The priest-rulers constitute what Lawrence terms an aristocracy—a natural aristocracy based on inherent life-wisdom, rather than on artificial discriminations based on wealth or pedigree. These rulers are to govern in such a way as to relieve their subjects of the burden of mental consciousness, immerse them in the "physical" flesh-and-blood kinship-medium of an organic community, and, through the mythic framework of their religion, put them in direct contact with the dragon of power at the heart of the cosmos. In Somers' phrase, man would then become subject to a "new, God-influx."[51] In the conception of Don Ramon, in *The Plumed Serpent*, man will again be a living shoot on the Tree of Life and will be able to send his tendrils down into the fund of life that is the root of the cosmos.[52] He will, in short, be able to live as "part of the great whole," social and cosmic, without being tormented by the pangs of individuation—usually false individuation—which the Christian ideal has imposed on all souls.

Lawrence's program was a long time taking shape. It apparently began to crystallize in the early war years, receiving its rudimentary formulation in 1915, in the course of a controversy with Bertrand Russell. At that point, Lawrence opposed to Russell's rational, liberal-democratic notions his own concept of a religious bond that would unite men and emancipate them from the imperatives of the modern liberal way of life and thought.[53] The same attitudes are expressed in a group of letters concerned either with the regeneration of the world after the war, or with the aims and values of the utopian community he wanted to found.[54] They receive more formal articulation in "Education of the People," which was written in 1918, and are repeated in the *Fantasia of the Unconscious* (1922).[55]

The fiction of the postwar years is less definite in its "solutions." In *Kangaroo* (1923) Lawrence's alter ego, Somers,

[51] Lawrence, *Kangaroo*, p. 299.   [52] See Chap. VII.

[53] H. T. Moore, ed., *D. H. Lawrence's Letters to Bertrand Russell* (New York: Gotham Bookmart, 1948).

[54] Lawrence, *Letters*, ed. Huxley, pp. 224ff.

[55] Lawrence, *Fantasia of the Unconscious*, Chaps. I and V; "Education of the People," *Phoenix*, pp. 607ff.

toys with all the ideas of Cooley and Struther, the novel's rival demagogues. The conclusions—tentative, to be sure—are embodied in *The Plumed Serpent*. The very latest fiction—including *Lady Chatterley's Lover* (1928) and *The Man Who Died* (1930)—abandons the communalist theme and even contradicts it. But the essays in *Etruscan Places* and the posthumous *Apocalypse* (1930) continue to echo the essential leadership ideas, though without the earlier emphasis on violence.

In the following discussion of the leadership solutions, I deal chiefly with the later, more fully elaborated formulations, overlooking the more tentative, earlier statements.

Both "Education of the People" (1918) and the *Fantasia* (1922) emphasize the problems of education and literacy; politics are central, however, because of the need to define educational objectives and the relation between the schools and society at large. Both works center on the urgency of putting a stop to mental stimulation, as well as the inculcation of the political "love"-ideal in the minds of children. Summing up his position in *Fantasia*, he writes:

Education means leading out the individual nature in each man and woman to its true fullness. You can't do that by stimulating the mind. To pump education into the mind is fatal. That which sublimates from the dynamic consciousness into the mental consciousness has alone any value. This, in most individuals, is very little indeed. So that most individuals, under a wise government, would be most carefully protected from all vicious attempts to inject extraneous ideas into them. Every extraneous idea, which has no inherent root in the dynamic consciousness, is as dangerous as a nail driven into a young tree. *For the mass of people, knowledge must be symbolical, mythical, dynamic.* This means you must have a higher, responsible, conscious class: and then in varying degrees the lower classes, varying in their degree of consciousness. Symbols must be true from top to bottom. But the interpretation of the symbols must rest, degree after degree, in the higher, responsible, conscious classes. To *those who cannot divest* themselves again of mental consciousness and definite ideas, mentality and ideas are death nails through their hands and feet.[56]

In the earlier "Education" study, Lawrence presents a more concrete image of his utopia. He conceives of society as stratified in classes.

The basis is the great class of workers. From this class will rise also the masters of industry, and, probably, the leading soldiers. Second comes the clerkly caste which will include elementary teachers and minor professionals, and which will produce the local government bodies. Thirdly we have the class of the higher professionals, legal, medical, scholastic: and this class will produce the chief legislators. Finally, there is the small class of the supreme judges. . . .[57]

Lawrence insists that these classes "will not arise accidentally, through the accident of money, as today. They will not derive through heredity, like the great oriental castes. There will be no automatism."[58] Even particular skills, talents, and aptitudes will not govern the placement of individuals within the castes.

The whole business of educators will be to estimate, not the particular faculty of the child for some particular job . . . nor even a specific intellectual capacity; the whole business will be to estimate the profound life-quality . . . his soul-strength and his soul-wisdom, . . . which cause him to be a natural master of life. . . . The first quality will be *the soul-quality, the quality of being,* and the power for the directing of life itself.[59]

Lawrence speaks in "Education of the People" of the mystery and sanctity of life as a religious quality. Though the later

[56] Lawrence, *Fantasia of the Unconscious*, pp. 112–13. Italics mine.
[57] Lawrence, "Education of the People," *Phoenix*, p. 607.
[58] *Ibid.*, p. 607.　　　[59] *Ibid.*

vitalistic and animistic doctrines are not explicit here, the
basic conception of values points toward the idea that the
dynamism of myth and symbol is necessary to life:

the system is primarily religious. . . . Our supreme judges and our
master professors will be primarily *priests*. Let us not take fright at
the word. The true religious faculty is the most powerful and the
highest faculty in man. . . . And by the religious faculty we mean
the inward worship of the creative life-mystery: the implicit knowledge that life is unfathomable and unsearchable in its motives, not
to be described, having no ascribable goal save the bringing-forth of
an ever-changing, ever-unfolding creation: that new creative being
and impulse surges up all the time in the deep fountains of the
soul, from some great source which the world has known as God;
that the business of man is to become so spontaneous that he shall
utter at last direct the act and the *state* which arises in him from
his deep being.[60]

Lawrence's religion of life affirms society as the matrix of
the individual existence; it affirms the fulfillment of lesser
individuals through greater individuals, of the "leaves of
grass" that are the mass of mankind through the flowering of
individual greatness at the summit of the tree of life. Men
cannot realize their full life-potential without the ministra-
tion of the life-priests. These are natural aristocrats who make
it possible for other men to fulfill their lives vicariously, in the
medium of the social organism. "All life is organic," and
organic life needs organization: to deny this organization is to
court anarchy or mechanism." "There must be a system; there
must be classes of men; there *must* be differentiation: either
that, or amorphous nothingness."[62]

In "Education of the People" and the *Fantasia*, the religious—that is, the social—center of experience is conceived in
fairly familiar and conventional terms. In "Education of the

[60] *Ibid.*, p. 608. Italics mine.   [61] *Ibid.*, p. 611.   [62] *Ibid.*

People," for example, Lawrence says that "State Education has a dual aim: (1) The production of the desirable citizen; (2) The development of the individual."[63] He indicates that: "You can obtain one kind of perfect citizen by suppressing individuality and cultivating the public virtues. . . . On the other hand, by the overdevelopment of the individualistic qualities, you produce a disintegration of all society."[64] Ideally, "you must have a harmony.. . . . Though man is first and foremost an individual being, yet the very accomplishing of his individuality rests upon his fulfilment in social life."[65]

The *Fantasia* makes evident the "conventional" nature of societal activity. Lawrence's examples of the "religious activity" which is "building a world" include the building of the Panama Canal and the construction of the medieval cathedrals: a pair of great engineering feats, the one undertaken in the service of imperial expansion, the other for the greater glorification of God and the medieval guilds.

This gives rise to certain difficulties. Man needs societal activity; he needs vital grounds for relationships with other men. Yet all the known forms of relationships, and especially the forms and expression of such relationships in the West, necessitate forms of consciousness and control that negate, from Lawrence's point of view, the possibility of individual self-fulfillment. Man needs societal outlets for his energies, and he needs the warm, intuitive relationships with other men that grow out of participation in the activities through which he discharges his energies. At the same time, he cannot, within Lawrence's scheme, relinquish the warm, somatic selfhood which is the seat of his true being and cannot be renounced if he is to remain sane and healthy.

In stressing Lawrence's communalism, it is altogether too easy to lose sight of this qualification. The problem, as Lawrence sees it, and as I have already indicated, is how to provide effectively for both sets of needs: those which satisfy the

[63] *Ibid.*, p. 613.   [64] *Ibid.*   [65] *Ibid.*, pp. 613–14.

social side of man's nature, and those which are indispensable
to the survival of a wholesome, balanced individuality. Lawrence, to be sure, rejects the prevailing conception of personality and of individualistic self-realization. As early as the Hardy
"Study" he had insisted that intellectuality and self-consciousness are not a means to self-realization. "All amount of
clumsy distinguishing ourselves from other things" through
consciousness cannot bring the self into being. Nor can individuality be achieved through the self-conscious and imaginative adding of objects and beings to the self—even by "adding
the world to the self."[66] Going to the opposite extreme and
negating mental consciousness or the controls it brings is no
more effective, from Lawrence's point of view; individuality
cannot be elicited by calling on young children to "express"
themselves. Nor can it be brought to birth by encouraging
adults to act on gross impulse, without conflict.[67] It can be
achieved, however, by allowing the deeper, integral needs and
desires of the "dynamic" unconscious to find expression in
both the private world of the family and the "religious" world
of communal activity.

One cannot emphasize too strongly the importance given
to individuality in Lawrence's communalist writings. Lawrence rejects only the ideal of individuality within the "love"-
mode. Referring to the ideal of brotherly love, he says:

Instead of finding our highest reality in an ever-extending aggrega-
tion with the rest of men, we shall realize at last that the highest
reality for every living creature is in its purity of singleness and its
perfect solitary integrity, and that everything else should be but a
means to this end. All communion, all love, and all communication, which is all consciousness, are but a means to the perfected
singleness of the individual being.[68]

[66] Lawrence, "Study of Thomas Hardy," *Phoenix*, p. 434 and "Democracy," *Phoenix*, p. 706.
[67] Lawrence, "Education of the People," *Phoenix*, p. 616.
[68] *Ibid.*, p. 637.

Such individuality

doesn't mean anarchy and disorder. On the contrary, it means the most delicately and inscrutably established order, delicate, intricate, complicated as the stars in heaven, when seen in their strange groups and goings. Neither does it mean what is nowadays called individualism. The so-called individualism is no more than a cheap egotism, every self-conscious little ego assuming unbounded rights to display his self-consciousness. We mean none of this. We mean, in the first place, the recognition of the exquisite arresting manifoldness of being, multiplicity, plurality, as the stars are plural in their starry singularity. Lump the green flashing Sirius with red Mars, and what will you get? A muddy orb.[69]

Lawrence likes to contrast the multifariousness of the starry heavens with the faded uniformity of the sunny sky:

Have done; let go the old connexions. Fall apart, fall asunder, each into his own unfathomable dark bath of isolation. Break up the old *incorporation*. Finish for ever the old unison with homogeneity. Let every man fall apart into a fathomless, single isolation of being, exultant at his own core, and apart. Then, dancing magnificent in our own space, as the spheres dance in space, we can set up the extra-individual communication. . . . [The goal is] not a mass of homogeneity, like sunlight, but a fathomless multiplicity, like the stars at night, each one isolate in the darkly singing space. This symbol of Light, the homogeneous and universal Day, the daylight, symbolizes our universal mental consciousness, which we have in common. But our *being* we have in integral separateness, as the stars at night. To think of lumping the stars together into one mass is hideous. Each one separate, each one his own peculiar ray.[70]

Man must realize his starry individuality at a level of being that lies below the socially-induced self-consciousness. Its realization is the goal of individual striving and of evolution

[69] *Ibid.*, pp. 637–38.
[70] *Ibid.*, p. 634. A parallel formulation appears in one of the "Democracy" essays, *Phoenix*, p. 709.

itself: "This is the true course of evolution:" Lawrence writes, "the great collective activities are at last merely auxiliary to the purely individual activities."[71] Nonetheless, it is not easy to subordinate the collective activities of mankind to the individual ones, since the collective activities are necessary to individual development. "Because, though man is first and foremost an individual being, yet the very accomplishing of his individuality rests upon his fulfillment in social life."[72] In modern times, as I have indicated at length, the problem of societal satisfactions is complicated by the fact that all social life is governed by the "lumping" and "merging" compulsions of the mental and psychic life. If man is to fulfill himself through communal activity, he must, in modern times at least, move into a realm that is defined by mentality and love. Whatever his individual preferences, he cannot escape the "love"-mode, whose greatest evil lies in denial of authentic individuality.

Nor is the Hardy "Study" solution possible. Man cannot escape the evils of the "love"-mode and the "social adhesion" by retreat into the intimate world of eros. Lawrence believes that societal values generally pervade the private recesses of the individual soul, so that one can escape it only through a supreme effort of will and consciousness—and even this is doubtful. Most men need the help of the life-priests, who have somehow overleapt the barriers of the corrupt civilized consciousness. Realizing the dilemma, the latter solve it by providing a framework of myth and symbol through which individuals can participate in the life of both community and cosmos without "merging" in the medium of "sun"- or "love"-consciousness.

Mythic religion, moreover, must assure satisfaction of the aggressive impulses which have been dangerously suppressed

[71] Lawrence, "Democracy," Phoenix, p. 702.
[72] Lawrence, "Education of the People," Phoenix, pp. 613–14.

—and repressed—within the "love"-mode. "Blood"-consciousness, the deep somatic consciousness that must be restored to its centrality in the dynamism of psychic and social life, must be acknowledged for its dual value. It is the "blood," signifying primarily the somatic, "female," premental unconscious life of the dynamic psyche, but also the integral, unfallen "male" dimension of the soul. It is, at the same time—at least in some of Lawrence's postwar formulations, like those of *Kangaroo* (1923), "The Woman Who Rode Away" (written 1924), and *The Plumed Serpent* (1926)— also the blood-*thirsty* consciousness, the consciousness that must find release in violence, even in human sacrifice. The necessary condition for the wholesome release and satisfaction of such an impulse is satisfaction of the "societal" blood-need within the pattern of religious, mythic enactment—enactment that must be instituted and governed by life-priests.

The Role of Myth

Altogether, myth and symbol are central here. Lawrence holds that (*a*) man cannot exist without conventions and without predetermined forms for consciousness to fall into, and (*b*) the thought-forms within which modern man is trapped are dead and no longer permit a total relationship with the self or the cosmos. Myth and symbol can help because, unlike the thought-forms of modern science and social thought, they are alive. They represent "embryonic realities of the living unconscious," reflecting the integral experience of the self at levels below ordinary consciousness. They embody, moreover, the reality of both the dynamic personal unconscious and the objective vitality of the cosmos. By expressing the objective powers that shape the personal unconscious, as well as the subjective reality of the radical self, symbols and myths can help attune man to the cosmos and permit him to draw the power of the cosmos into himself. They also provide a ground for shared experience, thus making it possible to satisfy the societal instinct.

Here we have the crucial motive for the radical affirmation of community which I have been discussing. The early Lawrence had insisted that it was possible to husk away commonplace forms of consciousness and to face the "unknown" on one's own. He had intimated that any vital individual might do this. The later Lawrence comes to insist that man always perceives the world through conventions (thought-forms or feeling-forms) and that he can see in the world only what he has learned to see. Lawrence insists this is so in the face of his own demand that man deliberately learn to live "breast-to-breast" with the cosmos.

In other words, Lawrence affirms culture as the necessary medium of human existence; it is the indispensable bridge between the individual and the worlds of man and nature. Though he tends to grudge acknowledgment of this and remains ambivalent to the end, his later works clearly assert it. In *Etruscan Places*, for example, he insists that "man can only see according to a convention." The other term of his ambivalence, to be sure, follows immediately. "We haven't exactly plucked our eyes out yet, but we've plucked out three-fourths of their vision." What he means is made clear by an earlier passage, where, commenting on the representation of horses in Etruscan frescoes, he says: "What is it that a man sees, when he looks at a horse?—what is it, that will never be put into words? For a man who sees, sees not as a camera does . . . but in a curious rolling flood of vision, in which the image itself seethes and rolls; and only the mind *picks out* certain factors which *shall* represent the image seen."[73]

[73] Lawrence, *Etruscan Places*, p. 119.

Words and images—again—involve an abstraction from the full scope of sensory and imaginative experience.[74] To the unsocialized, unself-conscious individual, able to use the full range of his powers, the world would be a "rolling flood of vision." One who experiences the world maximally experiences it expansively; he lives within an unspeakable rich explosion of subjective responses. One imagines that Lawrence has in mind a sensory responsiveness akin to the responsiveness necessary for perception of Blake's maximal sun, which is not a sun at all, but rather a band of angels crying "Holy, holy, holy!" As in the eyes of Wordsworth's infant babe, the world is enveloped in "clouds of glory." It is a kind of heaven, a "truth" of infinite experience. The power of "vision"—in Lawrence, sense-response—so to speak atom-smashes reality, so that a world of energy can be contained in a grain of sand, eternity in an hour. As Blake writes in *The Marriage of Heaven and Hell*:

How do you know but ev'ry Bird that cuts the airy way,
Is an immense world of delight, clos'd by your senses five?[75]

The state in which one is able to perceive this is, in Lawrence as well as in Blake, the realm, or state, or mode in which "energy is eternal delight."[76] Any limitation that is placed on the "infinite delight" of the perceptive moment is, for Lawrence, a travesty on experience. All the limitations imposed by the selectivity of language or conventional representation, in art or in consciousness itself, represent such a travesty. It is a travesty of experience, but also of the world, since the world, presumably, is seen as it really is only when the organism is able to bring to bear on it the full power of its inwardness—of its intuitive-sensory-imaginative self. Only when such power

[74] Lawrence's conception is very close to that of Ernest Schachtel, cited in Chap. V.
[75] William Blake, *The Marriage of Heaven and Hell*.   [76] *Ibid*.

of subjectivity is brought to bear on the world is the power that is in the world accessible to the self.

Yet there is no escaping the limitations of language, conventions, and myth. "The savage in a state of nature," Lawrence wrote in the *Fantasia*, "is one of the most conventional of creatures. So is a child."[77] Thus he disposes of our most familiar repositories of freedom and spontaneity, the child and the noble savage. He goes further in the late essay, "[The Good Man]," where he writes:

When Oscar Wilde said that it was nonsense to assert that art imitates nature, because nature always imitates art, this was absolutely true of human nature. The thing called "spontaneous human nature" does not exist, and never did. Human nature is always made to some pattern or other. The wild Australian aborigines are absolutely bound up tight, tighter than a China-girl's foot, in their few savage conventions. They are bound up tighter than we are. But the length of the ideal bandage doesn't matter. Once you begin to feel it pressing, it'll press tighter and tighter, till either you burst it, or collapse inside it, or go deranged. And the conventional and ideal and emotional bandage presses as tight upon the free American girl as the equivalent bandage upon the Australian black girl in her tribe. An elephant bandaged up tight, so that he can only move his eyes, is no better off than a bandaged-up mouse. . . .

And this we must finally recognize. No man has "feelings of his own." The feelings of all men in the civilized world today are practically all alike. Men *can* only feel the feelings they know how to feel. . . . This is true of all men, and all women, and all children.[78]

Lawrence goes on to say, "This is the agony of our human existence, that we can only feel things in conventional feeling-patterns."[79] The essential basis of this agony was acknowledged relatively early in Lawrence's work. Even in

[77] Lawrence, *Fantasia of the Unconscious*, p. 105.
[78] Lawrence, *Phoenix*, p. 752. [79] *Ibid.*, p. 753.

Women in Love, Birkin insists, in the "Class-room" scene, that "consciousness comes upon us willy-nilly"; he makes the point that ideas in themselves are not pernicious; only the wrong ideas are. To Hermione's affirmation of sensuality and the "savage" or primitive mode of experience he objects that those who attempt to revert to a savage sensuality are merely indulging the pornographic wish to observe themselves in the throes of a more thrillingly self-conscious experience than they might otherwise have undergone. There is, Birkin reflects, in the novel, an African mode of experience and of sun-sensuality—but this, too, would seem to be accessible only within the forms of subjectivity available to Africans.[80]

"Education of the People" and the postwar leadership novels amplify the idea that consciousness *must* emerge and be shaped. In the "Education" treatise, Lawrence insists that man "must have beliefs and foregone conclusions, and conceptions of what the nature of life is, and the goal thereof."[81] Hence, "It is useless to think that we can get along without a conception of what man is, and without a belief in ourselves, and without the morality to support this belief."[82] The particular beliefs to which modern man has been subject are pernicious, to be sure, and it is necessary, at any price, to escape the stranglehold of the modern consciousness and the modern values. "Why does this happen? Because we have become too conscious? Not at all. Merely because we have become too fixedly conscious. We have limited our consciousness, tethered it to a few great ideas, like a goat to a post."[83] In the formulation of Somers in *Kangaroo,* "being an animal saddled

---

[80] I must note, however, that in "Education of the People," Lawrence does speak of specifically racial predispositions when he suggests that Negroes have difficulty in transmuting sense-consciousness into mind-consciousness. *Phoenix,* p. 629. Some of Birkin's remarks in *Women in Love* suggest the same idea.
[81] *Phoenix,* p. 614.   [82] *Ibid.,* p. 615.   [83] *Ibid.,* p. 629.

with a mental consciousness, . . . man *must* have some idea of himself."[84]

This point is still more strongly taken in a review (1920) of *All Things Are Possible* by Leo Shestov, in which Lawrence writes:

The human *soul* itself is the source and well-head of creative activity. In the unconscious human soul the creativity issues first into the universe. Open the consciousness to the prompting, away with all your old sluice-gates, locks, dams, channels. No ideal on earth is any more than an obstruction in the end, to the creative issue of the spontaneous soul. Away with all ideals. Let each individual act spontaneously from the forever incalculable prompting of the creative well-head within him. There is no universal law. Each being is, at his purest, a law unto himself, single, unique, a Godhead, a fountain from the unknown.

This is the ideal which Shestov refuses positively to state, because he is afraid it may prove in the end a trap to catch his own spirit. So it may. But it is nonetheless, a real, living *ideal* for the moment, the very salvation.[85]

Lawrence insists that the ideal must be espoused, because it is only through some ideal that man can apprehend and realize himself. More positively, in a letter written in 1927 to Rolfe Gardiner, he writes. "You see, one cannot suddenly decapitate oneself. If barren idealism and intellectualism are a curse, it's not the head's fault. The head is really a quite sensible member, which knows what's what: or *must* know."[86]

As I have already indicated, there is quite obviously a tension between Lawrence's rage at the limitations imposed by ideals and his awareness of the need for them. His call in "Education of the People" for the institution of a clearly stratified social hierarchy headed by priests and organized within a framework of myth is in fact a way of resolving the

[84] Lawrence, *Kangaroo*, p. 295.
[85] Beal, *Selected Literary Criticism*, p. 244.
[86] Lawrence, *Letters*, ed. Huxley, p. 679.

tension. Myth, as Lawrence conceives of it, erects the framework of consciousness within which man apprehends himself,
or conceives of himself. Yet it does so in a nonmental, or
nonideal way. Furthermore, through myth man achieves a
community of consciousness. His loneliness is thus alleviated,
though he at the same time remains free of the mechanical
compulsion of the modern modes of social experience and
intellectual self-awareness.

Definitions of Symbol and Myth

One must, at this point, ask what Lawrence means by myth
and symbol, and what role he would assign to them in the life
of individual and society. Such definition is not altogether
easy. Although Lawrence makes some very clear formulations
with reference to both, it is difficult to integrate the personal,
or emotional, content with which Lawrence, the artist and
literary critic, endows them, and the broader scope that Lawrence, the constructor of utopias, would bestow upon them.
Bearing in mind this difficulty, I shall examine Lawrence's
concept of myth and point out some of the problems it
presents as a prospective instrument of social integration, if
not as a vehicle for literary expression or as a category of social
and historical analysis.

The earliest elaborated discussion of myth is to be found in
the first published version of his essay on *The Scarlet Letter*
(1917). There, Lawrence establishes a scale of modes of consciousness and of literary types that express (or accompany)
them. The basic distinction there, as in the "Education of the
People" and the treatises on the unconscious, is between the
"ideal" or "upper" consciousness and the "primal" consciousness. He holds that beasts, like birds and bees, act from their
primal consciousness, which is their instinctual consciousness.
The ideal consciousness, "thought" and "mental cognition,"

which is a later development, is a "sublimation of the great primary, sensual knowledge located in the tissues of the physique and centered in the nerve ganglia."[87] Human evolution involves a shift from the dominance of the lower centers to that of the upper centers. At the beginnings of civilization, he writes, the primary consciousness is so strong as to overcome the "upper mind." "Then we have myths, legends." Other literary modes express other—and later—forms of consciousness. Romance, for example, follows legend. "And after romance, pure art, where the sensual mind is harmonious with the ideal mind. The progression of man's conscious understanding is dual. *The primary or sensual mind begins with the huge, profound, passional generalities of myth, and proceeds through legend and romance to pure, personal art.* . . . The nearest approach of the passional psyche to scientific or rational reality is art."[88]

"Education of the People," which was written at about the same time (1918), echoes this concept but adds the notion that certain images enhance the unity of sensibility and of consciousness, allowing the socialized individual to experience deeper strata of the self. Lawrence writes, "Fairies are true embryological realities of the human psyche. They are true and real for the great affective centres, which see as through a glass, darkly, and which have direct correspondence with living and naturalistic influences in the surrounding universe, correspondence which cannot have mental, rational utterance, but *must express itself, if it be expressed, in preternatural forms.*"[89]

What Lawrence says of fairies he says, in the early versions

[87] Arnim Arnold, *D. H. Lawrence and America* (New York: The Philosophical Library, 1958), p. 69.   [88] *Ibid.*, p. 69.
[89] *Phoenix*, p. 626. Italics mine. The "naturalistic" influences, with which fairies "correspond," are the effluence of the "cosmic power" or the vital life of the environment.

of his *Studies in Classic American Literature*, of symbols: "Art speech," he writes (1918), "is . . . a language of pure symbols. But whereas the authorized symbol [one presumes, a flag, or the cross] always stands for a thought or an idea, some mental concept, the art-symbol, or art-term stands for a pure experience, emotional and passional, spiritual and perceptual at once."[90] This notion persists in Lawrence's literary criticism. "You can't give a symbol a 'meaning,' any more than you can give a cat a 'meaning,' " he writes in "The Dragon of the Apocalypse" (1929). "Symbols are organic units of consciousness with a life of their own, and you can never explain them away, because their value is dynamic, emotional, belonging to the senses—consciousness of the body and soul, and not simply mental."[91]

In the same essay, he defines myth in the course of distinguishing between allegory and symbolism:

It is necessary for us to realize very definitely the difference between allegory and symbol. Allegory is narrative description using, as a rule, images to express certain definite qualities. Each image means something, and is a term in the argument and nearly always for a moral or didactic purpose, for under the narrative of an allegory lies a didactic argument, usually moral. Myth is likewise descriptive narrative using images. But myth is never an argument, it never has a didactic nor a moral purpose, you can draw no conclusion from it. *Myth is an attempt to narrate a whole human experience, of which the purpose is too deep in the blood and the soul, for mental explanation or description.*[92]

Myth and the symbols of which the narrative-myth is made, in other words, attempt to express a primordial experience.

---

[90] D. H. Lawrence, "Spirit of Place," *English Review*, Nov., 1918, cited by Arnold, *Lawrence and America*, p. 40.
[91] Beal, *Selected Literary Criticism*, p. 157.
[92] *Ibid.*, p. 158. Italics mine.

Presumably, just as art and religion, in the theory of the Hardy "Study," represent the externalization in image and act of the integral experience of desire and its object, so the symbol expresses both the nature of the object represented and a subject's response to that object. Just as it expresses the "whole" experience of its creator, it has the power to elicit and cathart that experience in those who experience it. "A complex of emotions is a symbol. And the power of the symbol is to arouse the deep emotional self, beyond comprehension."[93]

If one studies these formulations closely, it becomes clear that Lawrence does not really distinguish between the creators of symbols and the experiencers of them. The crucial point is that a symbol is a "unit of experience," which at once embodies the emotion that went into creating it and has the power to release that emotion in anyone who is exposed to it. In this sense it is, in function, rather like the symbolism of the Freudian dream-work, in which an image is at once created by the urgent need of an unconscious impulse to make its way into consciousness, and evocative of the emotion that is attached to that impulse in the unconscious.

Myth and symbol are important for Lawrence because they are able to arouse and implicate the "deep emotional self, beyond comprehension." The role he attributes to them is rooted in the antagonism between the "deep emotional self" and the "comprehending," ideal self. Implicit in Lawrence's opposition of myth and symbol to the allegorical "unit of meaning" is the opposition, which we have already explored in the preceding chapter, between the feeling self and the thinking self, between blood-consciousness and mind-consciousness, between the "nuclear self" and the "social self." Thought, mind, the social self, and all the forms of culture, including language itself, negate or deny the submerged affec-

[93] *Ibid.*

tive-cognitive experience. Myth and its symbols, springing from the depths of the unconscious self, express the lost dimension of selfhood and make possible a restoration of the wholeness which modern civilization and its thought-forms destroy.

In one of its aspects, the opposition between myth-symbol and abstract thought involves a distinction which I drew in the preceding chapter in the course of examining Lawrence's critique of modern society. Discussing myth and the symbolism of ancient myth in *Apocalypse*, Lawrence insists that we moderns have almost lost the ability even to conceive of what myth meant to the ancients.[94] He points out that for us thought, together with the other mental functions, is always directed at some object. It always wants to get somewhere, it progresses, it is intrinsically instrumental. The sense-consciousness of the ancients, on the other hand, had no goal: it was an end-in-itself, an experience, purely in and for itself.[95]

This distinction is explored in the seventh and eighth chapters of *Apocalypse:*

We have not the faintest conception of the vast range that was covered by the ancient sense-consciousness. We have lost almost entirely the great and intricately developed sensual awareness, or sense-awareness and sense-knowledge of the ancients. It was a great depth of knowledge arrived at direct by instinct and intuition, as we say, and not by reason. It was a knowledge based not on words but on images. The abstraction was not into generalizations or into qualities, but into symbols. And the connection was not logical but emotional. The word "therefore" did not exist. Images and symbols succeeded one another in a procession of instinctive and arbitrary physical connections . . . , and they "get nowhere" be-

[94] Lawrence, *Apocalypse,* pp. 75–80.
[95] Again, Schachtel's remarks on memory, as well as Jung's notion of the dual movement of consciousness, cited at the end of "The subjective dimension" section of Chap. V, seem relevant. Jung's distinction is basically the same as the one that Cassirer makes. See below.

cause there was nowhere to go, the desire was to achieve a consummation of a certain state of feeling-awareness.[96]

. . . .

All our mental consciousness is a movement onwards, a movement in stages, like our sentences, and every full-stop is a milestone that marks our "progress" and our arrival somewhere. On and on we go, for the mental consciousness. Whereas of course there is no goal. Consciousness is an end in itself.

. . . .

[In ancient times] men still thought of the heart or the liver as the seat of consciousness, they had no idea of this on-and-on process of thought. To them a thought was a completed state of feeling-awareness, a cumulative thing, a deepening thing, in which feeling deepened into feeling in consciousness till there was a sense of fulness. A completed thought was the plumbing of a depth like a whirlpool, of emotional awareness, and at the depth of this whirlpool of emotion the resolve formed.[97]

Lawrence's description coincides with some recent anthropological theory. It avoids the excesses of Lévy-Bruhl's notion that primitive man had independently prelogical modes of thought, but it insists that his experience of the world necessarily differed from ours. It distinguishes, as the anthropologists have, between the rational scientific mode of consciousness and the mythic one. Ernst Cassirer, who speculates upon the anthropologists' material, formulates conclusions much like Lawrence's. He defines science as a mode of pure instrumentality. It tries to suppress all affects in its interpretation of nature. Myth affirms feeling. It has no ulterior purpose and necessarily projects affects and fantasies into the world.

Cassirer's formulation illuminates Lawrence's. Cassirer writes:

Nature, in its empirical or scientific sense, may be defined as "the existence of things as far as it is determined by general laws." Such

[96] Lawrence, *Apocalypse*, p. 75.   [97] *Ibid.*, p. 80.

a "nature" does not exist for myths. The world of myth is a dramatic world—a world of actions, of forces, of conflicting powers.
. . . Mythical perception is always impregnated with these emotional qualities. Whatever is seen or felt is surrounded by a special atmosphere—an atmosphere of joy or grief, of anguish, of excitement, of exultation or depression.[98]

Lawrence, more than Cassirer, speaks not only of the projection of feelings and purposes onto nature, but also of the fact that man transforms nature into a sphere of power. Man perceives the natural world as bathed in power because it elicits certain affects in him. The power in question is what anthropologists have called "mana," and which, Mark Spilka notes, can be referred to as any "highly relative force or flow: say Wordsworth's religious flux, Nietzsche's Dionysian force or Bergson's *élan vital.*"[99]

Lawrence differs from the anthropologists in one respect. He insists on the objective existence of mana. Lawrence's quarrel with science is based in part on the fact that it has trapped us in our "tight little cage of a universe," shutting out the preternatural, mana-saturated world. It has therefore denied us the "deep" experience which lives on in symbols and myth. Lawrence invokes myth as a means of restoring the

[98] Ernst Cassirer, *Essay on Man* (New York: Doubleday Anchor Books, 1953), pp. 102–103. See also Richard Volney Chase, *The Quest for Myth* (Baton Rouge: Louisiana State University Press, 1949), Chap. VII. Chase suggests that the mythic world is created by the projection outward upon the world of the emotional turmoil created by the conflict between the inner dread of the world-as-it-in-reality-is and the inner, magical fantasies of fulfillment in spite of the world-as-it-in-reality-is. "Myth," Chase writes, "is an aesthetic device for bringing the imaginary but powerful world of preternatural forces into a manageable collaboration with the objective facts of life" (p. 97). "We may . . . think of both myths and dreams as compromises between man's demonic impulses and objective facts" (p. 98).
[99] Mark Spilka, *The Love Ethic of D. H. Lawrence* (Bloomington: Indiana University Press, 1957), p. 14.

magical world, and with it the deeper experience of self to which it is related.

In calling for a revival of myth, Lawrence is calling for a reunification of sensibility, as he conceives of it. He wants to restore the quivering wonder of a naive response to the world. The element of wonder is crucial to Lawrence. Its absence characterizes the modern world.

The sheer delight of a child's apperception is based on wonder; and deny it as we may, knowledge and wonder counteract one another. . . . The great and fatal fruit of our civilization, which is a civilization based on knowledge, and hostile to experience, is boredom. . . . Modern people are inwardly thoroughly bored. . . . They are bored because they experience nothing. And they experience nothing because the wonder has gone out of them. And when the wonder has gone out of a man he is dead. He is henceforth only an insect.[100]

Lawrence's vision of a resurrected humanity is also a vision of a world to which wonder has been restored. Myth can renew man's religious sense of the unity and continuity of life, a unity that binds men to each other in communities. For Lawrence, the loss of man's sense of the unity of life is associated with social self-consciousness "While a man remains a man, before he . . . becomes a social individual, he innocently feels himself altogether within the great continuum of the universe."[101] "Paradoxical as it may sound, the individual is only truly himself when he is unconscious of his own individuality, when . . . he is not split into subjective and objective, when there is no me or you, . . . but the me

---

[100] D. H. Lawrence, "Hymns in a Man's Life," ed. Beal, *Selected Literary Criticism*, p. 7. Lawrence's concern with wonder puts one in mind of the Romantics, but also of Tylor, who regards myth as the expression of a Wordsworthian noble primitive's wonder-filled reactions to nature. See William Tylor, *Primitive Culture* (London: Murray, 1929), Chaps. VIII–X, esp. pp. 274ff.
[101] D. H. Lawrence, "Galsworthy" (1928), *Phoenix*, p. 541.

and *you* . . . is a living *continuum*, as if all were connected by a living membrane."[102]

The old religions, dominated by myth and marked by ritual, made possible a sustained kinship with the cosmos. Lawrence stresses this point in writing about the Etruscans, the New Mexican Indians, and the star-worshipers of *Apocalypse*. Of the rituals of the Indians of New Mexico, he writes:

> It was a vast old religion, greater than anything we know: more starkly and nakedly religious. There is no God, no conception of a god. All is God. But it is not the pantheism we are accustomed to, which expresses itself as "God is everywhere, God is in everything." In the oldest religion, everything was alive, not supernaturally but naturally alive. There were only deeper and deeper streams of life, vibrations of life more and more vast. So rocks were alive, but a mountain had a deeper, and vaster life than a rock, and it was much harder for a man to bring his spirit, or his energy, into contact with the life of the mountain, and so draw strength from the mountain, as from a great standing well of life, than it was to come into contact with the rock. And he had to put forth great religious effort. For the whole life-effort of man was to get his life into direct contact with the elemental life of the cosmos, mountain-life, cloud-life, thunder-life, air-life, earth-life, sun-life. To come into immediate *felt* contact, and so derive energy, power, and a dark sort of joy. This effort into sheer naked contact, *without an intermediary or mediator*, is the root meaning of religion. . . .[103]

Lawrence is intent on restoring unmediated contact with the cosmos. Man must shed the boredom and the deadness of knowledge; he must re-enter a life-giving communion with both the cosmos and with his creative self. Myth and symbol, as I have already noted, are the means of restoring this lost unity. They evoke a numinous experience of the living universe through mediating public forms of consciousness.

[102] D. H. Lawrence, "[The Individual Consciousness *v.* the Social Consciousness]," *Phoenix*, p. 761.
[103] D. H. Lawrence, "New Mexico," *Phoenix*, pp. 146–47.

Hence, to speak of "sheer naked cosmic contact," without intermediary or mediator, is to enter into self-contradiction. On the one hand, man can renew his vital *immediate* contact with the cosmos only through the intervention of myth. On the other hand, myth is a *mediate* public entity.

As at so many other points, it would be unprofitable to press the issue. At this juncture I merely wish to indicate the difficulty and to suggest that what is involved here is again not so much a refusal to think things out, as a deep and pervasive ambivalence toward civilization and its modes of existence and awareness. Lawrence craves direct, unmediated contact with the cosmos; he wants to be free of the social adhesion. Yet he recognizes that it is impossible to be so and is torn between the terms of his ambivalence. Myth seems to provide a ready answer by synthesizing the objective virtues of community with the subjective richness of unconstrained, fluid feeling response.

In the late works it is the communal term that dominates, however. Lawrence turns to myth because it is implicated in ritual and forges bonds of community between individuals. To understand him in this way is, assuredly, to stress the prophet in Lawrence rather than the artist, and to see a side of him which many critics overlook. Lawrence tends to speak of myth in terms of its impact on individual sensibilities and inevitably to speak of it in terms similar to those which describe the impact of art works. He also speaks of all art as "*au fond* symbolic." Hence the critics' temptation to speak of myth and of mythic consciousness chiefly as an artistic matter, as they must in connection with the work of Joyce and Eliot.[104]

[104] Eugene Goodheart, *The Utopian Vision of D. H. Lawrence*, Chap. II, "Art and Prophecy: The Mythical Dimension." Goodheart is primarily interested in Lawrence's ideas, but his treatment of myth blurs the prophetic and redemptive role of myth and treats Lawrence's myth-making merely as a matter of artistic evocation.

To do so, however, is to miss the point. Lawrence, to be sure, assumes that art is closer to myth than to science and the mental-moral consciousness. Since it is symbolic, it speaks to the deeper, the "nuclear" self. Yet it represents a movement away from the undifferentiated primordial consciousness. Through art man can undergo some of the deeper experience that knowledge, science, and the social self exclude. Yet, since art represents too attenuated a mode of experience, it can in reality restore neither the wholeness of selfhood nor the sense of kinship with the living universe. Even nature cannot be apprehended without mediating forms—in Lawrence's view, without mediating *religious* forms.[105] Man needs the primordial myths which are the vehicle of religious experience; he must find the ligatures that bind him to the life of the world.

This emphasis is marked. The passage where Lawrence describes the God-pervaded world of the old religions is followed by the statement that: "this effort into sheer naked contact . . . is the root meaning of religion. . . . At the sacred races the runners hurled themselves in a terrible cumulative effort, through the air, to come at last into naked contact with the very life of the air, which is the life of the clouds, and so of the rain."[106] This is the contradiction we have run into before. A ritual contest, undertaken within the framework of communal myth, is the condition for "naked," individual contact with the cosmos.

Such a reading gives rise to difficulties. I have already touched on the problem of the relationship between art and myth, a problem that is compounded by the fact that Law-

[105] This notion has been prevalent since the Romantic period. See, for example, Spengler's insistence that "even" science represents a "mythic," mediating construct (see *Decline of the West* [New York: A. Knopf, 1950], I, 3–18), and Cassirer's neo-Kantian notion that all things are mediated through forms of consciousness.

[106] Lawrence, "New Mexico," *Phoenix*, p. 147.

rence, as an artist, tried to perform the function of myth-maker. He tried to "lead our sympathies" out toward new forms of life and to revivify a world gone stale and dead within our "squirrel cage" of a universe. Himself an individual, he spoke to the individuals who constituted his public. Hence, to stress the communal basis of myth is to overlook the meaning of what he was trying to do in his fiction. For even insofar as his novels were designed to evoke qualities of mythic consciousness, their very nature as novels—works to be read in the privacy of one's chamber—contradicted the aim of creating a public art.

There is no remedy for this. All we can do is acknowledge his ambivalence and the difficulties he encountered, both as prophet and as artist. Much more important is the fact that the communalist emphasis opens the way to the charge that Lawrence was an incipient fascist. The fascists enunciated a vitalist creed, and they used myth as an agency of social cohesion. And they, like Lawrence, wanted to lead man away from the namby-pamby softness of Christianity and a post-Christian democratic civilization, and toward a more virile, more aggressive style of life. The charge of fascism is an important one, often asserted and often refuted.

Eric Bentley, in A Century of Hero-Worship, points out that the heroic-vitalistic tradition contributed some ideas to the fascists, but that it is foolish to call all heroic vitalists fascists: then Carlyle and Yeats, Nietzsche and Stefan George would also be fascists.[107] The same may also be said of the vitalist communalism, which often accompanies the development of nineteenth-century nationalism.[108]

[107] Eric Russell Bentley, A Century of Hero Worship (Philadelphia and New York: J. B. Lippincott Company, 1944) pp. 7–9, and the chapter on Lawrence, pp. 231ff.
[108] Peter Viereck, Metapolitics: The Roots of the Nazi Mind (New York: Capricorn Books, 1961), Chap. IV.

It has been pointed out, moreover, that Lawrence was not only an incorrigible individualist, but that he also was afflicted with a Puritan conscience and quickly recoiled from seemingly attractive fascist ideas.[109] This experience of attraction and recoil is the subject of *Kangaroo*, where the hero is drawn to a para-fascist movement but then rejects it. Still more to the point is Eliseo Vivas' insistence that Lawrencean "blood-consciousness" is not the blood-thirsty consciousness of the fascist ideologist. Vivas points out that Lawrence himself was fundamentally concerned with healing the breech between flesh and spirit, between "mind" and "blood."[110] Goodheart, moreover, has noted that the "personal and passional" relationship between the leader and the led in Lawrence is a far cry from the impersonal fascist power-machine.[111]

It is clear that Lawrence was not a fascist. He did refuse to align himself with nascent English fascism, and the overall imaginative pattern of his work suggests a real aversion to the instrumentalities of the fascist state.[112] Acknowledgment of this fact however, should not lead us toward wholesale denial of Lawrence's sustained affinity with certain ideas and attitudes held by a variety of fascist thinkers.

The points of such affinity are telling, though none is decisive. The Lawrence who momentarily celebrates a mystic ritual of human sacrifice in *The Plumed Serpent* and who pondered the need for socially sanctioned outlets for repressed blood lust comes close to fascism. So does the Lawrence who,

[109] H. T. Moore, *The Life and Works of D. H. Lawrence* (New York: Twayne Publishers, 1951), p. 238.

[110] Eliseo Vivas, *D. H. Lawrence: The Failure and Triumph of Art* (Evanston: Northwestern University Press, 1960), pp. 106ff.

[111] Goodheart, *The Utopian Vision of D. H. Lawrence*, p. 141.

[112] For the most telling direct, negative, formulations on fascism, see *St. Mawr, The Tales of D. H. Lawrence* (N.Y.: Viking Press, 1936), p. 613, and the letter to Rolf Gardiner, March, 1928, *Letters*, ed. Huxley, pp. 704–705.

at moments, diverts himself with *Blut und Boden* sentimentality. Yet these were passing—and, even at their shrillest, tentative—commitments, internally consistent solutions to problems of alienation and repression that he had observed in his culture. One may regard them as aberrant moments in his development to be outgrown, or as logical responses to the postwar situation as he grasped it.

More sustained in his thought was the communalist bias, which is the focus of our concern here. From the time of his intellectual and psychological crisis of 1915–1916 onward, Lawrence affirmed community and the need for community. He proposed, more or less consistently, the recommunalization of the individual psyche within the framework of extrarational myth. And the "personal-passional" relationship to a leader—so different from the mechanism of fascist self-subordination, yet formally so like the formulation of the leadership principle in fascist ideology—remained one of the central articles of his quasi-mystic, mythic creed. The important late fiction, to be sure—mainly *Lady Chatterley's Lover* and *The Man Who Died*—seems to recant, returning to the old themes of erotic self-fulfillment and reaffirming a qualified version of the old Lawrencean individualism. Yet *Apocalypse* and the "Introduction" to Dostoevsky's parable of the Grand Inquisitor reassert the necessity for community and for myth, and they are the very last of Lawrence's ideologically oriented writings. Hence I think it fair to say that the formulation from the *Fantasia of the Unconscious*, which I have already cited, seems to establish the frame of reference which, with adjustments and even major changes, defines his fundamental attitude until the end of his life. "For the mass of people knowledge *must* be symbolical, mythical, dynamic."[113] The inference that follows is the crucial one: "This means

[113] Lawrence, *Fantasia of the Unconscious*, p. 113.

you must have a higher, responsible, conscious class: and then in varying degrees the lower classes. . . ."[114]

In fact, *Apocalypse* and the "Introduction" to the parable of the Grand Inquisitor carry the notion of immersion in the forms of communal consciousness to its farthest limit. They go even further than had *The Plumed Serpent*. In his notes on the parable, Lawrence insists that the inquisitor was telling the truth when he said that Christ had shown a real lack of love for humanity in refusing Satan's worldly gifts of "miracle, mystery, authority" and offering his love instead. Lawrence writes that the ordinary man is too frail for freedom. To expect that he depend on his own instincts and his own consciousness for direction is to damn him outright. The Inquisitor, in other words, is right. Lawrence goes so far as to hold that Jesus' kiss at the end of the story is the kiss of assent.[115]

The thesis is more carefully spelled out in *Apocalypse*, which like the notes on the parable confronts Christianity and affirms Jesus even while rejecting The Christ. Whereas the notes on the parable could be taken as affirming a political vision, with mystic elements, *Apocalypse* refers very clearly to a mystical rather than a political community. Lawrence defines love as the opposite of power. Power is the mystic, vital-electrical bond between men in the communal realm. Love is the force that makes for individuality and withdrawal into the private world of isolated being. Lawrence argues that Jesus, in affirming love, affirmed the individual. He also affirmed the individual's freedom: a man must be free to realize his uniqueness.[116]

In Jesus Lawrence finds the historical roots of a radical

---

[114] *Ibid.*

[115] D. H. Lawrence, "Introduction" to *The Grand Inquisitor, Phoenix*, pp. 283–91.   [116] Lawrence, *Apocalypse*, Chap. III.

individualism that is not very different from what he himself
once espoused. In arguing with "Jesus," Lawrence argues with
his own former position. He now holds that to demand of
each individual human being the emergence into self-conscious individuality is to court anarchy or tyranny. Most men
do not need and cannot achieve individuality. Rather, they
need a sense of belonging to the societal whole. Beyond that,
they need a sense of the greater life and power of the universe.
This can be attained within a societal whole that is in possession of religious life-wisdom akin to that of the Etruscans and
the New Mexican Indians.

Thus Lawrence affirms a societal instinct and all that it
implies. But it is not merely a societal *instinct* that is in
question. Instinct is something that exists in each individual,
alone, and Lawrence seems to think of a sociality that completely cuts across modern notions of individuality. "My individuality is really an illusion. I am part of the great whole, and
I can never escape. But I *can* deny my connections, break
them, and become a fragment."[117] The "great whole" is, to
begin with, the community, but finally the "greater world" of
life itself. The community, in this sense, is no longer an entity
that is mediated through the needs and desires of individual
human beings, but rather a directly natural entity—what
Lawrence terms an organic one—which is continuous with
the "great living universe."

Hence, we have the most dramatic aspect of the shift in
orientation in the course of Lawrence's development. It is not
only that work, thought, art, and religion are direct and natural expressions of man's deeper nature. This much had been
affirmed, though ambiguously, in the Hardy "Study," as I
have suggested in detail in Chapters II and III. In *Apoca-*

[117] *Ibid.*, p. 200.

lypse, as in the writings of the early postwar years, the community itself becomes, not something that emerges in the course of the expression by individuals of their societal needs, but rather something natural in itself.

The position may be put otherwise. In the earlier work, Lawrence had held that the radical individual self was consanguineous with nature and entered the "fourth dimension" of "being" in the moment of orgastic-individual experience. At that moment it stood free of all the limitations of the social and the mental consciousness and was one with the life, or "being," that *is* nature. Now he holds that the community is consanguineous with nature and that the individual experiences his own bond to nature through the communal links. Hence he need not emerge from the societal adhesion in order to "be." His coming-into-being takes place in the matrix of community, which is conceived along quasi-racial, quasi-geographic lines. Myth is the "ligature" or web in which particular selves are joined. Priests or leaders administer the rituals prescribed within the myths and in this role serve as the medium of individual communion with the dragon of power which lies coiled at the heart of the cosmos. Within the mythic nexus, they serve as transmitters of a mana-like, vital-electrical power and, in the language of the earlier novels, a gateway to the greater life that is symbolized by the dragon of power. This is the meaning of the theory of polarities and of vital magnetism, at the communal level.

The Harmony of Man and Nature

The main achievement of the mythic mode will be the re-naturalization of man that Lawrence has sought from the very outset. Under the new mythic heavens, on the face of the new mythic earth, men will walk with each other even as the other creatures do—or, rather, will walk as birds fly and fish swim, in schools, gracefully careening in the wind or cutting their way through the eddying sea.[118] Alternatively, in an image as old as the Hardy "Study," they will naturally come together as a melody, realizing, or enacting, the harmony that emerges from the play-in-conflict of nature itself.[119]

Obviously, men are not birds or fish or notes in a scale. Nor are they terms of a natural dialectic. They are particular beings, moved by natural, instinctual needs but shaped by pressures from other beings in society. This, however, would seem to be Lawrence's point. A myth-defined society cuts across the distracting and disruptive impulses of particular men and joins them within a harmonic pattern in the rhythm, or pattern, of nature.

The crux, of course, is that Lawrence wishes, though ambivalently, to affirm such a pattern in nature. Nature can be spoken of as more than a source of normative judgments and values. It is a "real" entity, or structure of entities, to which man must relate. The heath of the Hardy "Study" formulations, which was largely a metaphor for the passionate, instinctive life of the individual, has become, unequivocally, an

[118] Such imagery figures often in the works of the middle and late years. For example, in "The Flying Fish," Lawrence writes, "What civilization will bring us to such a pitch of swift laughing togetherness as these fish have reached?" (*Phoenix*, p. 795). In "Education of the People," he writes of sheer, leaping movement, like fish, hawk, and deer. In "Autobiographical Fragment," he describes how the men of the future dance with "incalculable unison . . . , by instinct, like the wheeling and flashing of a shoal of fish or of a flock of birds dipping. . . . They were dancing the sun down, and dancing as birds wheel and dance, and fishes in shoals. . . . I wanted to . . . be one of them. To be a drop in that wave of life." (*Phoenix*, p. 832). *The Plumed Serpent* is full of such imagery of the instinctive, spontaneous harmony of movement among primitive dancers. This is, as I have indicated in this chapter, part of Lawrence's vision of the way the old religions represent man's "profound attempt . . . to harmonize himself with nature" (*Etruscan Places*, p. 123).

[119] Lawrence, "The Study of Thomas Hardy," *Phoenix*, p. 432.

objectified reality somewhere "out there," and man must adjust to it. The means of adjustment to the pattern or within the pattern is myth, and with myth, ritual.

Closer to Lawrence's essential meaning than the image of birds and fish, in which he formulated his sense of the close harmony between man and man and between man and nature, is the structured formulation, made in "A Propos of Lady Chatterley's Lover," of the advantages that the medieval church offered medieval man. Lawrence is writing of the need for a renewal of marriage, "the true phallic marriage."

And, still further, it will be marriage set again in relationship to the rhythmic cosmos. The rhythm of the cosmos is something we cannot get away from, without bitterly impoverishing our lives. The Early Christians tried to kill the old pagan rhythm of cosmic ritual, and to some extent succeeded. They killed the planets and the zodiac, perhaps because astrology had already become debased to fortune-telling. They wanted to kill the festivals of the year. But the Church, which knows that man doth not live by man alone, but by the sun and moon and earth in their revolutions, restored the sacred days and feasts almost as the pagans had them, and the Christian peasants went on very much as the pagan peasants had gone, with the sunrise pause for worship, and the sunset, and noon, the three great daily moments of the sun: then the new holy-day, one in the ancient seven-cycle: then Easter and the dying and rising of God, Pentecost, Midsummer Fire, the November dead and the spirits of the grave, then Christmas, then Three Kings. For centuries the mass of people lived in this rhythm, under the Church.[120]

"A Propos of Lady Chatterley's Lover" sums up all the relevant Lawrencean doctrines. In it, we find the notions of the vitality and sexuality of the cosmos; of the "blood" or of sexuality in man as the link to the cosmic life; and of commu-

[120] D. H. Lawrence, *Sex, Literature and Censorship*, ed. with introduction by Harry T. Moore (New York: Viking Compass Books, 1959), pp. 104–105.

nity, with its integrating forms of consciousness as the medium in which man can be put back in touch with the life of the world. With *Apocalypse*, this is Lawrence's great last word:

> the greatest need of man is the renewal forever of the complete rhythm of life and death, the rhythm of the sun's year, the body's year of a lifetime, and the greater year of the stars, the soul's year of immortality. . . . It is no use asking for a Word to fulfil such a need. No Word, no Logos, no Utterance will ever do it.

. . . .

It is a question, practically, of relationship. We *must* get back into relation, vivid and nourishing relation to the cosmos and the universe. The way is through daily ritual, and the re-awakening. . . . For the truth is, we are perishing for lack of fulfilment of our greater needs, we are cut off from the great sources of our inward nourishment and renewal, sources which flow eternally in the universe. . . . We must plant ourselves again in the universe.

It means a return to ancient forms.[121]

In "A Propos," Lawrence is directly affirming marriage as the "clue" to the universe; as in *The Rainbow*, the rhythm of marriage is closest to the rhythm of the year.

Sex is the balance of male and female in the universe, the attraction, the repulsion, the transit of neutrality, the new attraction, the new repulsion, always different, always new. The long neuter spell of Lent, when the blood is low, and the delight of the Easter kiss, the sexual revel of spring, the passion of midsummer, the slow recoil, revolt and grief of autumn, greyness again, then the sharp stimulus of winter of the long nights. Sex goes through the rhythm of the year, in man and woman, ceaselessly changing: the rhythm of the sun in his relation to the earth.[122]

But though sexuality and marriage are, as in the very early writing, the direct point of contact, they must have a com-

[121] *Ibid.*, pp. 105–106. [122] *Ibid.*, pp. 99–100.

munal-ritual frame of reference. Marriage is marriage only when the Church provides the necessary frame of reference for contact with the cosmos, so that in the end nature, or the cosmos, dictates the forms.

Such marriage, to be sure, cannot really solve the problems of the "love"-mode as presented in the novels of the middle years. Marriage does not provide a solution to the grinding problem of violence and repressed aggression; it does not release individual or community from the ingrown psychic life of those who have matured within the given—that is, the fallen—world. The vision of the redeemed world abounds in images of the harmonies that Lawrence sees in nature; the elaborated record of the unredeemed world, as set down in the novels, indicates that such harmonies are inaccessible to men in their present state. Men are too clogged with accumulated hatred and resentment; they suffer from a thwarting of their societal instinct that issues in further violence; and they suffer from oppressive subordination to ideas that suppress their vital life and impulses.

Only in *Aaron's Rod*, *Kangaroo*, and *The Plumed Serpent* does Lawrence confront the problem of the hostility and violence that must be overcome, even as he deals with the dangers to the psychic life of marital exclusivity, at the expense of communal ties. In those novels, violence figures as a prime issue, both in the given world and in the imagination of a regenerated one. *Lady Chatterley's Lover* and *The Man Who Died* turn away from such matters; so, in part, do the last discursive writings. The latest fiction is dominated by the questions of marriage and erotic fulfillment. It does not moot the questions of society's place in the life of the individual, or of society's needs in its own right. And what dominates "A Propos of Lady Chatterley's Lover," *Apocalypse*, and the Introduction to *The Grand Inquisitor* is the conception of an abstruse, utopian communalism, which I have just outlined.

That conception catches up impulses and themes that animate all of Lawrence's work, and it has its own intrinsic imaginative and salvationist interest. But it sidesteps the most radical of the difficulties that Lawrence sees in the world-as-it-is.

Ironically, it is the novels that are most problematical artistically, and that lean most strongly toward fascist ideas, that most fully confront the entire range of issues that engage Lawrence at his most vigorous. These are the novels that also articulate most fully the communalist fantasy that was designed to deal with these issues. Among these, *The Plumed Serpent* is perhaps the most coherent and self-consistent, dealing with the full range of Lawrence's concerns. It is therefore to *The Plumed Serpent* that I turn in the following chapter, with a view to examining the way in which the communalist vision is imaginatively embodied in a more or less (often less than more, by the standards of Lawrence's best fiction) realized work of fiction.

VII

The Communalism of The Plumed Serpent

The Plumed Serpent is the only one of Lawrence's novels to embody in fictive terms the redemptive vision which I have outlined in the preceding chapter. Despite aesthetic deformities and ideological absurdities, it renders more concretely than any of the other novels Lawrence's vision of the "new heaven and new earth" of a redeemed humanity. Even more than the essays, it particularizes the conception of community and of cosmos which is the center of Lawrence's terminal vision of the world.

The last of the leadership novels, *The Plumed Serpent*, sums up the insights that Lawrence had amassed in the course of the preceding years. In it he affirms: (*a*) the life (power) of the cosmos; (*b*) the duality of that life, and the need to affirm both terms of that duality; (*c*) the exhaustion of the "light" or "spirit" term of Western consciousness; (*d*) the historical pattern within which that exhaustion is to be understood; (*e*) the need for an elite of natural aristocrats to renew the community's relation to the life of the cosmos; (*f*) the role of myth and ritual in such renewal. In the pages that follow, I follow out, schematically, the treatment of these themes in the novel, with a view to indicating the way the novel embodies the notions touched upon in the preceding chapter.

a. The Cosmic Snake and the Life of the Cosmos

Don Ramon's regenerated society is based on the idea that the cosmos is alive. The "plumed serpent" is, among other things, the dragon of power that is coiled at the heart of the cosmos, a symbol of the pervasive animistic power that is the world. The religion of the Mexican Indians, as formulated by Don Ramon, is based on this idea. Don Ramon tells his peons that "the earth you dig is alive as a snake that sleeps. . . . The earth is alive."[1] Don Ramon's hymns praise the cosmic snake-dragon "that is father of stone . . . of the silver and gold, of the iron, the timber of earth from the bone of the father of earth, of the snake of the world, of the heart of the world, that beats. . . ."[2]

The dragon life imagery is scattered throughout the novel. Don Ramon says that "the universe is a nest of dragons with a perfectly unfathomable life-mystery at the centre of it." Elsewhere, however, he speaks of the cosmos as a tree of life, and Kate Forrester comes to experience the world as a great tree,[3] "She wished . . . to shut doors of iron against the mechanical world . . . to let the sunwise world steal across her, and add its motion to her, the motion of the stress of life, with the big sun and the stars like a tree holding out its leaves. . . ."[4] Kate also experiences the cosmic life as an ocean that carries her on its tide into a realm of cosmic sexuality. Listening to Don Ramon's snake-incantation, Kate feels part of "sex, but the greater, not the lesser sex." When she experiences the uplift of the "greater sex," she feels "her sex and her womanhood caught up and identified in the slowly revolving ocean of nascent life. . . ."[5]

[1] D. H. Lawrence, *The Plumed Serpent* (London: William Heinemann Ltd., 1955), pp. 193–96.   [2] *Ibid.*, p. 124.   [3] *Ibid.*, p. 75.   [4] *Ibid.*, p. 100.   [5] *Ibid.*, p. 127.

The notion that the cosmos is an ocean of life is central to the Yoga-like mysteries of communion which are the source of Don Ramon's power.[6] "['] I put off the world with my clothes. . . . ['] He stood soft and relaxed, staring with wide eyes at the dark, feeling the dark fecundity of the inner tide washing over his heart, over his belly, his mind dissolved away in the greater, dark mind. . . . He . . . stood still, in pure unconsciousness . . . like a dark seaweed deep in the sea."[7]

To say the cosmos is alive (vital) is, in actual fact, to distort the picture somewhat. The universe, as rendered in *The Plumed Serpent*, is animist rather than vitalist.[8] Its life is the mana-life that pervades and envelops things, not the vital life that is *in* all things. It is, in fact, the "fourth dimension" of "The Crown" essays and the *Reflections on the Death of a Porcupine*, the realm of "power" of the "New Mexico" essay. The singers and drummer of Don Ramon's Quetzalcoatl community sing themselves "into the other dimension of man's existence, where he finds himself in the infinite room that lies inside the axis of our wheeling space."[9]

b. The Duality of the Cosmic Life

Quetzalcoatl, the plumed serpent who presides over the religion of the new Mexico in the novel, is identified with the cosmic dragon and with the "nest of dragons" at the center of the cosmos. In the community that Don Ramon establishes,

[6] See Chap. II, pp. 69–72. William York Tindall points out the influence of Yoga and of theosophical speculation in the novel. He writes: "Lawrence's most animistic novel, *The Plumed Serpent*, is also his most theosophical. Its theme is that of Mme. Blavatsky's *Secret Doctrine*: the recovery of Lost Atlantis by means of myths and symbols" (*D. H. Lawrence and Susan His Cow*, p. 143).

[7] Lawrence, *The Plumed Serpent*, p. 190.

[8] Tindall, *D. H. Lawrence and Susan His Cow*, p. 108.

[9] Lawrence, *The Plumed Serpent*, p. 122.

Quetzalcoatl is a symbol of the preternatural cosmic life that man shares with nature. Just as the griffin of medieval iconography symbolizes the dual nature of Christ, Quetzalcoatl symbolizes the dual nature of man and cosmic life itself. The plumed serpent, as depicted in the old Aztec carvings and reliefs, is a griffin-like monster with a snake's body and the head and wings of an eagle. In his snake-nature he epitomizes the flesh-and-blood aspect of man and of man's harmony with the heavy, dark, lower world of earth. In his eagle-nature he symbolizes man's "light"-aspiring, pinion-thrusting, spiritual striving toward the heavens. Birds, Lawrence had written in the *Fantasia of the Unconscious*, are the symbols of the other-directed needs of the upper nervous system.[10]

The symbolism restates the old dualisms of Lawrence's cosmology and psychology. The plumed serpent represents the possibility of synthesis between antagonistic modes of human and cosmic experience. In Don Ramon's resurrected snake-god of the blood-darkness, Lawrence imagines the possibility of the seamless unity of the human faculties.[11] In the imagery of the later Lawrencean iconography, man is resurrected in the flesh. Resurrection, obviously, means redemption from the state of perpetual "crucifixion" on the "cross" of mind and blood. The resurrected man is one who lives in the flesh, without conflict between body and mind. He is also one who, implicitly, is freed from the conflict of severance from the mother-womb of nature. Whole in himself, he is at one with nature.

The vision of the earlier works is suggested here in the symbolism of the cosmic snake. This vision in its earlier forms is still more directly suggested by the novel's symbolism of the morning star. The novel's hymns of praise to Quetzalcoatl include hymns that celebrate the morning star, which hangs

[10] Lawrence, *Fantasia of the Unconscious*, p. 134.
[11] Lawrence, "[Autobiographical Fragment]," *Phoenix*, p. 830.

suspended between night and day. Night and day, in the Lawrencean manner, represent female and male, but also flesh and spirit and Father and Son in the Trinity. The morning star is analogous to the Holy Ghost of the personality that comes into being between the "male" faculties of the human individuals and the "female"; it is also the divinity that flickers into being "between" lovers; it is also the point of harmony between the community of worshipers who celebrate the morning star and the cosmos of which the morning star is the essence.

c. The Exhaustion of the Light-Term

Don Ramon's religion of Quetzalcoatl reveals a new heaven and a new earth and "places" man within it. In the novel, Lawrence tries to represent the achievement of the harmony that the religion of Quetzalcoatl can bring to the peons of Mexico. This harmony is never fully achieved; it is merely the desideratum of the new religion, adumbrated in the novel but never realized. The novel is interesting, ideologically and imagistically, because it pits a richly articulated vision of the fallen world against an almost but not quite fully developed vision of the redeemed world. Its effectiveness as a work of art depends on its success in rendering the conflict between the two. It is, after all, about a revolution and a struggle for power, and its strength, for all the limitations of Lawrence's politics, lies in rendering the necessity for that struggle. Such necessity arises, not from conflict over control of desirable worldly goods, but rather from a purely spiritual clash with reference to the means through which man's spiritual needs can be satisfied.

In this, Don Ramon seems to speak for Lawrence's view of Western civilization itself. The conflict in the novel is pitched at an unusually abstract level, even for Lawrence: between the

Catholic Church, which represents the "white," repressive Christian consciousness, and Don Ramon, who speaks for the "dark" Quetzalcoatl consciousness. In Don Ramon's view, the Church can no longer minister to the needs of its communicants. It has exhausted the emotional possibilities of the Mexican people in the direction of the white consciousness. Quetzalcoatl, synthesizing the white consciousness and the dark consciousness, can help renew the psychic life of the people.

The abstract assertion that the white consciousness (that is, the "love"-mode) is exhausted is expressed within the novel in several ways. In fact, the novel recapitulates most of the assertions with regard to the white consciousness enumerated above, in Chapter VI. The most concrete of these is rendered through the characterization of Dona Carlota, Don Ramon's wife. Carlota is a tormented, vindictive, guilt-ridden woman, whose life is devoted to good works within the Church, and who is full of impotent rage at Ramon's political and religious aspirations. Lawrence wants us to see her as a being who has died in the flesh, as a kind of vampire who would wish to suck away the life her husband still can lead in the flesh. Her love, once sincere and sweet, has turned into a tormenting hate. Lawrence suggests that a woman like Carlota is incapable of loving a vigorous man in the flesh because of her commitment to the "love"-mode.

Less concretely, he tries showing the way that the democratic ideal, joined to the Christian way, has broken down the integrity of the peasant personality, depriving the individual of the proud independence that had once been possible even in poverty. Socialism, communism, fascism—all the political panaceas—are seen as enforcing a deadly depersonalization, divesting the individual of his natural needs and responses for the sake of abstract, social goals—or uniform socioeconomic ones. The peasant no longer walks in proud isolation in his poncho, attuned to demons that invade him through the "lower gates." Instead, he buys a cheap ready-to-wear suit and congregates with other nonentities in the village square.

Along the same lines, Lawrence suggests, again quite abstractly, that the Christian ideal of charity, sacrifice, and identification with the suffering Christ is perverse. He implies that it is merely an inverted expression of cruel and barbaric impulses. The masochism is real, however—and the ecstasy of pain is shown to have played a part in perpetuating the exploitation that the peasants have suffered since the dawn of history.

Lawrence dramatizes the exhaustion of the white "Jesus" consciousness by showing us how the Mexican peasants must rebel against their Christianity. Ramon, the natural aristocrat and the thought-adventurer, expresses the people's revulsion from the Christian and Western ideals and points the way to the resurrection of the old, dark gods, of Quetzalcoatl and his pagan compeers. Ultimately, the primordial unconscious may be said to be rising in revolt against a superimposed consciousness and a repressive civilization. Man must re-establish contact with the dark and demonic side of consciousness in order to restore his psychic balance and regain contact with the power of nature (the cosmos).

d. The Historical Pattern

The problem of how the world has fallen into its "degenerate" Christ ("white") phase no longer vexes Lawrence. By the time of *The Plumed Serpent* his concept of history had changed, along with his changing conception of the life of the cosmos. In the novel, as in the bulk of the later work, Lawrence assumes that the cosmos is alive and that man is alive. He assumes, moreover, that human life and cosmic life are both dual, and that the dualities are coordinated. As in the *Fantasia* scheme, there must be correspondence and communication between the aspects (essentially, the poles) of the psyche and the aspects of the cosmic being.

In the *Fantasia*, Lawrence had taken as his major premise the assumption that history was the expression of man's experience in the matrix of nature. Hence, it was not completely engulfed and determined by the cosmic life and its demands. Rather, it represented what I have termed an outcropping of nature, or life. In *The Plumed Serpent*, on the other hand, history is largely a reflex of nature, or of the cosmic life. The all-engulfing, almost deterministic force of the environing life is stressed. The life of the cosmos is seen as the source of all human life, so that human life necessarily falls in with the patterns of that life, or at least expresses its needs. The life of civilizations—any civilization—depends on the cosmic life outside it and is ultimately controlled by that life.

This idea is ordinarily expressed in the imagery of the ocean or tree of life—of the great oceanic womb of all things, or the tree of life whose roots reach down into the nest of dragons at the heart of the cosmos. The tree-of-life imagery figures more often in the novel. "The Tree of Life is one tree," Lawrence writes, and insists that all the "flowers" of civilization, however different in appearance, are really the flowers of one tree: "When our souls open out in the final blossoming, then as blossoms we share one mystery with all blossoms . . . something transcendent. . . .[For] the mystery is one mystery, but men must see it differently."[12]

The fully developed tree-of-life imagery directly implies a cyclic conception of history. We are familiar with such a conception in the work of Spengler, who conceives of history in terms of the cycle of organic life. Each civilization passes through a series of necessary phases—phases of youth, maturity, and old age.[13] The sequence of phases is "coded" into the

[12] Lawrence, *The Plumed Serpent*, pp. 245.
[13] H. Stuart Hughes, *Oswald Spengler: A Critical Estimate* (New York: Charles Scribner Sons, 1952), Chap. I.

organism. Hence development in a given direction is a necessity in the life of the organism.

One becomes aware, in contemplating the metaphor, of the way in which an image adopted in the name of freedom becomes the vehicle for a conception of necessity. In the Romantic period writers had posed organism against mechanism with a view to affirming the possibility of life-movement as opposed to mechanical restraint. Yet the life cycle of any organism is itself fixed; if the metaphor is carried far enough, it necessarily implies a pattern of necessity. In Spengler's work, the sense of the inevitability of such a pattern becomes the basis of dire pessimism. Spengler fatalistically affirmed the decadence of Western civilization on grounds of necessity.[14]

The later Lawrence, but especially the Lawrence of *The Plumed Serpent*, leaned toward such a pessimistic, if not deterministic, view. He arrives at it, moreover, by way of the effort to affirm spontaneity and freedom. The early Lawrence, we recall, had spoken of the individual as a leading shoot on the Tree of Life.[15] Now, Don Ramon asserts that "men are still part of the tree of life."[16] The emphasis has changed, however. In the earlier writings Lawrence had stressed fresh budding and flowering, and with it the necessity of new leaps into the future and the unknown; man was a leading shoot into the unknown. Now he stresses the element of decadence and a confining rootedness in the soil of life. "The roots go down to the centre of the earth," Don Ramon continues. "Loose leaves, and aeroplanes, blow away on the wind, in what they call freedom. But the Tree of Life has fixed, deep, gripping roots."[17]

Obviously, the theme is not altogether new in *The Plumed Serpent*. "Old leaves have got to fall," he writes in *Fantasia of*

[14] Oswald Spengler, *Man and Technics*, trans. Charles F. Atkinson (New York: Alfred A. Knopf, 1932), p. 135.   [15] See Chap. I.
[16] Lawrence, *The Plumed Serpent*, p. 75.   [17] *Ibid.*

the Unconscious. "Old forms must die. . . . And dead leaves make good mould. And so dead men."[18] Civilization, he continues, is passing through a "winter period," a period of "death and denudation."[19] The reason: the emptying out of meaning within the old forms.

In *The Plumed Serpent,* the reason given is more external and more objective. The Christian phase of Mexico's civilization is over. This is so because the tormented psyche of the Mexican peasantry protests. An objective factor is also at work, however. The dark gods, who have existence in the cosmos, demand the casting away of old forms. After two thousand years (*sic*) of Christian dominance in the "love"-mode of white consciousness, the dark gods return. The cosmic life itself demands, through them, that Western man cast off the modes of consciousness within which he has been tormenting himself since the coming of Christ and adapt himself to its rhythms. At one level the dark gods symbolize an aspect of the human psyche. At another they embody a cosmic reality, and man must adapt to that reality if he is to survive.

The pattern of history (and of nature) is very clear and painfully simple—as it had been in the Hardy "Study" vision, but within a slightly different pattern. In the present scheme the rhythm of nature itself demands that man welcome the dark gods. The rhythm, apparently, is one in which all things are reduced to the basic dark-light dualism of Lawrence's world-picture. Despite all Lawrence's assertions of faith in the "strangeness" and "shimmering" variety of rainbow-colored civilizations, the rhythm of civilization dictates that a dominant dark mode be replaced by a dominant light mode which must in turn be superseded by a dark mode. It is as though there are alternating cosmic tides to which man's life in history must be adjusted. Don Ramon's Quetzalcoatl cult strives toward such adjustment.

[18] Lawrence, *Fantasia of the Unconscious,* p. 208.   [19] *Ibid.*

e. The Elite of Natural Aristocrats

The adjustment in question is not and cannot be achieved by individuals in and for themselves; it is achieved by a community that participates in a given mode of consciousness —albeit one that is enunciated by extraordinary individuals. We encounter something of a contradiction here. In *The Plumed Serpent*, as in the *Studies in Classic American Literature*, human communities are thought of as natural entities. Even their historical development is conceived in terms of vital but natural powers emanating from the souls of the dead and interacting with the souls of the living.[20] Yet human communities inevitably generate forms of consciousness that are not "natural" in the meaning of spontaneous, instinctive, and without *a priori* meaning. Such consciousness, even at its radical "blood"-body level, is in this sense at least partly historical and therefore conditioned by the experience, thought, and feeling of the men who have gone before and created the environing world, with both its cultural and its animistic energies. Myth itself, the most natural and unself-conscious of the forms of civilized consciousness, is in part both historical and self-conscious in its nature. The symbols of which it is made do not spring directly from the roots of the tree of life or from the nest of dragons that emit cosmic vitality. Rather, they come into being within history, through the instrumentality of great and creative men.

I do not mean to suggest that Lawrence thinks men can consciously and willfully create symbols. I merely wish to note that Lawrence, for all his insistence on the naturalness and unconscious roots of symbolism, nonetheless places symbols in a context of historical experience.[21] He writes: "It takes

[20] Lawrence, *Fantasia of the Unconscious*, p. 64.
[21] See Chap. VI.

centuries to really create a significant symbol. No man can invent symbols. He can invent an emblem, made up of images: or metaphors; but not symbols. Some images in the course of many generations become symbols, embedded in the soul and ready to start alive when touched, carried on in the human consciousness for centuries."[22]

Hence, the active role of Don Ramon in *The Plumed Serpent*—the role of leader and explorer. He does not create symbols out of the whole cloth, but he is needed to manipulate them to achieve the ends of accommodation between man and the cosmos. The materials he uses are a historical residue of the old myths which have survived in the unconscious life of the people at a level far below the white, Christian consciousness. In formulating the myths and rituals of the Quetzalcoatl community, he has taken up what Lawrence, in *Fantasia of the Unconscious*, had termed the "living clue to the universe." Discussing the "death period" of the West, Lawrence had written: "This time . . . we have consciously and responsibly to carry ourselves through the winter-period, the period of death and denudation. . . . For there are not now, as in the Roman times, any great reservoirs of energetic, barbaric life. . . . This time the leading civilization cannot die out. . . . It must suffer a great collapse, maybe. But it must carry through all the collapse the *living clue* to the next civilization."[23]

Ramon's role is in a sense opposite to the role of the lawgiver. Rather than legislate a way to the future, he cleaves a way to a lost past as a means of discovering a life-mode for the future.[24] In effect, he resurrects the residue of a more effective way of relating to the universe and, in doing so, satisfies the primordial needs of his people. As one of Law-

[22] Lawrence, *Selected Literary Criticism*, ed. Beal, p. 18.
[23] Lawrence, *Fantasia of the Unconscious*, p. 208. Italics mine.
[24] Lawrence, *The Plumed Serpent*, p. 238.

rence's natural aristocrats and as a thought-adventurer to boot, he has thrust himself beyond thought to a pure, dynamic, mythic way of relating to the cosmos.

Ramon conceives of his role in just such terms. "I would like . . . to be one of the initiates of the Earth. One of the initiators. . . . The First Men of every people, forming a Natural Aristocracy of the World. One must have Aristocrats . . . natural ones, not artificial."[25] Ramon is a sort of Platonic guardian of his society, or—closer to Lawrence both historically and in terms of the role assigned him—a Brave-New-World governor of it. He not only makes laws and enforces them but also constructs the framework of consciousness within which his people live. To do so, he deciphers the symbolic possibilities of consciousness within his culture and evolves a structure of symbols and rituals that connect his people to their past, their passions, and the circumambient universe.

Ramon is more than this, and his role is more vital. William York Tindall long ago defined Lawrence's conception of the leader as the bridge to the cosmos—as a sort of conductor for the power that man can, under optimal conditions, draw from the cosmos.[26] All the more recent expositions of Lawrence's ideas add nothing to this perception. The leader, in *The Plumed Serpent*, not only discovers the clues to the living universe but in the active, ritual context of its mythic life bridges the distance between his followers and the divine life of the world.

Within the cult established by Ramon, an elite of leaders, and not Ramon alone, fills this role. These leaders impersonate, within the ritual forms of the cult, the dark gods who are the object of cultic worship. They are able to do this because the gods are "in" them, having entered into them in

[25] *Ibid.*, p. 244.
[26] Tindall, D. H. *Lawrence and Susan His Cow*, Chap. IV.

the course of their trance-like submersion in the "Ocean" of power that is the cosmos. They are, in other words, inspired, or even possessed, though their possession is subject to the rational control of consciousness. In this state they carry their followers into a state of consciousness where cosmic life and being are accessible.

This function is most clearly enunciated in the treatment of Don Cipriano. Cipriano is Kate Forrester's husband; through her, we directly experience the sense of power that he "conducts." First we see him as the link between his wife and the vital world and then, by extension, are to imagine him as the bond between his men and the world. I propose tracing, through quotation in the main, the stages of Kate's experience with Cipriano, with a view to suggesting the nature of his role as mediator between his people and the cosmos.

Kate's development in the novel involves a husking away of her social ego and her imprisoning white consciousness, permitting the discovery of new possibilities of relationship to men and to nature. Toward the end of her quest for new and viable identity, she muses: "Now, must she admit that the individual was an illusion and a falsification? There was no such animal. Except in the mechanical world. In the world of machines, the individual machine is effectual. The individual, like the perfect being, does not and cannot exist in the vivid world. We are all fragments. And, at the best halves. The only whole thing is the Morning Star. Which can only rise between two: or between many."[27]

Kate's crucial development begins when she realizes the futility of the individuality she has always cherished. She first experiences the intimation of possibilities for extra-individual wholeness as she travels into the Mexican interior, on the shores of Lake Sayula. There she hears the tom-toms of Ra-

[27] Lawrence, *The Plumed Serpent*, p. 388.

mon's followers, who are chanting the "theme-song" of their religion: "Who sleeps shall wake! Who treads down the path of the snake in the dust, etc." It is at this point that she begins to experience

sex, but the greater, not the lesser sex. The waters over the earth wheeling upon the waters under the earth. . . . . She felt her sex and her womanhood caught up and identified in the slowly revolving ocean of nascent life. . . . Herself gone into her womanhood. And where her fingers touched the fingers of the man, the quiet spark, like the dawn-star, shining between her and the greater manhood of men. . . . How strange to be merged in desire beyond desire, to be gone in the body beyond the individualism of the body, with the spark of contact lingering like a morning star. . . .[28]

Later in the novel, Kate is able to give herself up to Cipriano because he fulfills this possibility for her. He transports her beyond her shell-self and her prison-like individuality into the morning star.

Kate felt she wanted to be covered with deep and living darkness, the deeps where Cipriano could lay her. . . . And Cipriano, as he sat in the boat with her, felt the inward sun rise darkly in him, diffusing through him, and felt the mysterious flower of her woman's femaleness slowly opening to him, as a sea-anemone opens deep under the sea, with infinite soft fleshliness. The hardness of self-will was gone, and the soft anemone of her deeps blossomed for him of itself, far down under the tides.[29]

The sexual imagery is embarrassingly blatant and betrays, to some extent, the metaphysical notions that Lawrence wants it to convey. Kate and Cipriano are "washed up" in the tide of sexual feeling, much as Paul Morel and Clara Dawes had been in *Sons and Lovers*. As in the earlier novel, but far more emphatically and affirmatively, the specific sexual expe-

[28] *Ibid.*, p. 127.   [29] *Ibid.*, p. 350.

rience involves not only pleasure but also a connection to the greater world. Thus, after her marriage to Cipriano, Kate experiences the following: "when Cipriano touched her caressively, all her body flowered. That was the greater sex, that could fill all the world with lustre. . . . But on the other hand, when she spread the wings of her own ego . . . the world could look very wonderful. . . . But after a while, the wonder faded, and a sort of jealous emptiness set in."[30]

Her feeble, self-generated wonder is very different from the experience that Cipriano affords her:

Cipriano . . . opened a new world to her, a world of twilight, with the dark, half-visible face of the god-demon Pan, who can never perish, but ever returns upon mankind from the shadows. The world of shadows and dark prostration, with the phallic wind rushing through the dark. . . . [Experiencing his presence, she feels that his blood envelops her:] Her limbs seemed to fuse like metal melting down. She fused into a sudden unconsciousness, her will, her very self gone, leaving her lying in molten life, like a lake of still fire, unconscious of everything save the eternality of the fire in which she was gone.[31]

The essential Cipriano-quality is rendered as follows:

Curious he was! With a sort of gloom of the ordinary world on top, and underneath a black volcano with hell knows what depths of lava. . . . The great part of his nature was just inert and heavy . . . limited as a snake or lizard is limited. But within his own heavy, dark range, he had a curious power. . . . She could feel the curious tingling heat of his blood, and the heavy power of the will that lay unemerged in his blood. She could see again the skies go dark, and the phallic mystery rearing itself like a whirling dark cloud. . . . The old, supreme, phallic mystery. . . . The mystery of the primeval world.[32]

The imagery recurs in a later passage, but with a significant magnification of certain elements: "A face like Cipriano's is

[30] Ibid., p. 437–38.   [31] Ibid., pp. 314–17.   [32] Ibid., p. 306.

the face at once of a god and a devil. . . . He had the old gift
of the demon-power. . . . When the power of his blood rose
in him, the dark aura streamed from him like a cloud preg-
nant with power, like thunder. . . . Language had abandoned
her. . . . Her self had abandoned her, and all her day was
gone. Only she said to herself: 'My demon lover!' "[33]

Demon, god, and devil—these are the key words here, distinguishing the quality and meaning of sexuality in this novel
from that which is rendered in *Sons and Lovers*. For Kate, the
European woman, Cipriano is the demon-god who denies the
values of her own mode of selfhood and relationship. Even
language, her mode of connection with others, abandons her
when she encounters his primeval erotic nature. The demon,
in this case, is not diabolically disintegrative of the bonds that
connect men to each other. He is demon in relation to the old
society, but god in relation to the new. He brings Kate the
possibility of rebirth and the renewal of her bonds with the
cosmos, and he brings these through the medium of sexuality.
As leader, he brings the same possibility to his people in the
medium of religious ritual. "We are all fragments," Ramon
had said. ". . . The only whole thing is the Morning Star.
Which can only rise between two; or between many."[34]

As god, or god-manifestation, Cipriano binds his people,
who are only fragments, to each other and to the greater life
of the cosmos. Cipriano, as Huitzilopochtli, the old Aztec
god, derives his divinity from contact with the cosmic life on
the one hand, and with the transpersonal reality of his people
on the other—their "blood" reality. "Not in the blood or the
spirit lay his individuality and his supremacy, his godhead.
But in a star within him, an inexplicable star which rose out
of the dark sea and shone between the flood and the great sky.
The mysterious star which unites the vast universal blood

---

[33] *Ibid.*, pp. 308–309.   [34] *Ibid.*, p. 388.

with the universal breath of the spirit, and shines between them both."[35]

In this, he is no different from any man who is able to achieve the transpersonal, transrational integrity of self. Nor is the way he links Kate to the cosmic life unusual, from Lawrence's point of view. Every man is a revelation of divinity to his woman. The morning star that rises within each man is the Holy Ghost of Lawrence's earlier formulations, and each man bears its potentialities within him, just as in the Christian view each man bears a spark of divinity.

Cipriano's special quality lies in his serving as mediator for his followers—in his religious-communal role, where he is a revelation of the godhead to the many. "The old Indians of the North," Lawrence writes in the novel, "still have the secret of animistic dancing. They dance to gain power; power over the *living* forces or potencies of the earth."[36] Cipriano, on the march with his army, dances:

He felt his limbs and his whole body immense with power, he felt the black mystery of power go out of him over all his soldiers. And he sat there imperturbable, in silence, holding all those black-eyed men in the splendour of his own, silent self. His own dark consciousness seemed to radiate through their flesh and their bones, they were conscious, not through themselves but through him. And as a man's instinct is to shield his own head, so that instinct was to shield Cipriano, for he was the most precious part of themselves to them. It was in him they were supreme. They got their splendour from his power, and their greatest consciousness was his consciousness diffusing them.[37]

Within the ambience of Cipriano's power, men are no longer at the mercy of their fragmenting individuality and of the instrumental will. Instead, they are caught up in the soft, organic life-flow within which life is lived on the boundary

[35] *Ibid.*, p. 387.   [36] *Ibid.*, p. 362.   [37] *Ibid.*, p. 363.

between night and day, flesh and spirit, action and passion. In
a sense, they exist at the point where "this" world joins the
"other," greater world of the "fourth dimensionality," which
is being. Through the religious practices of their leaders, the
Mexican people experience themselves as having come into
being, as living in the "sea" or "ocean" of the greater life,
which includes death and all "eternity."

The vision of the new heaven and the new earth is rendered
concretely in terms of two elements. One is the cessation of
clock time, which measures life out in mechanical units, dis-
joined from the organic flow of consciousness. The other is
the absence of the metal element of the machine: even time
is measured, not by the ticking metal mechanism which we
know, but by the organic, timeless rhythms of animal-hide
drums. With the return of the old gods, "the church remained shut up, and dumb. The clock didn't go. Time suddenly fell off, the days walked naked and timeless, in the old,
uncounted, manner of the past. The strange, old, uncounted,
unregistered, unreckoning days of the ancient heathen
world."[38] Still later, when the new regime is running
smoothly,

the world was somehow different; all different. No jingle of bells
from the church, no striking of the clock. The clock was taken
away.
And instead, the drums.[39]

.   .   .   .

Strange, the change that was taking place in the world. Always
the air had a softer, more velvety silence, it seemed alive. And
there were no hours. Dawn and noon and sunset, mid-morning, or
the up-slope middle, and mid-afternoon, or the down-slope middle,
this was the day, with the watches of the night.

.   .   .   .

[38] *Ibid.*, p. 285.   [39] *Ibid.*, p. 355.

It was as if, from Ramon and Cipriano, from Jamiltepec and the lake region, a new world was unfolding, unrolling, as softly and subtly as twilight falling and removing the clutter of day. It was a soft, twilit newness slowly spreading and penetrating the world. . . . Now, even in the cities the blue serapes of Quetzal-coatl were seen, and the drums were heard at the Hours, casting a strange mesh of twilight over the clash of bells and the clash of traffic. . . .[40]

For those who are drawn into the aura of power and the soft, twilit peace of the revolutionary regime, life becomes a slow but passionate unfolding of relationships in the context of nature. For Kate these relationships remain a problem. Her marriage to Cipriano is relatively firm, but her old, white, individuated consciousness resists the final submission to his maleness and to the god-demon in him. At the end of the novel, she is indecisive, unable fully to commit herself to staying and yet unwilling to return to the arid world of old, drawing-room "graymalkins" that England holds in store for her.

Insofar as Lawrence is identified with Kate, he is obviously questioning the universal validity of Don Ramon's solution to Mexico's problems. In itself, however, this does not wholly negate the validity of Ramon's solution for Mexicans. Ramon writes, in a proclamation, that

different peoples must have different Saviours, as they have different speech and different colour. The final mystery is one mystery. But the manifestations are many. . . . Men are fragile, and fragments, and strangely grouped in their fragmentariness. The invisible God has done it to us, darkened some faces and whitened others, and grouped us in groups, even as the zopilote is a bird, and the parrot of the hot lands is a bird, and the little oriole is a bird. But the angel of the zopilotes must be a zopilote, and the

[40] *Ibid.*, p. 357.

angel of the parrots a parrot. And to one, the dead carcase will ever smell good; to the other, the fruit.[41]

Even this much was to be renounced, for all practical purposes, within a year of publication of *The Plumed Serpent*. *Lady Chatterley's Lover* and *The Man Who Died* are, essentially, concerned with other solutions. And *Apocalypse* would pitch the mythic-communal issues on so abstruse and so largely unhistorical a level as to leave politics and history behind. Yet the problems confronted in *The Plumed Serpent* color Lawrence's sense of the world to the very end, though they never find so rich and consistent an embodiment as here, and this despite all its reservations and contradictions.

f. The Role of Myth

Our entire discussion has taken for granted the role of myth in the rehabilitation of the Mexican peasantry under the leadership of Ramon and Cipriano. This has been possible—and necessary—because the construct supporting political action assumes the existence of myth in the sense given in the preceding chapter. It assumes, furthermore, the accessibility of myth in that meaning to the consciousness of twentieth-century man. When Ramon and Cipriano resurrect the old Mexican gods, they are drawing upon a residue of experience that lives on in the unconscious of contemporary Mexicans. That experience lives on for several reasons. First, it is an organic outgrowth of the deeper nature of the Mexican "race" and therefore cannot fade away, even when it is overlaid with Christian and European culture. In addition, it has, as a historical product, impressed itself upon the communal psyche, so that what began within that psyche has found its objectification in cultural modes and, from without, has again rooted itself in the psychic life in a form that insures its

[41] *Ibid.*, p. 358.

survival. Finally, it is prompted to do so by the rhythms of the cosmic life itself.

The survival of the old gods, and the ability to embody them in the "manifestations" which are Ramon-Quetzalcoatl and Cipriano-Huitzipochtli, are the condition for the entire process of political and religious rehabilitation which the novel explores. This is the unprobed, unchallenged donnée of Lawrence's entire vision—the assumption that renders the entire novel so abstract and so far removed from any assumptions we might ordinarily make about the immediate psychic reality of the people who are said to be redeemed within it.

I think that the novel essentially fails because it is so remote from what we ordinarily know and accept about men and their communities. Even if we are willing to grant Lawrence his assumptions with regard to race, myth, historic survivals, and cosmic vitality, the novel fails to embody the vision that Lawrence is trying to project because it never engages with the accepted commonplaces of experience— with what we know, intuitively, about the world. The reader who is willing to renounce the possibility of meaning within the novel and who seeks only the aesthetic shape of such experience of myth and symbol as Lawrence renders will be able to say the novel is an artistic success. And even then he is likely to recoil from the garish masquerade that the myth-and-ritual performances of Ramon and Cipriano present.

However we judge it—and I, for one, judge it rather harshly —The Plumed Serpent is probably the best possible vehicle for Lawrence's vision of a reconstituted world. Indeed, its failure as a novel probably arises from the failure of the vision it seeks to embody. Throughout his "communalist" phase, Lawrence pretty largely severs nature from history and then tries to build a bridge between them. But the bridge buckles; the materials of which it is made are both too weak and too crude.

Specifically, The Plumed Serpent buckles under Lawrence's

rejection of the given world. Lawrence gives short shrift to the historical world, the world within which men make things in relation to other men and relate to each other in terms of words, objects, gestures, and commonly acknowledged reciprocities. Of all the arts, the novelistic art concerns itself most largely with such reciprocities. Even in its more symbolic, more "romance" forms it works, not with chaos and cosmos, nor with nature and history, but with the revealed immediacies of the known human world. Individuality, in whose absence the novel grows stale, can be made known only in terms of particularized human desire: desire for objects, people, approbations affirmed by the social and historical worlds in which it unfolds. Even the richly subjective worlds of the early twentieth-century novel orient themselves to historical and social reality—even when they challenge it radically.

Lawrence, to be sure, largely rejects the normative notions of individuality affirmed by his contemporaries. Stories like "The Man Who Loved Islands," "None of That," "Things" —even St. Mawr and "Sun"—expose the deathliness and de-individuation that Lawrence saw in the waspishly self-conscious individualism of his peers. One may argue, moreover, that there is no ultimate need for the novelist to cling to the world of familiar individuality, to the "social and moral ego" that is formed within the terms of manners and morals, as conceived in the nineteenth century. Indeed, one may hold that the real challenge for such as Lawrence was to move beyond people, as people conceived of themselves, and to take hold of the forces, psychic and historical that moved them. And one may insist that extreme forms of the "romance" novel, such as Lawrence himself explored, are the best vehicle for exploring them.

Yet the fact is that, however rich in poetic evocation of the non-human and the pre-human world, much of Lawrence's fiction lacks the embodied physical and psychic immediacy of

realized fiction, in any mode. Lawrence's fictive journey into
the Unknown is a measure of his plucky rejection of all that
irked him within the social encampment. But the novels that
reflect that journey are, however we try to think of them,
at least partial failures. And their failure is interesting, not
only because of the courage they reveal, but also because
of the way they catch up the problems of any writer in
Lawrence's position. Lawrence's problem was essentially that
of the theorist who seeks an Archimedean point from which
to view history. Such a theorist attempts to envision utopian
potentialities almost wholly divorced from the historical present which he negates. Because of his negations, he may well
lack embodied images of the thing he has, in the present and
in negation of it, been able to imagine.

This, I think, was Lawrence's essential difficulty, and I think
he was deeply aware of it. The works of his last years have a
very different tone from any that preceded them. Critics have
attributed the change to Lawrence's weariness, to his ap-
proaching death, to the mellowness with which he embraced
both it and the world in which it overtook him. I think these
things do bear on the changes that came about on his return
from America to Europe in 1926. But I think his shift in
mood is also conditioned by a heightened awareness of the
value that existing things had for him—and for the human
consciousness. He writes, from Italy in his last years, of the
pleasure he derived from a richly cultivated historical scene: a
world whose past is rich and palpable, which surrounds one
with the beauty and softness of millenia of cultivation and
care.

It is within such a perspective that both the tone and the
style of his fiction change radically. Lady Chatterley's Lover
works in the mode of quasi-pastoral romance with an una-
bashedness inimical to the strenuousness, say, of Women in
Love—with which it has so many affinities. And the late

essays, collected in *Assorted Articles*, have a lightheartedness alien to the Birkinish rantings of the author of *Fantasia of the Unconscious*. *The Man Who Died* turns our attention to problems in the exhaustion of an entire mode of civilization —the problem of *The Plumed Serpent*. But it does so in terms of an imagery and an evocation of erotic experience both less ambitious and less factitious than the Love-and-Power emphases of the earlier work.

Lawrence, I would insist, does not abandon his interest in either politics in our sense or Power in his. Indeed, his interest in politics and his kind of Power is—as I hope I have shown —implicit in his earliest discursive writings: it animates the Hardy "Study" and is already full-blown in the letters to Bertrand Russell and Ottiline Morrell in the earliest War years. But the emphasis shifts. Toward the end of his life, Lawrence abandons the strenuous effort to work out the thorniest problems of all: the problems of how to restore the social cement in a world where—as in *Women in Love*—it has crumbled, and where the mere bonds of *eros* between man and woman provide no substitute or ground for it. The works of the *Wanderjahre*, involved with the communalist vision, as I have called it, directly confront that problem, though they cannot solve it; they can only explore varieties of strangeness in relation to it. I think we can be pleased with the aesthetic achievement of the work that precedes *Aaron's Rod* and that follows *The Plumed Serpent* because we would rather not be vexed with the unpleasantness, substantive and artistic, of the effort. But an admirable, and internally consistent effort it was—and one necessitated by the presuppositions of earlier, more attractive works.

AFTERWORD

To consider Lawrence in terms of his shifting view of self and society is to become aware of certain affinities. It is also to confront questions of larger scope within the history of our times.

It becomes clear that Lawrence, as both individualist and communalist, is essentially an optimist with strong affinities for writers like Shelley, Emerson, and Whitman. This characteristic tends to be obscured by what has been termed Lawrence's perversity, for it is hard to reconcile it with the fact that his most striking fiction concerns itself largely with lust, hatred, and death. The latter part of *The Rainbow*, *Women in Love*, and all the major writings of the *Wanderjahre* depict hate-ridden and compulsive types. Lawrence often blames the corruption of civilization itself for the violence its denizens undergo. Yet we often feel a deep exultance in that violence —an exultance that is open and unabashed when Lawrence comes to show how nature destroys those who violate her. It is this exultance that Middleton Murry deprecates when he mourns Lawrence's failure to become a prophet of love.

Lawrence's identification with the less pacific aspect of nature is of a piece with Aldous Huxley's critique "Wordsworth in the Tropics." Like Huxley, Lawrence mocks the "nature pure and simple" of Rousseau and "the other romanticists"; he is contemptuous of the eighteenth-century moralists who conceived of the "good man." Yet he himself seems to fall subject to the sentimentalism of which both he and Huxley accuse Wordsworth. William York Tindall noted this long ago, pointing out that Lawrence mocks those to whom his affinities are greatest. Professor Tindall suggests that Lawrence's duplicity is a matter of whimsical perversity. It is my impression, however, that the contradiction stems from the fact that Lawrence is one of the most deeply ambivalent of writers and that this duplicity reflects his ambivalence.

I would go further, and in a direction that leads away from Lawrence's art and thought and involves us with his life. If such a procedure needs justification, I would do so on the grounds that neither Lawrence's artistic nor his speculative projections of his conflicts are wholly self-validating. Even if they were, however, the issue would remain a real one: why *did* Lawrence—or, for that matter, any writer—come to see the world as he did? With Lawrence, it seems to me, much can be elucidated by the fact that he was never able to resolve his uncommon ambivalence toward his parents, and, by extension, to nature and society, but most of all to that creature of both—Lawrence himself. Lawrence's faith in the innate goodness of nature and goodness of man—"Man," he wrote, "is moral, is by his very nature moral"—seems to reflect a deep need to believe in the goodness of Mother-reality, on the one hand, and in the goodness of what he experienced as his own very evil self, on the other. At the same time, his "demonism" and his exultation in evil and destruction, as manifest in stories like "The Princess" and "The Woman Who Rode Away," are a dramatization of his own hostility, a dramatization that may have helped him to evade the real experience of his own feelings and of the hostility that was at their center.

If this is so, the emotional logic of his speculations on good and evil, on nature and society, is interesting, for it affirms "evil," in the meaning of cruelty and discord, together with "goodness," in the meaning of mildness and harmony. Within his broadest scheme for harmonizing nature, Lawrence insists that "destruction is the opposite equivalent of creation." He preaches destruction as a means of overcoming the destructiveness of a corrupt and "evil" civilization and demands that we exult in the annihilation of "The Woman Who Rode Away" on the grounds that the woman is enacting a cosmic rite: "Thus power passes from race to race."

Graham Hough suggests that Lawrence does not write tragedy because, like Nietzsche's Dionysiac reveler, he identifies with pain, dismemberment, and death as aspects of the world-process, but never really goes beyond them. Yet, assuredly, his relationship to tragedy is very different from the optimal Nietzschean one. As we read his stories of violence and lust for destruction, we feel that the "evil" is not merely the corruption that is in the world. Rather, we perceive it as part of the corruption in Lawrence's soul and sense that his vision of a harmonic universe within which love and hate, creation and destruction, god and demon are locked in perpetual but fruitful struggle is a way of attempting to render his own insoluble conflicts tolerable and productive.

To understand the ambivalence underlying his vision of cosmic harmony-in-dissonance is perhaps to cast light on the main problem of my essay. I refer to the tendency first to conceive of the individual *sui generis*, and then to conceive of him as something that grows out of the matrix of society. One is tempted to suggest that Lawrence's near-anarchic sense

of individual being as the be-all and end-all of existence is the
product of an intense desire to be swallowed by the "being" of
the whole, and that the later reversion to what I have termed
communalism represents a capitulation, an acknowledgment
that the pains of individuation are too keen, that the candle is
not worth the burning.

I must insist at this point that to direct attention to the
unresolved ambivalences reflected in Lawrence's work is not
necessarily to reject the perceptions that arose out of them.
Whatever the source of Lawrence's perception of the terrible
fragmentation the self undergoes in society, the perception
presses itself upon us as a valid one. Whatever peculiar satisfaction he derived from his near-apocalyptic vision of our
doomsday world of industrialism and of the Protestant ethic
and its nemesis in mass culture, the fact is that his vision
embodies perception of the known world. It embodies, moreover, a creditable interpretation of that world, even where it
proves finally inadequate.

If Lawrence's violent rejection of the world of creeping
industrialism and of the totalitarianization of civilization is
colored by his unresolved aversion from himself and his own
aversions, it remains one of the most richly articulated visions
of that world in its *psychic* implications. Its value, moreover,
lies perhaps not so much in what he actually came to see as in
the *effort* to see as he did. For in Lawrence, as I have been
insisting, we have a prime example of a writer whose art is
governed by the impulse toward apocalyptic speculation upon
the utopian possibilities of both self and society, without
acquiescence in the frames of reference that have ordinarily
characterized ethical thought in the Western tradition.

Albert Camus has suggested that metaphysical rebellion—
that is, refusal to acquiesce in the condition of the world as it
is—is one of the characteristic trends of modern times. He
cites the Marquis de Sade, Byron, Baudelaire, and (in fiction)

the nihilistic Dostoyevskean hero. I would include Lawrence in a countermovement, among writers like Blake and Nietzsche, who are not so much metaphysical rebels as metaphysical reconstructionists. These are writers who attempt to reconstruct the world they reject, to reform the deity they negate, and to enunciate a radical vision of possibilities within the world even while shattering the very foundations of self and society as we know them.

Such vision recurs again and again in modern letters—so much so that if one affirmed man's innate religiosity, the visionary strain might seem part of the "spilt religion" T. E. Hulme sensed in Romanticism. In contemporary America, for example, Norman Mailer and some of the radical, visionary writers sustain the ardently antitraditionalistic tradition of apocalyptic speculation. They continue to reject the "world" because of its repressiveness, and they seek viable alternatives. The spirit of Lawrence, not to speak of Blake, lives on in Mailer's assertion that "The nihilism of Hip proposes as its final tendency that every social restraint and category be removed, and the affirmation implicit in the proposal that man would then prove to be more creative than murderous and so would not destroy himself."[1]

Yet the apparent similarity between Mailer and Lawrence serves mainly to dramatize one essential difference—a difference close to the heart of Lawrence's intellectual failure. Like Mailer, Lawrence believes man's capacity for creation exceeds his capacity for destruction, but he also believes that the cosmos is a pattern of natural harmonies. Lawrence is the chief exponent among twentieth-century writers in English of the concept of nature as an incipiently moral order—and this despite his reiterated disavowals of morality itself. For Lawrence sets up the natural as the moral and insists that morality,

[1] Norman Mailer, *Advertisements for Myself* (New York: Putnam, 1959), p. 354.

like societality, is "instinctive." In fact, it is such faith in the
ultimate order and harmony of nature that permits Lawrence
to swing so freely from a radical individualism grounded in
the order of nature to a radical communalism grounded in the
same order.

Lawrence is, as I have indicated, not the only writer to
negotiate the movement from anarchic individualism to totalitarian communalism. The movement, as it happens, seems
endemic in modern social and political thought. What sets
Lawrence apart from Rousseau and Marx, from St. Simon and
Durkheim, or from D'Annunzio and Jung, is the freedom that
his faith in nature allows him. Assuming the natural sociality
of man, he twists that conception of sociality to suit his
immediate need. He can wield nature against society, against
history, or against traditional humanistic individualism, without concern for consistency or logic.

Lawrence, as I have shown, was not completely arbitrary in
his change of position: I have tried to sketch the urgent
problems that led him to shift his conception so radically.
The fact remains, however, that Lawrence's failure as a
thinker stems from his inability to integrate the harsh facts of
historical reality with the abstract constructs and images
against which he sought to judge that reality and through
which he sought to understand it. Lawrence's vision, essentially an antitragic one, fails even in its own terms to explain
the phenomena which it sets out to grasp. It cannot apprehend the logic of a fallen world grotesquely at odds with the
golden world of nature from which it has fallen. All he can
do, therefore, is contemplate the horror of the world-as-it-is,
on the one hand, and mutter incantations toward the world-
that-could-be, on the other. He can call for a magical transformation of it through language and feeling—the domains in
which his own power was considerable.

Looked at in its totality, his position, in its weakness, bears a remarkable similarity to Jung's. Like Jung, he assumes the natural "goodness" and wholeness of the psyche, and the naturalness of social man's journey through history. Like Jung, moreover, he is unable to deal theoretically with the racking tension of the human animal, who is perceived to be trapped between the claims of nature and the claims of history, the urgencies of self and the urgencies of society, and who can maintain both integrity and understanding by acknowledging heroically the tragic dividedness of his own nature. As a consequence, like Jung but unlike Freud, he oscillates between an atomistic sense of the radical claims of the pre-conscious, pre-social self in its isolation, and a totalitarian sense of the validity of civilization.

I do not mean to equate Lawrence with Jung. It seems to me that the aims of Lawrence's "therapy" and of Jung's are often antithetical in their implications for both individual and society. If one seeks analogues to Lawrence's psychic cosmicism, one would find them in the late work of Wilhelm Reich, not in Jung. Yet the comparison to Jung is, it seems to me, ideologically and paradigmatically the more significant one. The similarity to be noted lies in the fact that both of them affirm the radical asociality of the self and then insist on its irrefutable sociality. Yet neither troubles to provide a dialectical scheme that might afford us insight into the real tension between the one and the other, and the unfolding of the one in and through the other.

I should add, in closing, that the problems that arise from Lawrence's dichotomization of self and society and his subsequent fusion of them are not synonymous with his having been "a fascist." I hope I have shown that this is not a real issue. Rather, the difficulty lies in the fact that, like Jung, he is not able to evolve a truly dynamic conception of the relationship in question. Just what such a conception would be I do not know. From all that I grasp, the Freudian view makes the closest approach to an adequate account. The difficulty of Freud's attitude, from the utopian point of view, is that there is no way back to nature: there is only the heroic struggle with and within history. But perhaps this is a necessary limitation of the human condition—the very limitation, in fact, that forces us to reach out for utopian alternatives.

APPENDIX A

I wish to point out several analogues of Lawrence's conception of the fourth dimension that "men used to call heaven" as a world that exists apart from but also within the everyday sense-world.

1 The Lawrencean concept bears comparison with reference to its form with Spinoza's idea of double worlds, that is, of the simultaneous existence of the material and the intellectual world as aspects of a single substance. The intellectualism of Spinoza's view would obviously have been repugnant to Lawrence. Yet Spinoza's identification of the intellectual substance of the world with both God and nature influenced the Romantic pantheists. Through them, though indirectly, it undoubtedly had its effect on Lawrence.

2. It bears comparison, from another point of view, with Blake's "heaven," or Albion. Albion could be described quite adequately in Lawrence's formulation as a condition wherein "souls are established upon all revelations." The revelations

that concern Blake are not, to be sure, "revealed relation-ships" in Lawrence's sense. They are, rather, the imaginative apprehension—or redemption—of the world and its possibili-ties. Blake's eternity is an eternity of desire that has been enshrined in the forms of art, which reveal the utmost poten-tialities of the world. One may also note that Blake's concep-tion of eternity, like Lawrence's, partakes of the paradox of intensified temporality. "Eternity," we recall, "is in love with the productions of time." "Eternity" seems to consist of the productions of time—of those works of art and consciousness which have arisen within time out of the clash and conflict of the "Contraries" that collide in time.

3. Other Romantic concepts bear approximately the same relation to the Lawrencean notion as does Blake's. Like Blake, Shelley believed that immortality lies, not in "another" world, but in the intensified experience of this one. In a note to *Hellas,* for example, he holds that eternity would lie in a moment which contained an infinity of experience. Keats's conception of eternity and of immortality would seem to have involved an analogous notion of intensified relationship, wherein the self coalesces with its object and transcends itself in its excruciatingly intense experience of the object.

4. The Lawrencean concept of the "fourth dimension" is still more closely related to the notion of entelechy in the writings of Hans Driesch, the vitalist. Driesch addressed him-self to the question of how living things direct their growth toward their natural ends, and how, within the ordered pat-tern of development, mutations come about. Driesch con-fronts the problem from within the deterministic framework of nineteenth-century science, which conceived of the world in terms of strict laws of matter and motion that admitted no variation and which provided no basis for explaining develop-ment, evolution, or what Lawrence terms "creative surprises." Driesch's view held that an "entelechical principle" intruded

upon the deterministic time-space medium from a dimension of creative existence that lay within it, and yet beyond it. The similarity to Lawrence's "fourth dimension" is self-evident.

5. Obviously, Bergson's *élan vital* and Jung's *libido*, which Lawrence mocked repeatedly, also have their affinity to the "fourth dimension," the principal difference lying in Bergson and Jung's conception of an energy that drives existents in a particular direction. The Lawrencean "fourth dimension" is, on the other hand, a state of existence toward which existents move, though it also is, at other times, identified with cosmic power.

APPENDIX B   LAWRENCE'S ME-
              DIATION OF EROS
              AND CIVILIZATION
              About a fifth of the
"Study of Thomas Hardy" is devoted to an analysis of the play
of "masculine" and "feminine" elements in the work of a
small group of Renaissance artists. Dürer, Botticelli, Raphael,
Michelangelo, and Correggio are examined with a view to
exemplifying the development from a medieval to a modern
attitude.

    Lawrence assumes that works of art express their creators'
erotic nature and experience. The work of art is assumed to
embody the experience of the artist both in its themes and its
formal qualities. Lawrence observes that in medieval painting
the Madonna is at the center of interest, while in Renaissance
painting, the child is the center of the painting. He interprets
this difference to mean that for the artist of each period and
implicitly for the culture as a whole one aspect of reality and
of his own nature predominates. He then reads from the

artifact to the life of the artist and interprets the phenomenon as referring (1) to the reality of woman for the painter; (2) the reality of the fleshly side of his own nature for the painter; and (3) the reality for him of the unconscious emotional aspects of his experience.

Lawrence seems completely uninterested in the actual biographies of the painters. His treatment is based solely on what can be inferred from the themes, projected feelings, and formal organization of the paintings. These are inferred from the works of art themselves, and interpreted on the basis of the assumption that all art expresses a tension between "Love" and "The Law," that is, between male and female, spirit and flesh, etc. Art, like life, depends on the tension between the "polarities" and must be interpreted in terms of them.

Lawrence begins with Albrecht Dürer, whom he treats as a transitional figure. Lawrence finds that Dürer places woman at the center of his work. She is not, as he sees her, necessarily sensuous in her pictorial representation, but she is naturalistically represented as a palpable being, and the surrounding world pivots upon her. The stable center of things, she is the hub around which whatever light and movement are present must revolve. The masculine principle, like the actual male in the sex act as Lawrence imagines it, circles the fixed axis of the woman.

In Botticelli Lawrence perceives a significant change. Woman remains at the center of Botticelli's pictorial world. Yet she is divested of the centralizing substance of Dürer's women, as well as of the solid fleshliness that characterizes them. In both the Primavera and the Nativity, the movement is centripetal. The splendor of movement flings outward toward the frame of the painting, and the woman around which it whirls is lost in her delicate, narcissistic, wind-blown loveliness. She has lost her primacy.

Yet in Botticelli woman remains an erotic and imaginative

reality. Movement and action challenge her, but they continue to have reference to her, to orbit around her, and at times even to emanate from her. All this is lost in Raphael. Raphael, in Lawrence's view, has no immediate experience of woman; she has no sensuous reality for him. Lawrence infers this from the lack of sensuality in the paintings and from their highly geometrical organization. Lawrence writes that Raphael substitutes for emotional, desirable, tender, loving, actual woman the organized, geometricized structure of space itself. He suggests that Raphael has to utilize space in this way to counteract the masculine thrust of his spirit, which has lost the stabilizing resistance of woman as an erotic object, as well as of his own flesh and feelings in relation to such an object.

Michelangelo is seen to represent a further distance from the centralizing woman. Lawrence finds that Michelangelo has completely lost the ability to contact woman as object. To find woman, the narcissistic, self-enclosed sculptor must react upon his own body and seek a substitute for woman in the intensified experience of its form and its musculature. Hence the heavy, tormented corporeality of his figures, and their sexual ambiguity. Hence, too, the peculiar absence of tenderness toward woman.

Michelangelo and Raphael represent different ways of reacting to the loss of woman and of the flesh as the immediate object of desire and experience. Both refuse to renounce her altogether, and seek substitute means of stabilizing their artistic worlds—and, we are to assume, their selves. In Raphael, the intellectual (geometrical) ordering of space represents the masculine will's need to create an antagonist for itself by simulating the feminine principle and to master it in the very act of creating it. In Michelangelo, the super-sensual but self-tormented fleshliness of the work represents the masculine will, generating the feminine principle out of itself.

As Lawrence sees it, Raphael and Michelangelo succeed in achieving stability through legitimate subterfuge. Their gambits are only gambits, but they are effective ones. Hence one is able to speak of the struggle and the balance of Renaissance art. It is only with Correggio that the balance is lost. For Correggio, woman is real, but only as an aesthetic object. He renders her with delicacy and occasional sensuality, but with a detachment and a theatricality that betray the lack of vital relation to her. In a passage I have already cited in Chapter III, Lawrence writes that Correggio

leads on to the whole of modern art, where the male still wrestles with the female in unconscious struggle, but where he gains ever gradually on her, reducing her to nothing. Ever there is more and more vibration, movement, and less stability, centralization. Every man is more occupied with his own experience, with his own overpowering of resistance, ever less and less aware of any resistance in the object . . . , less and less aware of any unknown, more and more preoccupied with what he knows, till his knowledge tends to become an abstraction because he is limited by no unknown.[1]

The shortcomings of Lawrence's approach should be evident. The terms "masculine" and "feminine" have no concrete referents in either the works he is analyzing or the experience of the painters who produced those works. We recognize, to be sure, the process he is describing: descriptively, the works can be said to make sense within his categories, and the attitudes that he attributes to their creators are conceivable within his frame of reference. Yet the frame of reference is arbitrary. It turns the paintings and their painters into a vehicle for an allegorical reading of history—a reading that is legible once we are given the cryptographic key, but is unintelligible without it.

The treatment of painters that I have summed up in this

[1] Lawrence, "Study of Thomas Hardy," *Phoenix*, p. 456.

Appendix is characteristic of Lawrence's entire approach to history in the "Study." It is, in fact, the most detailed of all the expository material; only the chapters on the Hardy novels are more extensive. The same problems that confront us here are encountered on a still more vexing scale throughout the "Study": the problem of a construct that is clear and symmetrical and cleaves to many of the phenomena it sets out to interpret, but is unable to ground itself in the particulars of historical experience. This is the final limitation of the Lawrencean "theory of history": it represents his way of seeing the world rather than anything necessary and fixed in the world.

INDEX